About the Author

Christopher Spencer (not his real name) has worked in the banking and construction sectors and as an Adviser to Government. He has over 50 years of experience in international business and finance and has qualifications in economics, accountancy and banking. He is still active in business and now works on promoting new "Green" technologies.

Christopher lives in London with his wife and has two grown-up children. He also has several grandchildren. He likes solitary walks and reading about international politics and world history. But he also reads modern poetry and detective stories. In 2021, Christopher Spencer published his first book "Manna from Heaven and other True Stories" which received 5-Star reviews. In 2023 he published his second book of autobiographical stories "The Sound of Guns and other True Stories." You can watch interviews with the author on YouTube; search for "@englishmanasks – Christopher Spencer"

Praise for "Manna from Heaven and other True Stories."

"Amazing and true insights into a fascinating life on the dark side of international business and politics."

"It really is like reading about James Bond's Accountant and I could not recommend this book more."

"A good insight into government and international business."

To my wife, with love.

GREEKS BEARING GIFTS AND OTHER TRUE STORIES

The Truth Is Too Often Stranger Than Fiction!

CHRISTOPHER SPENCER

Copyright © 2024 by Christopher Spencer

All rights reserved. No part of this publication may be reproduced, stored in any form of retrieval system or transmitted in any form or by any means without prior permission in writing from the publishers except for the use of brief quotations in a book review.

The moral rights of the author have been asserted for this work in accordance with the Copyright, Designs and Patents Act 1988.

ISBNs:
978-1-80541-646-3 (Paperback)
978-1-80541-645-6 (eBook)

Published by Publishing Push Ltd.,
30 Stamford St., London SE1 9LQ.

Contents

Preface vii
Greeks Bearing Gifts 1
Casablanca 25
Egyptian Roulette 41
Bumiputras 63
Club Talk 93
The Journalist 125
A Walk in the Woods 141
In the Spotlight 173
The Iron Lady 199
Manoeuvres 217
Heart Strings 241
The Playboy 271
Spooks 291
Highland Games 309
Alarm Bells 341
Postscript 371

"The World will not be destroyed by those who do Evil, but by those who watch them without doing anything."
— *Albert Einstein.*

"Those who cannot remember the past are condemned to repeat it."
— *George Santayana.*

"Intelligence is based upon how efficient a species became at doing the things they need to survive."
— *Charles Darwin.*

PREFACE

"Those that the Gods wish to destroy, they first make mad"–derived from the play Antigone by Sophocles.

I am pleased to say that this is the third volume of true stories that I have produced, and that I appear to have, somehow, created an unusual genre. All my stories are autobiographical; they are about events that actually happened to me. But rather than creating an autobiography detailing my life from my childhood to the present day, I have instead written a number of true stories covering certain episodes in my life, and detailing what I have really experienced. These stories have covered both my parents' background, and my childhood, because so much of what happens to your parents, and indeed to your grandparents, must reflect on your own life. But, most of my stories are actually about my over fifty years of experience in international business and finance, and what I have seen and learnt from this process of constant travel and immersion into the culture, politics, and business of other countries.

I have now reached 80 years of age. From my point of view I have been very fortunate; the first stage of my childhood was stable, but then it unravelled as a result of my father's unfortunate addition to gambling. There followed years of family breakdown, struggle, and real poverty. I lost a whole year of schooling because of moving around the country, and then had to leave school early in order to support myself and my mother. I joined a major bank and worked and studied hard to get on; eventually I completed my banking examinations at a fairly early age. If I had not had to leave school early, I imagine that I would have become a Scientist, because the rigorous scientific method, and its logic and reasoning, appealed to me. After my mother came into an inheritance, I was then able to leave her and move to London to attend university and read for a degree in Economics, as a mature student. Then work followed in several merchant banks in the City of London, followed by over a decade in a major international construction group. Finally, I became an Adviser to a government department which covered the promotion of exports, and then, following that, I was appointed as an Adviser to a leading, previously government-owned, high-technology group.

I am still writing under my non-de-plume of Christopher Spencer, which is compiled from Saint Christopher, the Patron Saint of travellers, and Spencer, which is the third of my given Christian names. This is not only because some of my stories are somewhat controversial or clandestine, and I want to hide my true identity, but also because I am still working and I want to separate out my continuing business life, from my writing. Although, financially, I do not have to work, I am trying to do some good for the world, and for the future life of my children and grandchildren. I now work on promoting new "Green" technologies, including renewable energy, which I feel is important work and something that I must do, in my own very small way, to help ensure a better future for us all.

The main character in my true stories is called Edwards; which is me. Edwards is my alter-ego; he travels to where I have travelled and he experiences exactly what I have experienced, either in this country or abroad. I use the name Edwards as this was the maiden surname of my maternal grandmother, a feisty and independent woman who, in 1934, left the cosseted life in her husband's large house, which included live-in servants, to live with her lover in a far-away, small and isolated bungalow. In my childhood days, I spent many happy hours of my school holidays at her new home, in a wild and beautiful place. She came from a well-off Welsh family, who had settled, long before I knew her, in Shropshire. I was also born in that beautiful county and am therefore a true "Shropshire Lad." Edwards also means "son of Edward" and my father's second Christian name was Edward. Although I was estranged from my father for many years, my mother and father eventually got back together again, to live in Devon. As time went by, and my father and I became older, I managed to begin to forgive him for what he had done to my mother and me. Then I began to realise that excessive gambling, just like alcohol or drug taking, is another form of serious addiction.

In all my writing I strive to write the truth as I remember it, and to be as accurate as I can be in what I write. I still work to meet the high standards of the logic set by my student days, and always aspire to follow the motto of The London School of Economics and Political Science, which I attended. This motto is derived from the Latin poet Virgil and it states: "Rerum cognoscere causas," or translated: "To know the causes of things." Unfortunately, the truth about the causes of many things is, too often, largely unbelievable to the majority of the population and, to a corrupt minority, it is also highly inconvenient for it to be widely known!

The title of this new volume is taken from the first story it contains and which originally is from a reference in Virgil's Aeneid. This reference is part of a quote attributed to the Trojan High Priest as he warned his people about the 'Trojan Horse,' gifted by the Greeks to the city of Troy. Unbeknown to the citizens of Troy, it contained Greek warriors and these were then used, by the Ancient Greeks, to capture the city of Troy! This true story is a lesson to us all: that what comes free, usually has some motivation behind it! These days many mobile or computer applications are offered to the population on a "free" basis. But people should not allow themselves to be tricked in such a manner, for these things are only offered so that corporate or government surveillance can be carried out, and many personal details and useful information is unknowingly extracted from their users. At university, one of my favourite sayings was "I used to be a Cynic, but now I do not believe in anything!" But, ironically, I do not believe in the concept of "Conspiracy Theory" either; it is too often a feeble-minded and paranoid attempt to explain events as the machinations of the "Rich and Powerful." That being said, versions of these Theories can also sometimes be created and offered up to serve the interests of government and corporate elites. However, the world is really just far more complicated than that, to enable such simple theories to be true, and for people to be allowed to believe in them.

In her brilliant book "The Age of Surveillance Capitalism" Shoshana Zuboff, of the Harvard Business School, laid out the history and process of how decades of marketing and advertising experience, coupled now with advanced computer technology, has enabled this new Age to happen. Now, one of the most quoted adages of the advertising world is "If your product is free, it is because you are the product!" The consumer's regular usage of such "free" computer applications produces data that can be sold to the highest bidder. The Conspiracy Theorist would claim that all this is just a well thought out plan by the rich owners of the "Big Tech" firms to control us, whereas we have arrived where we are now through at least five decades of slow development that has often taken many wrong turns. This case shows that any Conspiracy Theory has to be very simple to appeal to the many, whereas the Reality of the world is far more complex. Strangely, most people seem to complain very little about this constant "Surveillance for Profit!" What they more often complain about is the surveillance used by our Western governments and which is needed to help fight crime, terrorism, child exploitation and pornography and the covert actions taken by our enemies against our democratic societies and our individual freedoms. This seems to me to be one of the best examples of "Double Standards" in the modern world!

I have included the earlier events of my life, in their correct sequence, within my second volume, "The Sound of Guns and Other True Stories", which was also named after the first story that it contained. However, with that volume, I also purposely tried to draw the allusion between life and war. For me, life, like war, seems to be a struggle for existence; it is fought against disease, violence, hunger, and ignorance. For those, like me, who live in a comfortable Western country, this is now largely forgotten. But I have travelled widely and I can attest to this continuing widespread struggle for existence. There is, however, a limit to what the Western "Nanny States" can now afford to do to support their populations; for many people in Britain this fact is, unfortunately, slowly becoming an obvious daily truth, but still the clamour to be helped rises to even louder proportions.

This is also an era of an unfortunate belief in "Entitlement;" a dangerous claim that takes away from our morality and from what it is to be human. Respect must always be earned through people's actions, and a good living obtained through study and hard work. We must learn that with Human Rights must also go Human Responsibilities! Some of those that feel "entitled" to many things, but fail to achieve them, become bitter, blame others for their own inadequacies, and then try to divide society further. Others descend into defeat, despair, and drug and alcohol abuse. Many more now share simple "Conspiracy Theories," fed by social media, to try and explain why they or others are failing. Conspiracies of course do exist but, as I have already shown, they are often more complex and particularly targeted. They do not generally concern a whole group of people, such as the "very rich." But these kinds of conspiracies are something that cleverly targeted social media would now want us to believe, and they are joyfully propagated by our internal and foreign enemies, along with false information, in a clear attempt to destroy our freedoms and our democracy. They soon begin to closely resemble the evil conspiracies put forward by the Nazis in Germany in the 1930s!

Most of the autobiographical narratives in my second volume, and in my first book, "Manna from Heaven and Other True Stories," were about my extensive experience in international business and finance. I have been fortunate in my various jobs, often trying to promote British exports to many different countries, working with people at the top of their societies, and with their government ministers and officials. But, I have found that the level of corruption in many of these countries is high and there is a real conspiracy to try and hide this. However, Britain is now, unfortunately, rapidly catching up and is in no way exempt from corruption or from trying to hide it. Recent press reports have made clear that all kinds of corruption in Britain are rising rapidly, along with the levels of injustice, in what was once a largely incorrupt and just country.

Above all, I strive to write the truth and what I have actually experienced. Because of my wish to protect them, I do change the names of some real people that I have encountered along life's journey. In only a few cases have I hidden where these events have actually taken place. The first few stories in this volume deal with corruption within a number of foreign countries, which I have actually experienced, and these are then followed by several stories illustrating injustice and conspiracy in Britain. Within the latter, I also put forward what seem to be logical conclusions, to solve the mystery of some high-profile deaths that have occurred. The stories that then follow become more personal, before returning to some true stories mainly routed in the field of espionage.

The pace of technological change in our world is now developing so fast that, in fact, it might be changing too fast for many human beings to ever catch up. We now live in a Post-God, Post-Truth, and increasingly Post-Reality world. I fear that those that immerse themselves in this "Virtual Reality," will soon lose their grip on Reality itself, unable to separate out what is the truth from pure fiction. They then become so easily led by the total lies promulgated repeatedly by politicians, and the social and mass media. These lies are also eagerly distributed by our enemies. I am fearful that this process could well lead to the death of democracy, and to the loss of human freedom. Unfortunately, the future seems to be all-powerful governments, and increasing autocracy around the world, including in Britain.

The Roman Empire has been accused of seeking only to provide "Bread and Circuses," just to keep the mass of the population well-fed and happy, and so that those in charge could more easily control them. How familiar this sounds to me in the present day! Food, much of it very unhealthy processed food, is becoming so important for our population; cooking programs and videos seem to regularly populate both the mass and social media. As for Circuses, "reality" television shows and so-called "influencers" now dominate both mass and social media. Couple this with the ever-growing industry of computer gaming, now extended into "Virtual Reality," and we have too many people just glued to their screens, as part of an unwholesome physical, and mental, lifestyle.

It is now becoming clear that this modern lifestyle is unhealthy, both physically and psychologically. It increases obesity, ruins both physical and mental health, and turns people into isolated and lonely souls. These people can then be so easily mislead by the lies and false information broadcast by the mass and social media. Those unfortunate enough to succumb to such a lifestyle, usually lack any real face-to-face experience with both other people and with nature. They soon find it impossible to participate in family and social life and to form any real friendships and intimate relationships. Now, really cut off from Reality, they become both scared and withdrawn, increasingly uneducated, and with psychological problems that leave them unable to confront reality, or even to face the smallest of challenges. Their common reaction to such real life experiences is often anger and increasing hatred of those that are unusual, or that they perceive as disagreeing with them. This can then lead to sick, mindless, and unmotivated violence; witness the increasing number of children now killing other children, not only taking their victim's lives, but also ruining their own lives, without seemingly any real motivation or any real understanding of the very serious results and consequences of their actions in the real world.

These increasingly isolated children or immature adults can so easily become immersed in the Internet, and websites that promote violence, terrorism, murder, self-harm and suicide. Unfortunately, these growing problems can then be easily exploited by the "Enemies of the West"; those that do not agree with our democracy and our wish for human freedom. Social media now enable these forces to carry out their undermining of our society much more efficiently with misinformation and downright lies and unfortunately, with the advent of Artificial Intelligence, the capability to do this has now increased exponentially. There has also developed the ability to influence the results of elections by targeted lies and by counterfeit announcements and speeches, using manipulated recordings of our political leaders. Our true enemies can now use these new technical opportunities, to promote our own destruction!

If this was not enough, we now face the phenomenon of Climate Change; I do not want to be drawn into an argument about its causes, except to comment that I cannot see how the burning of fossil fuels, over several hundred years, representing the Sun's energy locked up over many millions of years, can fail to affect the Earth. But Climate Change has always been with us; at certain times the level of the sea has been higher or lower than it is today. The Earth itself has been hotter or colder than during current times; witness the great Ice Ages. So Humankind, which has fortunately faced a period of comparative Climate Stability up to now, must somehow learn very quickly how to adapt and survive! The recent ravages of the Covid Pandemic pale into insignificance, when compared with the immense challenge that now faces humanity, as a result of the imminent, severe Climate Change, which confronts us as a species.

What is already clear is that these changes will seriously undermine food production. Long droughts and uncontrollable fires, followed by violent storms and severe floods, will both wipe out food crops, and possibly even prevent them from being planted, let alone grow to be harvested. I believe that gone is the era of plentiful and cheap food; indeed there may well soon be an increasing need for some kind of international food rationing. In terms of international migration, this will now increase exponentially, as many millions try and flee land that can no longer support even a small population. The so-called "West" must quickly become fully aware of these future trends and start planning for them now. The ludicrous wars that are currently raging, can only take away our collective attention from the "Express Train of Climate Change coming down the track." There is already no chance of stopping it now, whatever strenuous efforts we may try to make to reduce our carbon emissions! Many of these efforts, I believe, will in any case be frustrated by the actions of those with vested interests; short-term profits and power will always prove to be more important than long-term survival!

But there is one other massive problem that has to be tacked and that is the one of Corruption. As some of the following stories illustrate, it is already widespread and, I fear, growing. Along with Injustice and Unreality, Corruption robs the Human Spirit and devalues Human Life. It is a real and immense theft of money and power from ordinary people, and it lowers their standard of living, and the services that governments can provide to their population. It is a widespread, insidious disease, sapping hope, justice, and the strength of Humankind! In Britain, which is increasingly mired in Corruption, I would call for a strong, statutory body, devoted, with proper resources, to track down and punish the criminals that engage in Corruption in every form. This body should be given extra-jurisdictional powers to also investigate international links in such matters that happen outside Britain, with the possibility of bringing criminal prosecutions against foreigners in British courts.

In all my writing I strive to tell the truth, based upon my own personal experiences. Sometimes I feel like a Village Elder in ancient times, sitting around a camp fire at night and telling my stories to any of the younger members of my community that will listen! Even in the modernised societies of Africa and Asia, older people are much more fortunate than in the West. They are listened to, and many people still come to them for help and advice, as it is clearly understood that they must be much wiser and more experienced than the younger generations. In the Capitalist societies of the West, unfortunately, this situation is reversed; older people are often deemed as incapable and therefore valueless and it is believed that they should be ignored because they are "out of touch." Even worse, it is believed that they should be put away by their families into isolated "old people homes." In more civilised societies in the world, older people are still cherished, respected, and looked after by their own families, within their own homes, and their experienced views are sought on many family and other matters of great importance.

I have studied Marxism and its effects and I view it, like all the other religions, as just another form of "Ideology." During my university days at The London School of Economics, I personally saw indoctrination and radicalisation at work. The Marxist student leaders that I knew were from privileged backgrounds, and were determined to keep their upper-middle class positions as "the Leaders of the Proletariat." They used lower-class, less intelligent and less educated students, from a poorer background, as their "cannon fodder." They were arrogant, potentially violent, totally dismissive of any other views except their own, and supported the then totalitarian Communist regimes in the Soviet Union and Central Europe. It must have come as a great shock to them when the Communist Soviet Union collapsed in 1991 and the countries of Central Europe gained their own independent democracies. For a while, no doubt, the world's Marxist community could not understand how Karl Marx's theory of Class Conflict, which would soon bring a violent revolution, and then to them coming to power, could have failed so badly!

But then they began to concentrate on, and support the remaining major, totalitarian country that still practised a form of so-called Communism: the People's Republic of China. The Chinese government saw the opportunity to undermine the West. They began to fund Western universities and sympathetic political leaders, academics and scientists, and gain top-level friends and influence. This was in order to try to demolish Western values of democracy and freedom, from the inside. The ancient Chinese military general Sun Tzu wrote in his book,

"The Art of War," that it was far better to first try to undermine your enemy peacefully, than to ever have to confront him in battle. But the concept of "Class Conflict," put forward by Marx, had so obviously failed and been devalued. Instead, some new means of trying to divide the population of your enemies had to be devised to replace it; a new way to produce a form of violent revolution had to be found. So, "Race and Gender Conflict" was devised, and the "Woke Culture" began to be promulgated to introduce schism, uncertainty, and division in the West. This was quietly funded by the Chinese government, wherever possible, using the universities, the education system, and the elites of Western society.

Western countries now seem to suffer from a form of group forgetfulness, indeed ignorance, about their own history, and the history of other countries. This also applies to even more recent history and even the "study of history" is derided because it is "the wrong kind of history!" This tragic phenomena results, I believe, not only in the undermining of our society but in an inability to try and plan for the future, or even to understand what is really happening in the present day. If you cannot understand your own past, how can you ever begin to try and consider what is to come? In Europe and the United States, this habitual myopia and inability to understand even the more recent past of the world, directly contributes to major and repeated errors. This is how the surreal circumstances of the fictional novel,

"The Manchurian Candidate," by Richard Condon, actually took place in the United States in 2016.

Those of us that have seen and actually experienced life in a Communist-dominated society, with their elite and efficient intelligence agencies, dedicated to protecting and propagating their creed and to influence other countries in the democratic world, cannot doubt what had actually happened. But, again, the West seemed ignorant of even recent history and many did not bother to return to, and investigate the circumstances of 1977, when it was a very different world. If they had done so, maybe the glaring truth would have become evident! The "Candidate's" first wife had a father who was a known agent of the Communist Czechoslovak intelligence service, and that service worked very closely with their Russian counterparts. The "Candidate" would have been immediately marked out as a "Person of Interest" and developed over the years as an agent, using the "Carrot" of money and profitable business deals, and the "Stick" of "Kompromat," being a portfolio of compromising material. As I write, it now seems that, maybe, this great error will be repeated, and that "The Manchurian Candidate" will be elected again by gullible American voters!

So, as Lenin once wrote: "What is to be Done?" There is another great quote that may well answer Lenin's question: "The price of freedom is eternal vigilance" is a saying generally ascribed to Thomas Jefferson, a Founding Father and third President of the

United States. Today, this last quotation must be repeated and repeated as it is of utmost importance; otherwise we will all just lose our freedom! But how can you have Vigilance if you live in a Post-Truth, and Virtual, imaginary World? How can you separate out the Truth, from the monstrous lies and propaganda fed to us by our enemies, and those of us that support them? These lies can then be repeated and peddled by the means of social, and mass media. What is needed is a continuous, cold Blast of Reality, so that we can glimpse the Truth and, in so doing, recognise Reality and all the lies, through the mists and confusion which are used in an attempt to defeat us. This must be the priority for us all. Otherwise, like the citizens of Troy, we will fall prey to the gift of the Trojan Horse which, so easily, has been brought into our midst!

In my true stories, I have always sought to try to pass on my experiences, and what I have learnt, to the next generations. This has been in an effort to try to teach and help them, so that they can avoid having to learn from the same mistakes that my generation has made. I have also tried to introduce a sense of Reality, and to show that this is how the world really works. I have also tried to remain true to this principle in this Preface. As I have tried to make clear with the true stories contained in this book, Corruption and Injustice are widespread. Unfortunately, they are also growing greater, particularly in Britain and in other Western countries. If this growing rot is not stopped, I truly fear that it will undermine our society and we will lose our once-great democracy, and our freedoms. In such a rapidly changing world, that is the task that I must now leave to the present and future generations, and I must wish them well, as it will be a most challenging task.

But in trying to carry out this task, I would urge them to remember that they can only base themselves on Truth and Reality; otherwise they will surely fail. There is no point in constructing solutions which are based upon Unreality, which are then impossible to implement. The great engineers, planners, and thinkers of the British Victorian era, were successful in finding solutions because many of them were people of a broad educational background, and they were willing to imagine and experiment until they found the solutions that would work. Their work was based upon the freedom to "think outside of the box," and that is what is now desperately needed again. Otherwise, Humankind will fail to find the solutions that are now really urgently needed and that will enable it to survive. These solutions will be needed to be found in the next few decades, in the face of increasing Climate Change, food shortages, mass Climate migration and growing autocracy, to enable us all to continue to prosper in democracy and freedom.

It is indeed a Great Task that we all have before us. I fear that it will be intense and harrowing, and that many millions will die from starvation, lack of water, wars fought over resources, and extreme temperatures and weather events. But Humankind must now evolve very quickly as a species, because if we cannot achieve these needed solutions and use them successfully, we will all most surely perish!

–Christopher Spencer.
London. May, 2024.

GREEKS BEARING GIFTS

"May the Gods protect us from living in interesting times" – attributed to Aristotle (384-322 BCE)

1

Edwards had just been handed a large, tall glass. It contained his favourite drink; a strong Gin and Tonic with a couple of floating ice cubes and a slice of lemon. It was September 1999 and the man who had just handed it to him and who had invited him to dinner at his home that evening, was one of his contacts. Edwards had been introduced to Gary many years before by his long-standing friend Brian, who was a Barrister in the Middle Temple. Gary had a rather unusual background; he had a Greek father and an English mother, but he had been born in Brazil, where he father was then working. He had been sent to a leading British Public School and then on to Oxford University, so he appeared to be a born Englishman.

He had worked for many years in the financial centre of the City of London, but had then started up several of his own companies offering financial advice to rich individuals, and companies. Then he had made the decision to move to Athens, where he had found a Greek wife. They had now produced a small son and owned several luxury apartment blocks in the city. Gary had started a Greek company which offered financial and investment advice, and also dealt in foreign currencies, for the many rich Arabs that now found Athens a convenient centre to do business in, particularly as it was within the European Union. But Gary's main claim to fame was that he was one of the very few people who drove a Rolls Royce car through the streets of Athens!

Gary and Edwards had taken their seats on two very comfortable chairs on the large balcony of the luxury penthouse flat, at the top of one of the apartment blocks that Gary owned. This was his preferred home in the city; it was built on a hill and the view over the roofs of Athens was stunning. They chatted quietly away, mainly about the potential business opportunities in Greece. Edwards had arrived in Athens that very afternoon in the comfortable Business Class section of the morning British Airways flight, from London. He had then taken a taxi to check in at the Hotel Grande Bretagne, probably the best hotel in Athens.

This hotel had started life as a house built in 1842 for a very rich Greek businessman. It had been converted into a hotel and given its present name by another Greek owner in 1874. It was the first hotel in Greece to have electricity, which had been installed in 1888. Since then it had been extended with a least two new wings added. It had served as the Nazi headquarters during the

German occupation of Greece and, when the Germans withdrew, the British forces had also taken it over for the same purpose. The original house had been finally demolished in 1954 and replaced by another new wing.

Just two weeks before Edwards had arrived in the city, Athens had experienced a strong earthquake and a large number of buildings had been damaged. Over 140 people had been killed and some 1,600 people had been injured. But the Hotel Grande Bretagne was very well built and had suffered no damage. This was Edwards's first visit to Greece and, as always, when visiting a new country, he liked to talk to reliable and knowledgeable people about their views on doing business there. As they sat talking, Edwards became very interested in what Gary was saying. He did not notice that the liquid in his glass had begun to vibrate. Suddenly the building began to shake! It was a strong aftershock from that main earthquake, but Edwards did not know that. Below, many people had run out of their homes and several women had begun to scream. Edwards began to feel a sense of panic, as the building continued to tremble.

"Should we all get downstairs as quickly as we can?" he asked Gary anxiously.

But Gary's British half had taken over. "If this building collapses," Gary replied calmly, "we will at least be on the top of the rubble."

Edwards took a very large swig from his strong Gin and Tonic and then, taking his cue from Gary's phlegmatic attitude, just continued his discussion with him about doing business in Greece.

2

Edwards was now employed as a Director of a company that covered the engineering, defence and security industrial sectors. As part of its business portfolio, it included the design and manufacture of an advanced material, which could be applied to navy ships and military aircraft, so that they could become virtually invisible to radar. The Greeks had one main enemy, the Turks, and the owner of Edwards's company believed that the Greek Air Force could be interested in this product to coat some of the American-built aircraft, that they had bought several years before. In this way, these military aircraft could become much more difficult for the Turkish radar bases to spot.

Edwards had consulted with his long-standing friend Richard who, he remembered, had done business in Greece some years before. Richard had many excellent contacts around the world. He had suggested that Edwards contact a man in Athens, that he knew, and who he thought would be ideally placed to help Edwards. His name was Stavros and Edwards had contacted him from London. He had arranged to meet him, at his hotel, the following morning. Soon Gary's wife called them in to the dining table and served a light, but very delicious, Greek dinner. After the meal was over and it was polite to do so, Edwards made his excuses to leave. He was tired from his early start from home to get to Heathrow Airport to be in time for his flight that morning, and he wanted to return to his hotel to sleep. By now, Edwards had recovered fully from the experience of his first earthquake. He was very grateful to Gary and his wife for their kind invitation to dinner at their Athens home, and also grateful to Gary for his most helpful advice on doing business in Greece.

The next morning Edwards was in his hotel's reception area at a quarter to ten. Stavros was due to arrive at ten o'clock and Edwards always believed in arriving early. He identified himself to the duty receptionist and said that someone would soon arrive and ask for him. He indicated where he would sit in the reception area and then took his seat to wait. As he waited, he remembered Richard's words to him, "You do know that if you want to make sales in Greece, you will have to add to your price some payments for outside parties to help the sale go through. Otherwise, no sale will happen!" He had also heard stories about Greeks; some of them had a reputation of very poor timekeeping. But he need not have worried; at ten o'clock precisely a man aged about thirty-five but rather short and already somewhat overweight, entered the hotel lobby. He had the typical Greek dark looks and was carrying a small briefcase. He marched quickly to the reception desk, and then the man behind it, pointed towards Edwards.

Stavros was a typically friendly Greek; he had a broad smile on his face and gave Edwards a very warm welcome to his city. They moved to a table in the ground floor bar and Edwards ordered them both some coffee. Edwards asked him some personal questions about where he lived and about his family. He always liked to learn a little more about the person that he was dealing with. Stavros then kindly asked about Edwards's family. They then compared notes about their mutual friend Richard. At this point, Edwards told Stavros about an amusing incident, when Richard and he had been trying to do some business together some years before, in another country. Edwards always found that, when dealing with new contacts, it was useful to cause them amusement, or even to crack a joke. Humour was always a good way to get some trust between one person and another, especially if they were of different nationalities.

But Stavros was also an astute businessman; he soon turned to the matter in hand. "With your permission," he said in his perfect English, "I would like to introduce you to my good friend Yannis, this afternoon. He is the Managing Director and owner of what you would call a consultancy company. They advise and do business, all the time, with our Ministry of Defence and our Armed Forces. You will understand that, in order to achieve a contract for your company, certain people have to be looked after, and this they will handle. That will take some extra money to be added to the contract amount."

Edwards did indeed understand; he had already had years of experience behind him of dealing in foreign countries, and he also remembered again Richard's words. While bribery and corruption certainly still happened in Britain, it was so very well hidden and was never talked about. But in the majority of foreign countries, it was an accepted part of life in the world of business, and it was most usually required to win any contract sale. This was particularly the case if you were selling to a foreign government.

"I have already asked my friend and he has advised me," continued Stavros. "He will require ten per cent of the price to be added to the contract sum. You understand that it will only be a small contract and that it will therefore require that kind of percentage figure, to get people really motivated. That ten percent will be paid by your company to Yannis's company, once you have been paid. Of that ten per cent, only a small part will be kept by Yannis's company, for its fee. The rest will be divided between some senior Air Force officers, who will approve and recommend your product, and some senior officials at the Ministry of Defence, who will pay out the money. To that must be added another three per cent to be paid to me; this will be the fee for my work, and I will give one per cent of that to Yannis personally, not to his company. You understand?"

Stavros completed his requirements with a broad smile. Edwards, rather reluctantly, indicated that he understood. He realised that, unfortunately, there had to be these kinds of arrangements, if his company was to get any business here. "But what about the politicians?" he asked.

Stavros laughed heartily. "They are very, very greedy," he said. "If they were in on this deal, there would be much, much more extra to pay. Fortunately, the price of this contract will come from a budget that has already been allocated by them for the improvement of our Armed Forces, so we do not need them to approve any more money!"

Edwards indicated that he agreed to these arrangements. "Should our afternoon meeting, with my good friend Yannis, now take place?" asked Stavros. Edwards nodded his agreement and Stavros left for a few minutes to call Yannis and confirm the meeting. "Now that we understand each other," said Stavros, when he had returned, "I will take you out for a long lunch. We have long lunches here in Athens, because we usually eat our dinners very late."

3

Stavros showed Edwards to his car, which was parked in the large square outside the hotel. Edwards had already experienced Greek driving, as a result of the number of taxis that he had already taken. But Stavros's driving seemed to be even a little more hair-raising! When he stopped, and he seemed to specialise in sudden and heavy braking, he seemed determined to get as close to the vehicle in front of him as possible. Edwards was sitting in the front passenger seat, and his right foot practically made a hole in the car's floor! Eventually they arrived safely at their destination. It was a restaurant at the top of a hill, with large picture windows. When they were shown to their reserved table, beside one of these windows, Edwards realised why Stavros had chosen it!

Sitting, looking out of the window, Edwards had a stunning view of the ancient citadel of the Acropolis, high on its own hill above Athens. Its main building, the Parthenon, was clearly visible, in all its classical glory. Completed in 438 BCE, at the height of the power of the City State of Athens, it was a temple dedicated to the goddess Athena, whom the people of Athens considered to be their patron goddess and holy protector. Edwards gazed at it in awe; he ached to visit it properly, but he knew that, like on so many of the trips he had experienced on business around the world, he would never have any time for mere sightseeing.

Edwards took Stavros's recommendations as to the Greek food and wine; it was excellent. They talked about things other than business and, inevitably, their conversation turned to the view from the restaurant. "Thank you for bringing me here," said

Edwards. "It is a wonderful view over that great monument to Ancient Athens."

Stavros smiled; "Yes," he said. "It represents a time when so much was invented that we know in our modern world: democracy, theatre, other arts and of course, philosophy."

"Yes, I know," replied Edwards. "At university I studied the Philosophy of Political Thought. My favourite part of that was to be able to read Plato, who wrote down so much that Socrates had said."

Stavros smiled again. "You must always remember," he said, "that all that achievement was only possible because the Greeks then had the time and leisure to think and talk about such things. The reason that they had that time, was because they had enslaved other Greeks, to work for them. For every two male Athenian citizens that had a vote, there was at least one slave. The women of Athens were not considered citizens, and had to work in, and hardly ever left, their homes. So it was on the back of slavery and using the subjugation of women, that the achievements of Athens were built!"

Edwards swallowed hard; he knew that Stavros was right. "But they were remarkable," continued Stavros. "Not too far from here is a high mountain. You cannot pass it easily to get into the next fertile valley. So our ancient ancestors made a tunnel, under that mountain. One team of miners started at one side, and the other team at the other side. They met in the middle of the mountain; the alignment of both tunnels, coming from those two different directions, was perfect." Edwards expressed his amazement, but Stavros then went on.

"About ten years ago, it was decided that a new tunnel was needed. Some of the major construction companies in Europe were involved. As before, one company started at one side of the mountain, and another company at the other side. When they met in the middle, the tunnel was ten meters out of alignment, so quite a lot of it had to be re-bored. So, with all our so-called modern technology, we could not achieve this task properly. But that task had been perfectly achieved, without any such problems, two and a half thousand years before!"

Edwards's view of Stavros had improved; not only was he very honest and efficient about business, but he appeared also to be a well-educated man. They took their time over lunch; Edwards could still not believe the magnificent view. But soon they were back in Stavros's car, heading for the suburb of Athens where Yannis had his company's offices. Maybe it was the wine with his lunch, or maybe he had just got used to it; Edwards now felt a little more relaxed with Stavros's driving! They arrived at a low, blue-glass building and went inside. The offices of Yannis's company seemed to occupy the whole building, and Edwards was impressed. To afford this, it appeared to be a very successful company. They were shown into the office of the Managing Director and then Edwards was introduced.

Stavros's friend Yannis was an older man; his dark hair was already beginning to turn grey. But he was as charming and as welcoming as Stavros himself. However, his English was not as good, and Stavros had to translate a few phrases from English into Greek, and vice versa.

"If you will excuse me," said Stavros politely, "I will speak to Yannis in Greek now about the financial arrangements that we have agreed." Edwards realised that this was about the additional sums that would have to be added to the contract price. There was then a short discussion in Greek and then Stavros and Yannis turned to Edwards. They were both smiling; everything seemed to have been agreed.

"Yannis has asked if you can please come back again tomorrow?" asked Stavros. "He will then introduce you to his Deputy, who speaks much better English then he does. He will also introduce you to some of his people, on the technical side, who deal specifically with the Air Force. They will want to ask you for some more details on the product."

"Of course," replied Edwards. "I have some technical information with me that I can let them have."

"Unfortunately," said Stavros, "I have to fly this evening to Corfu. That is where my parents now live, and tomorrow is my father's birthday. I hope that you will understand. But I will be back early the following day, and we can meet again at ten o'clock, at your hotel, to review matters. Yannis and his colleagues will look after you tomorrow. Will that be alright?"

"Of course," replied Edwards, knowing full well how important family life was for the Greeks. "But I have to go back the day after tomorrow."

"Yes, I know," said Stavros. "You are on the late afternoon flight. I will take you in comfort to the airport myself."

Edwards thanked him. Stavros seemed to have a conscience about not being available for him the next day, as he then asked Edwards if he could drive him back to his hotel? He assured Edwards that it was easy for him, as it was on his way to the airport. Edwards accepted, and then spent the evening, by himself, over an enjoyable dinner. He so rarely had time to himself, on these intensive overseas visits. It was so pleasant to relax, and not to have to think and to talk to someone else, as you tried to eat your food!

4

The next morning, Edwards took a taxi to Yannis's offices. There he was introduced by Yannis to his Deputy, and to several more of his colleagues. They occupied a large meeting room. Yannis's Deputy spoke excellent English and so did his three colleagues, who all appeared to be engineers. Yannis himself chaired the meeting, to show, Edwards thought, that he considered this matter to be very important. They spoke about the requirements of the Air Force, and how the product made by Edwards's company could be important to them. Edwards handed over all the technical information that he had with him. He felt that he had to apologise that it was not in Greek. "Don't worry," said one of the engineers. "We all speak and read English, and so do all of the people that we deal with."

Another round of coffee was brought in to the meeting room at about half past eleven. It was just after that, when Yannis's secretary entered the room, and approached Yannis. She whispered urgently into his ear. He nodded and then stood up.

"Will you please excuse me," he announced. "My mother has just been taken to hospital and I must go and see her immediately!"

Edwards was shocked; he gave Yannis his best wishes for his mother's quick recovery. As Yannis left the room, Edwards noticed a strange smile on the face of his Deputy. He was rather put off by it; he could not understand why the man was smiling at so serious a matter. They continued their discussions. An hour later they were asked to clear their papers, and a light lunch was brought in and laid in front of them by some of the more junior staff. Then glasses and some wine bottles were brought in.

In this more relaxed atmosphere, Edwards turned to Yannis's Deputy. "I was so sorry to hear about Yannis's mother," he said. "Was this sudden or had she been ill for a long time?" Thinking about his reply afterwards, Edwards could really not understand it.

"Yes, it was sudden," the man had replied. "But you should not worry about it. I am sure that she will get better very quickly."

By the middle of the afternoon they had finished their discussions. Edwards thought that it had gone well. They all stood up and Edwards shook the hand of each of the engineers. Then he turned to Yannis's Deputy and shook his hand; "Let me take you to Reception," the man said." You can wait there and we will call a taxi to take you back to your hotel."

Back at his hotel, Edwards decided to telephone Gary and invite him and his wife to dinner. Gary replied that his wife would have to stay at home to look after their child, but he could certainly make it. They fixed a time to meet at the hotel at eight o'clock. Over dinner, Edwards told Gary, in strict confidence, what had happened on the previous day, and earlier on that day. He asked his opinion of Yannis's company?

"I have heard of them," Gary replied. "But I do not know of them myself. What I have heard about them is that they are well established and that they are very close to a number of Government Ministries and Ministers, including the Ministry of Defence." The dinner over, Gary now wanted to return home to his family. Edwards thanked him warmly for all his help and sent his best regards to his wife. They parted with promises to meet again, on Edwards's next visit to Athens.

The next morning, Edwards took the lift down to the Dining Room for the excellent English Breakfast that, appropriately, the Hotel Grande Bretagne provided to their guests. Every morning, there was a table placed at the entrance to the Dining Room, on which various English language morning newspapers were set out for the hotel guests to take with them, if they wished. Edwards selected a local Athens newspaper, which was printed in English. He always liked to catch up on any local news when he was staying in a foreign country. He started reading it, as he was waiting for his main breakfast to be served. He turned to the second page, and what he saw there, nearly put him off his bacon and eggs, that he had just ordered!

In the middle of the second page was a formal photograph of Yannis, followed by an article which stated that he had been called to report to the Central Police Station in Athens, the previous day. There he had been arrested, questioned and then charged with bribery and corruption! The charges seemed to relate to certain transactions at the Ministry of Defence! Yannis had finally been released, on bail, the previous evening. Edwards finished his breakfast, as quickly as he could. He washed it down with several cups of strong coffee and then sat in the Reception area to wait for Stavros.

Promptly at ten o'clock, Stavros entered the hotel; fortunately his domestic flight back to Athens had been on time. Edwards said nothing to him; he guided him to a quiet, corner table in the ground floor bar and ordered some more coffee. Only when they were seated, and the coffee had been served, did Edwards pass him the newspaper, opened at the relevant page, and pointed out the photograph of his good friend, Yannis.

5

Stavros read the newspaper article carefully and then smiled. "We knew that something like this could happen, but not so quickly," he said. "The European Union is indulging in one of its periodic drives against corruption, and this time it has chosen Greece. They have forced the local police to do this," he continued. "Do not worry yourself about it. My good friend knows, how do you say it?" He thought for a moment and then smiled again. "He knows where all the skeletons are buried!" he said.

"But we can't use him now," spluttered Edwards, thinking that Stavros was really not taking the situation seriously.

"But this will soon pass," replied Stavros. "You will see. The politicians will intervene. He knows far too much about them, and where all their money is hidden. These charges will never be proceeded with. They will be formally cancelled and he will be a free man able to carry on his business again." Stavros laughed. "Why he even knows where the Chief of Police has buried all his many skeletons!"

Edwards shuddered; how was he going to explain this to the owner of his company back in London? He asked Stavros if there was any alternative to Yannis's company, that he could use, for an alternative approach to the Ministry of Defence? Stavros replied that he knew of none. In any case, Yannis's company was the best company in Greece to get business done with the Ministry of Defence. Everybody, who knew anything about Greece, knew that! This temporary problem would pass, and Yannis would soon be back in business again and now even stronger and better placed to do these kinds of deals.

It was not a happy Edwards who boarded the British Airways flight back to London, that afternoon. On the other hand, he was quite relieved to be going home. Given his recent meetings, if he stayed, he might even just get caught up in the investigations too, and be questioned by the Athens Police. He had been driven to the airport by Stavros; they had not said much in the car.

"I do not know what will happen now," he had said to Stavros, as he had shaken his hand, in farewell. "I will get back to you as soon as I can."

Back in the office, the next day, he had a meeting set up with the owner of the company, to report on his visit to Athens. He outlined the people that he had met, and then gave a brief summary of his conversations. He did not mention about the strange incident of Yannis suddenly leaving their second meeting.

"Everything seemed to be going so well," he said. Then he produced the English language Athens newspaper that he had brought back with him. He showed the owner the photograph of Yannis on its second page. The owner read the article next to it and was suitably horrified.

"We cannot deal with them now," was all that he had said.

"I am afraid not," replied Edwards. "It would be too much of a risk to the reputation of this company to do so. I will inform

Stavros accordingly. I am afraid that, for the moment, we will have to forget any prospect of selling our product to the Greek Air Force."

But Edwards did not forget what had happened, and kept his eyes open for any further news. A few weeks later, it came in a short article in the London Financial Times. As Stavros had predicted, the article reported that Yannis had been released from all charges made against him, because of a total lack of evidence! Edwards showed the owner of the company this new article and he read it. But he refused to change his mind.

"We cannot now try to do any business in Greece, through him, or his company," was all that he would say. Edwards sent Stavros a final message to this effect; he did not hear back from him and the potential sale never happened.

But Edwards, having visited there, was now interested in the fate of Greece. For years, he followed newspaper reports on that country and any news reports on both radio and television. What he saw really saddened him. The Greeks had joined the Euro, along with other European countries, at too low an exchange rate with their old currency, the Greek Drachma, in 2001. This meant that goods from the major manufacturer in Europe, Germany, were now cheap, and for years German goods flooded into Greece, supported by very large loans from the German banks. Many Greek politicians and government officials bought, or were given, new houses, cars and other German goods, and their very private bank balances soared, thanks to bribes from German companies.

In 2004, the Olympic Games were held in Athens; this provided another opportunity for German construction companies to win large contracts, to construct the major projects that were needed for this major international event. It proved to be just another, huge "Rip Off" of Greece, and the country was eventually left bankrupt! The country that mainly benefitted was Germany, who controlled the European Union, by virtue of its political, economic and financial power. The German banks then demanded the repayment of the very large loans they had given, but Greece, by now, could just not afford to repay these vast loans that had been offered to it, and which the greedy politicians in charge had accepted.

The European Union, prompted by Germany, then insisted that a major economic austerity program, should be introduced. Civil unrest broke out in Greece, as the economy collapsed, and large parts of the Greek population were reduced to poverty. A succession of democratically elected Greek governments tried to demand financial help from the European Union, even using the threat of leaving the Euro and the Union, in a desperate attempt to recover control of their own country.

But the power of Germany and the other North European countries was too strong. Slowly, they managed to force out of power any elected Greek politicians, who were both radical and honest, but who had proved too difficult in their dealings with the European Union. In the country where it was invented, Democracy itself was being undermined! The more conservative and corrupt Greek politicians, who had so largely prospered from the demise of their country, merely waited to be returned to power. Then they could reinstate their large private incomes, based on bribery and corruption!

To Edwards it was a true tragedy; the current sufferings of the ordinary Greek people, were worthy of the tragic dramas produced in the fifth century BCE, by the three great play writers of Ancient Greece: Aeschylus, Sophocles and Euripides. Generations of corrupt Greek politicians had combined, with the overbearing trans-national state of the European Union, controlled by its most powerful member Germany, to rob a people, not only of their national wealth, but also of their pride, their established traditions and their humanity.

There is a very ancient saying, "Beware of Greeks bearing Gifts," which is quoted by the Latin poet Virgil in his Aeneid, written in the first century BCE. It is attributed to the Trojan priest Laocoön, referring to the Trojan Horse, gifted by the ancient Greeks to the city of Troy during the Trojan War. But it contained some Greek soldiers who, at night, opened the city's gates to let the

Greek army in to capture the city. But now, perhaps, for the modern Greeks, it should have been rewritten in order to be more truly a warning for them in their current, more unstable, times. It should now read: "Beware of Non-Greeks, bearing, so-called, Gifts!"

CASABLANCA

"An Ambassador is an Honest Gentleman sent to Lie Abroad for the Good of his Country" – Sir Henry Wotton in 1604.

1

Edwards sat in his comfortable Business Class seat looking out of the aeroplane window next to him. It was a bright, cloudless day outside and the British Airways Captain had just announced that they were flying over Cape Trafalgar, on the coast of south-west Spain. Edwards could just see below the long headland, stretching out into the Atlantic Ocean, with its prominent lighthouse at its end. It was off this headland that, in 1805, the great British Admiral Horatio Nelson, had defeated the combined French and Spanish naval fleets at the Battle of Trafalgar, using the new and unconventional naval tactics which he had invented. It was in that Battle too, that Nelson had been shot and killed, by a French musketeer. Being without a legitimate heir, his titles had passed to his brother William.

Beside Edwards sat Henry, usually Edwards's chosen colleague to accompany him on some of his more difficult overseas visits. Henry had escaped the Nazi death camps by being put, by his parents, on to one of the special trains leaving Prague that had brought young Jewish children to safety in England in 1939. These trains had been organised by a British stockbroker, Sir Nicholas Winton. Henry had lost both his parents and his sisters in the Nazi Concentration Camps, in which they had been imprisoned. On his arrival in England, he had been placed in the care of a British family. A few years later, his new family had also been wiped out, when a German bomb had fallen on their house, while Henry, fortunately, had been out at school. He had then been given to a second British family, who had brought him up as an English boy.

Henry now spoke at least six languages, plus English, and had a subtle, logical and clever brain which Edwards found very useful to compare notes with; especially while on what had often proved to be complex overseas visits, full of challenges and intrigue. It was now the late 1980's and because of his language skills, his excellent mind and his Central European background, Henry had often been sent to market and negotiate in Eastern Europe, which was then behind the "Iron Curtain" and dominated by a Communist Soviet Union. Edwards knew that Henry had often been in real danger and under threat there but, having escaped death several times in his younger days, he did not seem to mind!

Henry was talking to their other colleague, who was sitting behind them, through the gap between the aircraft seats, in the two abreast Business Class cabin. This colleague represented the mining construction company, within the group of contracting companies that employed them all. The three of them had been sent by that mine construction company on a reconnaissance mission, to examine the possibility of the company bidding for a particular construction contract, in a foreign country. Edwards's mind was wandering; it sometimes had the tendency to do that, back to people and events in his past lives. He smiled to himself as he made a mental connection and a face and a name came into his consciousness. It was the face of a Viscount, who he had once worked with, over fifteen years before, in a merchant bank in the City of London. Edwards had been privileged to join this elite financial institution; after some time working in a large open plan office in their International Banking Department, he was transferred to work on some special projects. He had been moved to a smaller room with three other men. The Viscount, who occupied a desk in this room, was a direct descendent of William, the brother of Horatio Nelson. He had inherited, in addition to his British titles, an Italian title given to Horatio Nelson by Ferdinand, the King of Naples and Sicily, in 1799.

Nelson had saved the King from a potential violent uprising of rebels supporting Napoleon Bonaparte and had then taken the King and the Royal Family, in a British naval vessel, to safety in Palermo in Sicily. They had been accompanied by Lady Hamilton, the wife of the British Ambassador in Naples, who, while staying in Palermo, had become Nelson's mistress. In return for his help, the grateful King had granted Horatio

Nelson a Dukedom and a large estate in Sicily, which apparently included the ownership of Mount Etna. One morning, Edwards's colleague had just returned from a long holiday, on his Italian estate, during which time Etna had spectacularly erupted. He spread out his holiday photographs on his desk; most of them were of Etna, spouting fiery lava and smoke. "Look at my volcano erupting!" he had said very proudly. Edwards had just remembered his thought, at the time; that there were very few people in the world that could have made, in all truth, such a seemingly ludicrous statement!

Edwards and his two colleagues were now flying to Morocco to discuss a potential mining project, for which the Moroccan Government were asking for competing bids. Half an hour later their aeroplane was due to land at the main Moroccan airport near Casablanca. Edwards had never been to Morocco before, but had carried out his research carefully. He had made a study of both the proposed mining project and the country that they were now visiting. He had briefed his relevant contacts in the British Civil Service carefully, including those in the Foreign and Commonwealth Office, in order to try and get their full support for his efforts. He was a little surprised when an invitation had immediately come back, via the Foreign and Commonwealth Office, from the new British Ambassador to Morocco, for the three of them to dine with him on the evening of their arrival at his Embassy in Rabat, the country's capital.

As they commenced their landing at Casablanca, Edwards continued to look out of the window; he saw below him the deep azure of the Mediterranean Sea, with a smattering of fishing boats and some larger vessels. Suddenly this turned into a view of the great, white city of Casablanca, which glistened in the strong sunlight. Then there was a flash of green vegetation and that quickly turned into the dark grey of the runway, as their aircraft landed safely.

2

As the three of them had only carry-on baggage for their two nights stay in Morocco, they were quickly through Immigration and Customs. Emerging from the one-way door after Customs, Henry quickly spotted his name being held up on a board by a driver. "I took the trouble of hiring a car and a driver for our visit," Henry said to Edwards.

"Good thinking, Henry," replied Edwards, who knew that they had been unable to find hotel rooms in the capital of Rabat. That city only had a limited number of hotels and these seemed to be all currently fully occupied by the delegates to an international conference that was taking place in the capital. Instead the travel agent, who worked for their company, had found them rooms in a rather down-market three star hotel in Casablanca.

This did not matter to Edwards, who had suffered hotel rooms in several other parts of Africa, which would probably prove to be far worse. The disadvantage of staying in Casablanca was that it was over a one hour's car journey to Rabat. Henry's decision to hire a car and a driver, which would be available to them during their visit, was therefore a wise one. They followed their driver to his car, piled their bags into the boot and sped off to their hotel to check in. There was only an hour to unpack and freshen up, before they were back in the car again, for the drive to Rabat, along the fast duel-carriageway road to the capital.

The then British Embassy was in a pleasant, but rather run-down, large, white villa of French colonial design. They were greeted by a junior member of the British staff there and escorted to a room where the First Secretary of the Embassy was waiting for them. "Drinks, gentlemen?" asked the First Secretary immediately. These were then served to them by the junior staff member. "The Ambassador will join us shortly for dinner," said the First Secretary. While they were waiting for his arrival, the conversation covered the reason for their visit and the comfort of the hotel where they were staying in Casablanca. The door opened and in walked the British Ambassador to Morocco; a slightly stooping, but avuncular figure in a three-piece suit, which had probably seen better days!

"This is our new Ambassador, gentlemen, His Excellency John William Richmond Shakespeare," said the First Secretary by way of a formal introduction. "As you will know he only took up his new posting here last week," he added. The three colleagues took it in turn to shake the Ambassador's hand.

A set of double doors were then opened and they were shown into the dining room by the junior official, who then left. They sat down at the table, which had been laid with the best cutlery and glass available at the Embassy. A Moroccan waiter then appeared to serve the first course of the evening. It was an excellent meal, complemented by fine French wines; first a clear soup followed by a small fish dish, then an aromatic Moroccan lamb casserole. The meal was completed with some Moroccan pastries and a tasty orange dessert. As an excellent coffee and a choice of digestifs and cigars were served, Edwards thought to himself "Well this dinner was paid for by the British taxpayer. But then I am a major British taxpayer too!"

Edwards, as the senior company representative present, had been seated to the right of the Ambassador and briefed him about their visit, and about the mining project that they wished to bid for, to the Moroccan Government. He realised that the Ambassador had already been well briefed by the Foreign Office in London. He had asked some very pertinent questions, which showed both knowledge and an intelligent understanding about what they were doing there. "I have not yet presented my Diplomatic Credentials to His Majesty the King of Morocco," said the British Ambassador. "But I have arranged for us all to meet the Minister of Energy and Mines, at his Ministry, tomorrow morning at eleven o'clock. My First Secretary will give you the address of the Ministry. I will meet you there at ten-thirty so that we can group our forces before going in."

Edwards was delighted; here was a man who took immediate action. He began to suspect that the Ambassador, because of his breadth of knowledge, had probably held some kind of responsible position in British Intelligence. "Thank you for your support, sir," he said. Then, because he could not help himself he asked the obvious question. "Tell me about your name. Are you actually related to William Shakespeare?"

The Ambassador looked at him and smiled. "That has always worried me too," he replied. "Some years ago my wife insisted that we look very carefully into this matter. She employed an expert to fully examine the position. Unfortunately, he came back with the answer that I am not, in any way, related to the Great Bard of Avon!"

3

After this excellent dinner, the three colleagues got back into their car, to be driven back to their hotel in Casablanca. Henry sat beside the driver, at the front of the car, and conversed with him all the way, in a mixture of French and Arabic. As they neared Casablanca, Henry turned around to his two colleagues, sitting at the back of the car, with a big grin on his face. "How about if we go and try to find Rick's Cafe and have a nightcap?" he asked them. Edwards knew that Henry liked classic films and that he was actually referring to the 1942 film of "Casablanca," in which Humphrey Bogart played Rick Blaine, an American expatriate living in Casablanca during the Second World War. He owned Rick's Café, the most popular nightclub in the city. One evening his former lover, played by Ingrid Bergman, arrived in his Café with her new husband. Her husband was fleeing from Nazi-occupied Europe and Casablanca was still a city controlled by the Free French government, and was on the much-used escape route out to America. The Casablanca of that time was filled with such refugees and with many spies!

"I don't want to disappoint you Henry, but I don't think that it exists," replied Edwards.

"Well we can go to a few places, to try and find out," said Henry.

"Well maybe one place," said Edwards. "We have an early start in the morning and we have to keep a clear head for the meeting with the Minister."

There was a torrent of French conversation from the front seats and then Henry turned around again. "This guy thinks he knows a good place to take us to," he said. "He says that usually there are a lot of pretty girls there as well!"

"Ok Henry, just one bar then," responded Edwards.

Suitably encouraged, Henry then gave his truly awful impression of Humphrey Bogart: "Of all the gin joints, in all the towns, in all the World, she walks into mine," he drawled.

"And he hasn't even had one nightcap yet!" Edwards joked to his colleague sitting next to him.

The next morning they were all trying to recover from a hangover; they had indeed sampled Casablanca's night life, by visiting a number of bars, as Henry had wanted. An early, large breakfast, washed down with lots of coffee, seemed to help. Soon they were in the car again, speeding back towards Rabat. They found the right Ministry building without difficulty and parked there to wait for the British Ambassador to arrive. There was no mistaking his car; a large Daimler with the Union Jack flying from its right-hand front wing. It was a fine sunny day and they spoke together in the car park, before entering the building, to plan their tactics. They decided that the Ambassador would speak first to introduce their company and then they would speak in turn, to explain how they could help with the mining project that the Moroccan Government had planned.

On entering the building, they were shown to the Minister's suite of rooms. There they were received by the Minister's Private Secretary, who asked them to sit and wait in the Outer Office, where he sat behind his own ornate desk. Around the walls, in typical Arab style, were a number of long, low sofas. Suddenly, the tall, double doors to the Minister's inner office burst open and the Minister himself, in an immaculate three-piece suit, strode forward towards the British Ambassador. He had a huge smile on his face and he shook the Ambassador's hand very warmly. He then embraced him and in the French fashion, kissed him on both cheeks! The Ambassador, like any Englishman, was clearly a little put off by such an intimate greeting!

"Your Excellency," said the Minister in a loud voice and in perfect English. "We, the Moroccan Government, are deeply honoured to receive you, as the direct descendant of the most famous Poet and Playwright in the World, William Shakespeare!" Edwards waited with bated breath; what would the Ambassador do now as he had been so wrongly identified? The new Ambassador decided that he would accept the Minister's adulation; after all, it might help in the future relations with his Moroccan Government!

He paused for a few seconds, then he smiled. "It is so very kind of you to say that to me, Minister," was all that he said.

The Minister then formally conducted the Ambassador into his Inner Office, followed by the three company representatives. He fussed around the Ambassador, making sure that he was comfortable on one of the large sofas inside his Inner Office and then, finally, took his seat behind his great desk. The three company colleagues sat on one of the other long sofas. His Private Secretary arranged for Arabic coffee to be brought in for them all. At last, the Private Secretary closed the great double doors behind him and sat down, on a hard chair beside the Minister's desk, to take some notes of the meeting. The Minister promptly forgot that he spoke fluent English and insisted instead on speaking in French which, after Arabic, was the second official language of Morocco!

4

The Ambassador's French was fortunately perfect. Edwards tried to follow his explanation of why he was here and the company that the three businessmen with him represented. Unfortunately, Edwards had, by now, forgotten most of his schoolboy French. Finally, the Ambassador finished his speech and the Minister responded. The Minister turned to the three company men sitting together on the large sofa, to hear what they had to say! Edwards paused as he really did not know what to do. Henry coughed. Then, in his perfect French, he took over their part of the meeting! Edwards merely nodded at what he thought was the most appropriate points. Soon the Minister and Henry seem to be having a most friendly and animated conversation. Edwards sat back. "It is a wise man who knows when to keep silent," he thought. He mused to himself. Suddenly some words came into his mind: "The perfect spy has one mainly closed mouth, but many active eyes and ears!"

The meeting over, the four British men came out of the building together. "Well I think that the meeting went very well," said the Ambassador. He had not seemed to notice that Henry had done all the talking and that neither Edwards, nor his other colleague, had said a single word. Edwards hoped that the Minister had not noticed this either. He made a mental note that, in the afternoon, he had to sit down with Henry in a quiet place and transcribe a note, translated from the French, of a summary of what the Ambassador had said at the meeting; he would also be interested to know the full content of Henry's long and friendly conversation with the Minister. The three of them said farewell to the Ambassador, who was now taking his car back to his Embassy, and thanked him warmly for all his help. They climbed back into their car for the drive back to their hotel in Casablanca. They were due to fly back to London the following morning.

International business is like war; you meet hostile, competitive armies and navies in the field. When you are working for a large group of companies, it is like a chess game, played on a very large board, which can cover the whole World. You certainly need inside information, when you can get it, and good judgement. You also need a consistent Strategy, but always flexible Tactics.

From Henry's conversation with the Minister, he reported that he thought that the Minister had been quite honest with him. The Minister had mentioned the names of two large and capable French companies, who had already been to Rabat to meet with him. Henry also reported that the Minister seemed particularly attracted to one of them and Henry had guessed that this particular French company had made some offer by which the Minister would most certainly benefit financially, if they happened to win the contract. Henry added that, in order to keep up the pretence of competition, the two French companies had probably already agreed which one would win the contract and the winner would then compensate the loser for its efforts in making a non-competitive bid.

This information was perhaps the deciding factor; the mining company, within Edwards's contracting group, decided not to pursue this particular contract. They would have had to be involved in getting a good and expensive translation of all the documents that the Moroccan Government had issued, in French. Then they would have had to get all the details of their bid proposal also translated into French. It would have been just a too expensive and time consuming operation. It was better perhaps to confine themselves to countries where English was a commercially acceptable language. In war, if the enemy already has stronger forces than you in the field, it is best not to attack, but to retire in order to fight another day!

But Edwards did not forget his entertaining visit to Morocco and his meeting with the then excellent British Ambassador there, who, without protest nor delay, and for the good of his country, bravely accepted the mantle of being the direct descendant of the great Bard of Avon!

EGYPTIAN ROULETTE

"From the heights of these Pyramids, forty centuries look down on us" – from a speech by Napoleon Bonaparte during his Expedition to Egypt in 1798.

1

The steady rhythm of its twin paddle wheels propelled the antique vessel along the river. It was late Spring in a year in the early 1980's. Edwards sat with his wife under the large white awning stretched over the rear, upper deck. He had checked the temperature a few minutes before, on the gauge which had been thoughtfully provided. It had been 120 degrees Fahrenheit in the shade! But the air was bone-dry and one hardly felt the intense heat at all. On both banks of the River Nile, the lush vegetation reached down to the water. But Edwards knew that this view was a chimera. As they had been landing at Luxor, the view from the aircraft's window had been spectacular. Desert, a narrow strip of green, then next the broad river, to be followed by another narrow strip of vegetation, and then the mighty desert again.

The waiter was dressed in a spotless, white jacket and a fez; he had brought them Afternoon Tea. A few small sandwiches, straight from the refrigerator, an apology for an English Scone with cream and strawberry jam, followed by some Dundee Cake, all washed down with a large pot of Assam Tea. As they slowly passed a small village on the West Bank of the river, the children came out to shout and wave enthusiastically at the vessel. Just as enthusiastically, Edwards and his wife waved back. "Despite their poverty, they are so friendly," thought Edwards.

This was a holiday, but he had already experienced several business trips to Egypt. He and his wife had been attracted to come on this holiday after they had seen John Guillermin's 1978 film of Agatha Christie's "Death on the Nile", with Peter Ustinov playing the famous Belgian detective Hercule Poirot. They had picked this paddle steamer, rather than a modern Nile cruiser, which usually had the luxury of a swimming pool on its upper deck, so that they could perhaps recapture the experience of a 1930's traveller to Egypt, who was visiting the country to see its wonders.

By now the routine of this trip had been established; the vessel moored overnight, at a convenient place, close to the next spectacular sight that they were to visit. They got used to getting up at 5 o'clock for a Continental Breakfast. Then it was out for the short journey to the next Ancient Egyptian site, to complete their viewing, before the heat of the sun became impossible to bear. Back on the vessel, a light lunch was served in the oak-panelled Dining Room, followed by an hour's rest in their small suite, which was equipped with its own lavatory and shower. Then it was up on deck, as the vessel got under way to the next site, at which point, Afternoon Tea was served.

As they travelled slowly south between Luxor and Aswan they had already visited the temples of Edfu, dedicated to the chief falcon-headed god Horus, Esna, dedicated to the ram-headed god Khnum, the god of the source of the Nile and Kom Ombo, which belonged to the crocodile god Sobek. Ahead lay the temple of Philae, located on an island and dedicated to the great goddess Isis, the brother of Osiris and the mother of Horus. After a dusty journey from Aswan, they would then see the temple of Abu Simbel, carved out of the solid rock, by the great Pharaoh Ramesses the Second.

Edwards smiled to himself as he remembered the first morning of their holiday. They had landed at dead of night at Cairo Airport and had been taken to their hotel for the first four nights of their visit. It was the Mena House Hotel at Giza, just outside Cairo. Built originally by the then Egyptian ruler as a hunting lodge in 1869, it had then been converted into a hotel by an English couple in 1886. In 1890, the hotel opened Egypt's first swimming pool. Since then the hotel had been renovated and expanded several times; its famous guests had included the future King George V, Sir Arthur Conan Doyle, Agatha Christie and Winston Churchill. Exhausted by their long journey, they had fallen into bed.

The next morning Edwards's wife had got up first; she pulled back the heavy curtains. Then she gave a gasp and tottered backwards in shock! Directly outside their window rose up the massive shape of the Great Pyramid of the Pharaoh Cheops! After that they just had to go inside it; the climb up the Grand Gallery had been hard but, to stand at last, in the bare stone King's Chamber, with its great empty sarcophagus and to feel the massive weight of stone above and around you, had been truly awe-inspiring!

They had visited the Egyptian Museum in the centre of Cairo and gazed at the golden death mask of Tutankhamun. They had also visited the Pyramids again one evening for the Son et Lumiere and had found out just how cold the desert could be at night. They had taken a trip to Saqqara to visit the even older "Step Pyramids" on which the Ancient Egyptian builders had learnt their craft. Then there had been the short flight to Luxor and the visit to its temple, and the adjoining Temple of Karnak. Edwards had stood awestruck among the great columns of Karnak's massive Hypostyle Hall. The Karnak Temple complex was so huge that the entire Vatican could be easily lost within it!

They had returned to Karnak, at night, for another program of Son et Lumiere. They sat in complete darkness, waiting for the show to start. Edwards gazed upwards. Surely, nowhere but in the desert, could the stars be so bright and so plentiful? Then the program started, illuminating each part of the vast Temple complex in turn. Edwards could not help it; the hairs on the back of his neck stood up and he started to tremble, not from the cold from the desert, but from the sheer magnificence of the floodlit scene.

The next day they had visited the Valley of the Kings, crossing slowly to the West Bank of the Nile on a felucca. They had visited a number of the magnificently decorated Pharaoh's tombs, but inside the smaller and plainer Tutankhamun's Tomb, there had been a strange incident. A female visitor had started screaming! The Egyptian guard outside had rushed inside, drawing a large, automatic pistol from his flowing robes. But this was no attack on a tourist; she had just seen a very large rat, scuttling its way, around the sarcophagus of the long-dead Pharaoh!

At dinner each evening Edwards and his wife had played a game together; which of their fellow travellers would not appear tomorrow morning for breakfast? Edwards called the game "Egyptian Roulette," and if one of them guessed correctly, then the other had to buy the bottle of wine at dinner the following evening. Edwards was by now almost virtually immune to the bacteria of Egypt, but you could never be sure who might suddenly be affected, and where and when that might happen. His worst experience had been after concluding a contract to build two new bridges over the River Nile in Cairo. They were working in partnership with an Egyptian company and its owner had taken him out for dinner, with his colleagues, to an excellent

Cairo restaurant to celebrate. He had woken up, during the night, with violent stomach cramps and severe diarrhoea. He was booked on an early morning British Airways flight back home the following day and he had just managed to pack and make it to Cairo Airport. Fortunately, he was booked into First Class and he had been able to occupy the First Class lavatory during most of the flight!

2

Nearly two years before, Edwards had been asked to visit Cairo to research the financial situation for this forthcoming project. The City of Cairo was to be the buyer for these same two new bridges over the Nile, but the whole project was to be supervised by the Ministry of Public Works, and would be guaranteed by the Government of Egypt. The Ministry of Public Works would take the lead on deciding who would build them. One of the construction companies that Edwards looked after wanted to bid for the project, and a full Finance Package was also required to be submitted at the same time as the bid. The provision of this Package was the responsibility of Edwards.

This had to provide finance for the full price of the project that they had tendered. Not having visited Cairo before, Edwards had asked for advice from some of his colleagues, who knew the country well. Their advice was clear; stay in the most recently completed Cairo hotel, as the older hotels had by now acquired the bacteria in their kitchens, which would lay him low with the so called "Gippy Tummy." So he booked himself into the most recently completed Ramses Hilton Hotel.

He arrived at Cairo Airport in the evening; he had a smooth journey through Immigration and then through Customs. Just to be sure, he had not checked in a suitcase. Instead he had all his needs in his "Carry-On Bag" which had already visited many parts of the World. He exited the Airport Terminal to look for a taxi; clustered around the door was a large mob of people who wanted desperately to sell things to this new visitor to their country. Edwards pushed his way through until a small, rather pathetic-looking boy of about ten years old, in ragged clothes, had touched his arm. He said something to Edwards in English; not hearing it properly the first time, Edwards leant down and asked him to repeat it. "Would you like my sister, sir?" was what the boy had asked.

Edwards was horrified: "No, No!" he said firmly.

The boy looked up at him with pleading eyes. "Would you like me then, sir" he had asked. Edwards quickened his pace towards the Taxi Rank.

During this visit Edwards had met with a number of Egyptian construction companies; it was necessary for them to choose an Egyptian company for them to partner with on this project, as they would carry out the simpler, but still essential, construction work. The Egyptian Government would want Egyptian goods and services to be used to the maximum extent possible, but there was not yet any Egyptian company that could design, build and take full responsibility for completing the two large, complex bridges that were required.

Edwards also had to meet the relevant officials from the City of Cairo's Engineering Department, and the officials from the Egyptian Government's Ministry of Public Works and Ministry of Finance. The latter Government department was relevant because they were responsible for advising on, and then finally approving, the Finance Proposal that had been put forward with the winning bid.

Edwards had found the Egyptians that he had met, to be friendly and talented; they knew what was possible and did not seem to indulge in outlandish demands. To his surprise a number of them were highly educated women, who held senior positions in the bureaucracy. They did not even wear an Islamic head scarf and seemed very relaxed meeting and talking alone with an Englishman. Slowly he began to understand the role of women in the liberal Muslim Egyptian society; as wives and mothers they were considered just as important as men and usually made all the final, important decisions in matters of home and family.

Returning to London, he began to put together the Finance Package that would be required. But he also had to answer many questions from his colleagues, particularly about financial aspects of the expected project, and the terms of any contract with the Egyptians. A large part of the British content of their bid would be covered by the British Government's Export Credit scheme, which would guarantee repayment to the lending bank. The rest of the British content, and the Egyptian content, would have to be covered with a bank loan on commercial terms. Hopefully, this would be given by the same bank, because the separate guaranteed Export Credit loan was a very attractive piece of banking business, which many banks were very willing to make available. Edwards carefully selected a British bank willing to lend the rest of the money needed to Egypt, on the best commercial loan terms.

3

Their bid for constructing the two bridges was finally submitted, together with the Financing Proposal that Edwards had produced. They had been asked to submit their bid in Pounds Sterling for the British content and in Egyptian Pounds for the goods and services that would be provided within Egypt itself. As always they were acutely aware of the competition and, fortunately, the Ministry of Public Works published a list of the bids that had been submitted. Their competitors came from four different countries: France, Holland, Germany and the United States. The Egyptian company that they had chosen as their business partner, seemed to be getting good commercial intelligence, and reported that the British bid was well favoured, but that the French contractor's price was just below theirs.

Then, one Monday morning, Edwards's telephone rang; it was the Project Manager responsible for their bid within the group's bridge building company. "Have you heard the latest?" he asked.

"No," replied Edwards, expecting to be asked to make some simple adjustment to what they had submitted. As the man continued, the impact of what he was saying hit Edwards like a sledgehammer!

"In their wisdom," the Project Manager continued, "the Ministry of Public Works has asked every contractor, who has submitted a bid, now to submit a separate bid for the overseas sourced element of the project, denominated in each of the four other currencies of their competitors, together with a Financing Package, in each of those currencies."

Edwards was amazed; he had never heard of anything so ridiculous. Just to be sure, he checked. "Do you mean," he asked "that we now have to submit four additional bids in French Francs, Dutch Guilders, German Deutsch Marks and United States Dollars, together with a Finance Proposal in each of those currencies?"

"That's right!" came the firm reply.

"They must be mad," said Edwards. "They will never be able to come to any decision on that basis in a thousand years!"

"Well, it is Egypt," was the quiet reply. "I personally think that there is something to do with corruption going on here!"

"It is just Egyptian Roulette," responded Edwards. "Put the ball into the wheel and see where it lands!"

"By the way, you have a week to do this before we have to resubmit our four additional bids and Financial Proposals!" replied the Project Manager.

Edwards was, by now, used to his "Missions Impossible," but this one took up all his time. He had to shut down all his other work and stayed in the office late every night, to tidy up details and to constantly rethink how he could complete this immense task. Within the first day he had worked very hard to identify a French, Dutch, German and American bank, with offices in London, who were able to take the British Government Export Credit guarantee for the British content of the project, and who also seemed willing to lend the extra sums needed to Egypt, without a British Government guarantee. Furthermore they seemed very willing to support him and his company, and provide all the finance needed in their own currency.

But much more was needed to be done than that. Because his company would now be paid in a foreign currency, while they wanted to be paid Pounds Sterling, Edwards had to work out how he could cover the foreign exchange risk between the Pound and the foreign currency involved. If the Pound appreciated in value against the foreign currency, over the period of the contract, his company would end up making a loss on the project! On the third day, the Dutch bank reported to Edwards that their Head Office in Amsterdam had been put under heavy pressure by the Dutch construction company competing for the project. They had asked the Dutch bank not to deal with their British competitor. But by then it was too late; Edwards had already got them committed to supporting the British bid!

Edwards worked hard on the question of recalculating their bid, denominated in Pounds Sterling, into the other four currencies required, having regard to future possible currency exchange rate movements. After all, they needed to end up with Pounds Sterling, as that was the currency in which their costs had to be paid. Edwards had to do a very quick study of the Forward Foreign Exchange Market in all four of these foreign currencies. This was the market, run by the banks, which offered to buy or sell various foreign currencies against the Pound Sterling, on certain future dates. The problem was that the market was reasonably efficient enough to be able to sell forward the foreign currency that they would gradually acquire over the four year construction period for the two bridges, for the first twelve months of construction. But then, the possibility of selling this currency forward over the longer periods required, became much more uncertain. Also the costs of carrying out such a major financial operation were heavy and had to be included in their price.

Edwards came up with a possible solution to this problem and spoke to the Project Manager about it; "If we win the contract in one of these foreign currencies," he told him, "then we could borrow all the future income in foreign currency at Day One, and convert it into the Pounds Sterling that we need at a known exchange rate. Then we could pay off the loan as we received the foreign currency payments over the contract period." But this scheme too could be costly, because the interest that they would be charged on the total contract sum they had borrowed, would be more than any interest they could earn on the Pounds that they could deposit, before they needed them. The conclusion of their discussions was clear; that for each foreign currency bid they now had to put together, they would have to increase their price to account for the extra costs and risks involved, in possibly being awarded the overseas part of the contract in a currency other than the Pounds Sterling that they needed.

Fortunately, the deadline for the submission of the rebids was then postponed and they were given another three weeks of time to put in their new multi-currency proposals. So it was that it was decided that Edwards had immediately to visit Cairo again;

this time, the owner of their Egyptian construction partner, would use his influence and contacts to get Edwards to meet the relevant officials at the Ministry of Finance. Then he could explain to them how this request, from the Ministry of Public Works, could only serve to increase the costs of the project, and the price that Egypt had to pay. Only the Ministry of Finance should be able to understand the financial implications of this major change in the bidding process.

The day after he arrived, he met with the owner of their Egyptian partner company. The man spoke excellent English and by now, Edwards had got to know him quite well. "I really cannot understand why the Ministry for Public Works has decided to ask for all this to be done," said Edwards.

The Egyptian looked at him wisely and smiled. "It is really quite simple, my friend," he said. "Ours is the best and cheapest bid but the Minister and his senior officials are working for our French competitor, and the Minister has decided to try and muddy the waters of the Nile, in this way. Out of all this confusion, he hopes that he can still push for the French to win the contract and he and his officials will then get their big pay-off!"

4

So Edwards had a fairly relaxed week in Cairo; he had to wait for his Egyptian business partner to arrange for him to meet the relevant officials at the Ministry of Finance, who hopefully would take an objective view of what he had to say. When it became clear that he had some free time, he was determined to use it. One free afternoon, he took a taxi from his hotel to the Egyptian Museum. He wanted to see again the ancient treasures, found by Howard Carter, in the tomb of the young Pharaoh Tutankhamun in 1922. Edwards had first seen some of these items at the British Museum, when they had been exhibited there, in 1972. He spent the whole afternoon in the Egyptian Museum and a lot of that time was spent looking, for his second time, at the marvellous Tutankhamun artefacts. When the Museum was closing, he had to leave; he then spent some time in the busy street outside, trying to hail a taxi. At last he got one to stop; it was an old, rusting vehicle, with several dents in its sides, and without any air conditioning. Cooling was supplied by keeping all the car windows completely open!

It was only after he had been driven a few hundred yards that he found out another major disadvantage of this particular taxi. Not only was the driver taciturn and uncommunicative, but his favourite occupation seemed to be violently spitting at other vehicles and their drivers that were passing him by. He was also driving at the top speed that the heavy traffic would allow. The result was that the slipstream caught hold of some of his discharges and directed them towards the back of the taxi. After a few minutes, Edwards moved to the other end of the back seat to try and avoid the flying spittle! Needless to say, when they at last arrived safely back at Edwards's hotel, he was not minded to give the taxi driver a big tip. His next action was to go up to his room, in order to carefully wash his face.

On the Thursday morning he, at last, got his opportunity. With his Egyptian business partner, they visited the Ministry of Finance. There they met with three senior officials and Edwards described to them, not only the complexity of the new demands from the Ministry of Public Works, but also how these new demands were bound to add to the old price that they had originally tendered. "It will be the same for all the other competing contractors," he had said. He added that this was not the way forward to try and get good value for the Egyptian people. One of the officials was making copious notes, and Edwards was encouraged because the officials seemed to fully understand what Edwards was telling them. He answered a few questions from them, which he thought were very sensible ones and then the meeting was at an end.

Outside the Egyptian contractor turned to him; "I thought that the meeting went very well," he said. "I will follow it up with a call on a good friend who is also a good friend of the Minister of Finance, and we will see what then will happen. Let me take you for a light lunch and then you can have my car and driver for the rest of the day. I will take a taxi back home." Over the lunch, Edwards told his Egyptian friend about his recent visit to the Egyptian Museum, but leaving out a description of his taxi driver!

They then discussed where Edwards could go that afternoon; "I think that a visit to the step-pyramids at Saqqara would much interest you," said the Egyptian. "My driver will take great care of you and deposit you back at your hotel. He is a good man." So Edwards had the use of an air-conditioned luxury car and driver to take him to the site of these pyramids that were much older than those at Giza.

Saqqara is only some twenty miles south of Cairo and is the vast, ancient burial ground for the Ancient Egyptian capital city of Memphis. It has a number of pyramids, some of which have now collapsed, which served as tombs for the Pharaohs of the Third Dynasty. Around the vast site are many older, simpler tombs, dating back to the First and Second Dynasties. The Saqqara pyramids are built up on a "step principle", with layers build up on layers, as the Ancient Egyptians had not yet perfected building the pure pyramid form. The most spectacular is the Step Pyramid of the Pharaoh Djoser, designed and built by the Royal Architect Imhotep. It was completed in about 2,660 BCE. Edwards was taken straight to the centre of the site by his driver, who stopped next to the Pyramid of Djoser. Nearby was a small low building, which the driver walked to and then knocked on its door. A man in a white flowing robe came out and the driver talked to him; still sitting in the car

Edwards noted the quick movement of some bank notes being passed over. Then the two men approached the car.

"This is the Superintendent of the Site," explained the driver in perfect English. "He is very happy to show you a few of the things that are here."

The Superintendent also spoke excellent English; so, while the driver waited in the car, he gave Edwards a short description of the site and pointed out several of its features. He took him to one of the several simpler tombs, or Mastabas, and explained that they were not the tombs of Pharaohs but of senior Court Officials, who had gained the great honour of being buried at this Royal site. A long, narrow tunnel, led to the burial chamber, and Edwards visited several of these types of tombs. Inside each there were carvings and paintings of domestic life and nature, which had not lost any of their bright colours, despite being over four thousand years old. After that, Edwards was taken on a visit to Djoser's Pyramid itself; inside was a labyrinth of tunnels and chambers which, fortunately, the Superintendent knew very well. The passageways were decorated with blue tiles and, inside the chambers, the decorations showed the Pharaoh participating in various royal ceremonies.

As they came out of Djoser's Pyramid, into the blinding light, Edwards looked at his watch. He realised that he had already been on this visit for nearly three hours. He thanked the Superintendent profusely; but the man was not finished with him yet. "There is something else I must show you," he said. "It is something that most visitors here do not see, but I will show you."

He led Edwards towards a smaller, ruined Pyramid and some distance away, led him down some steps, and then unlocked a large iron door, with one of the keys from the bunch that he had tied around his waist. They had to bend forward to walk down a long, sloping passage with a low ceiling. They arrived into what seemed a burial chamber; the Superintendent illuminated the walls of the chamber with the powerful torch that he carried. Edwards gasped! All the walls were totally covered by magnificent, deeply-carved Hieroglyphs!

"This is the Pyramid of the Pharaoh Unas," said the Superintendent. "For him they built the first straight-edged pyramid, but it was not well built and now, as you saw, it is in ruins. But below it are these Hieroglyphs. They are taken from the Egyptian Book of the Dead."

"But how old are they?" asked Edwards.

The Superintendent made a quick calculation; "They are nearly four thousand, five hundred years old," he said. Edwards gazed in awe; the Hieroglyphs looked as if they had only been cut just yesterday!

Back in London, he waited to see if his last visit to Cairo would have any effect. Two weeks went by and they were now ready to submit their new bids in five different currencies, with five different Finance Proposals, that Edwards and his colleagues had worked very hard to prepare. They had used the extra time given to them with effect. Many things had been tidied up, but the four bids in the foreign currencies, still had to be increased because of the costs and risks involved to his construction group. One morning his telephone rang; it was the Project Manager.

"What do you think has happened now?" he asked.

"Tell me?" said Edwards, anxiously expecting some new demand from the Egyptian buyer.

"They have just cancelled their request for Bids and Finance Packages in the other four currencies of our competitors," was the reply.

"Thank God!" exclaimed Edwards, despite the fact that a lot of his recent work would now be wasted.

"And there is more news," continued the Project Manager. "Our Egyptian partner tells us that the Minister for Public Works has been removed, and demoted to be a Junior Minister in another Department."

"That is good news!" replied Edwards happily. "So his corruption has at last found him out."

"I don't think that this will help our French competitors," added the Project Manager. "I think that he was very much in their pocket!"

Two days later Edwards received another telephone call; it was from a senior civil servant, that Edwards knew well. "Don't ask any questions," said the civil servant, "but I want to tell you something in strictest confidence, of course." He then gave Edwards a list of figures which represented an adjusted final price and a new breakdown of the French contractor's final bid that they had just resubmitted! Edwards carefully wrote all this down; it was obvious to him that somehow this critical information had been intercepted from some kind of telephone communication, by the British intelligence services.

The call over, he telephoned the Managing Director of the group company involved, and fed him the figures. As a result, the British bid was readjusted, and then resubmitted. Not surprisingly, the company that Edwards looked after, won the competition for the work! Two weeks later, Edwards was back in Cairo to start the final negotiations for this construction contract, to build the two new bridges over the River Nile in Cairo.

BUMIPUTRAS

"I cannot accept this country being destroyed by selfish people who only think about themselves." – Doctor Mahathir Mohamad, Prime Minister of Malaysia.

1

Edwards was shocked. The loud, Yorkshire accented voice of the Group Director, that most people in the group of companies he worked for, despised, had been reduced to a rather pathetic whine. In fact, it was worse than that, he did not seem to be able to get his words out in a logical sequence. It was one Friday afternoon, in the late 1980s. Already people had started to drift off home early for the weekend. "Whatever is the matter?" Edwards had asked him. Like all bullies, when he was properly challenged, he collapsed and just did not know what to do!

Gradually, Edwards managed to get the full story out of him; he had been on the telephone to Kuala Lumpur, the capital city of Malaysia. He had been talking to the very powerful "bagman" of the Prime Minister of that country; the man who arranged all the Prime Minister's personal affairs, including the secret arrangements for him to receive bribes for projects awarded to certain international contractors and suppliers, by the Malaysian

Government. He also arranged for the careful handling of those bribes, so that they would remain untraceable, but still be safely invested. The subject of this telephone conversation had been a new major construction project in Malaysia, which one of the companies that Edwards assisted, was bidding for in potential competition with several other international companies.

Edwards had arranged for the financial package for this project, which enabled the Malaysians to pay for it on easy financing terms. This finance package involved an element of British Government aid money as a grant, and a long term loan backed by the British Government's Export Credit organisation. By some careful questioning of the distraught Group Director, Edwards slowly began to understand what the current problem really was. The Group Director had been told, pretty forcibly, by the Malaysian "bagman", that the terms of the loan currently on offer, were not good enough. It had to be offered for a loan period of an additional three years, and the repayments would not have to begin for at least another two years, after the so-called Grace Period currently on offer.

Furthermore, this new improved finance offer had to be with the Malaysian Prime Minister by tomorrow morning, in Malaysia. Being a Muslim country, Saturday and Sunday were normal working days. At the end of this long telephone conversation, Edwards had simply said to the Group Director, "Leave it with me," and had then put the telephone down on the miserable creature at the other end of the line.

Edwards thought quickly; what could he do now? It was already past four o'clock on a Friday afternoon. He picked up his outside line and started dialling. He managed to locate a junior civil servant, who he knew well, in the Overseas Development Administration, then the government department which administered the total British aid budget. He explained the situation quickly, and extracted a promise from the official to remain at his desk, on standby, for at least another hour. His next call was to the Government's Export Credit Guarantees Department, where he was fortunate in finding a senior official that he knew, still in his office, and who handled the entire South East Asian region. He managed to extract an offer to help get a new proposal together, on the improved terms required by the Malaysians, provided that the other relevant government departments were in agreement.

Edwards's next call was to the Foreign and Commonwealth Office, where he managed to locate someone fairly junior to speak to about this project. He explained the situation, and again, extracted from them a promise to stay at their desk. Then he called the Department of Trade and Industry; he managed to locate a senior civil servant there that already knew about this project and supported it. From this official, he obtained a promise of full support. Edwards had by now geared himself up, to make the last and most difficult call of all, to Her Majesty's

Treasury! In the "Corridors of Power" of the British Government, within which Edwards worked, the in-joke about the Treasury was that if you called them you would always get the same response: "The answer is No! What was the question?"

Governments of various Political Parties and their Ministers might come and go, but the Permanent Government of the Civil Service continued. Just then his telephone rang; it was the Group Director, who seemed to have begun to recover a little from the verbal beating he had received on the telephone line from Kuala Lumpur.

"What is happening?" he asked.

"I am dealing with it," replied Edwards. "There is no point in calling me. I will call you just as soon as I have a result."

"I think that I had better call the High Commissioner in Kuala Lumpur," said the Director.

"There is absolutely no point in doing that," said Edwards. "The decision will be made here in London, and if there is one made tonight, then the High Commissioner will be informed by a secure, overnight message!"

Before speaking to the Treasury, Edwards had already obtained the tacit support of the officials he had already spoken to, in the four other Government departments. He therefore had some ready "ammunition" which he could now use, in what, he knew, would be a difficult conversation. Fortunately, he managed to find a relevant, but, again, fairly junior, Treasury official still at his desk. The man probably regretted ever picking up his telephone! He, of course, first tried to put off any decision until Monday. "That is no good," Edwards told him. "We are dealing at the highest level in Malaysia and they are demanding an answer immediately." He then went through, very carefully, his four previous conversations with the officials in the other British Government departments.

The Treasury official began to crumble; he demanded to speak to the officials responsible for the government aid, and the long-term loan. Edwards suggested that he did that, at once, and gave him their names and telephone numbers. He then asked him to call him back immediately, with the final decision. It was just twenty minutes later, when his direct line rang. It was the Treasury official saying that, between them, they had taken the positive decision that Edwards needed. Edwards thanked him profusely; he now knew that, in certain circumstances, and if forced to do so, the "Wheels of Government" could work very quickly if needed!

Edwards's next call was to the Foreign and Commonwealth Office, to arrange for the secure, encrypted message to be sent out to Kuala Lumpur overnight, giving the new improved financial terms that the British Government would now offer. Since Malaysia was a Commonwealth country, the British Ambassador there was known as a High Commissioner, and it was to the current High Commissioner, Sir Nicholas Spreckley, that this confidential, encrypted message would now be sent. It would contain instructions to deliver the new improved finance terms, tomorrow morning in Kuala Lumpur, to the Malaysian Prime Minister's office. Out of courtesy, Edwards then telephoned the senior official at the Department of Trade and Industry, to tell him the good news.

Having completed his task, Edwards called the Group Director to report to him that the new improved terms were, even now, on their way to Kuala Lumpur, and that the High Commissioner would be asked, as an absolute priority, to deliver these new terms to the Prime Minister of Malaysia in the morning. The Group Director seemed to almost sob with joy down the line but, as always, he did not thank Edwards for what he had achieved!

He was beginning to recover his composure. "I will have to send a case of Champagne to Lady Spreckley," he said. "I called the High Commission and they woke her up to speak to me!" Edwards realised with horror that, because of the major time difference, it was actually the middle of the night in Kuala Lumpur. "Sir Nicholas was not in the High Commission," went on the Director. He laughed nervously. "He was actually down in Malaysia's Port Klang, in his full dress uniform, as the Royal

Yacht Britannia is just docking there, with the Queen on board! They are all beginning to assemble for the Commonwealth Heads of Government Meeting next week."

Edwards was appalled; "I told you that I would deal with this, and that there was no need for you to call the High Commission!" he said sharply. He found it very difficult to hide his contempt for this man! Edwards slammed his telephone down and sat back in his chair; he felt pleased with himself. Another of his "Missions Impossible" had been achieved, and done very quickly.

Then a picture came into his mind; it was of Lady Spreckley, perhaps in her hair curlers and nightdress, trying to get her "Beauty Sleep" before meeting Her Majesty the Queen, the following day. Then she had been woken up with an annoying, unnecessary and inconsequential telephone call from Edwards's pompous Group Director. Edwards laughed out loud! He then tried hard to imagine the disjointed and irrational telephone conversation that would have taken place. He would certainly have liked to have listened in to it. He smiled to himself: he had concluded that, even a case of the best Champagne, was not really sufficient to fully compensate Lady Spreckley for this totally frustrating and irrelevant, late-night interruption, to her slumbers!

2

It was only some six months later, that Edwards again became involved, at the front end, with another project in Malaysia. One of the companies that he looked after, was in joint venture with another major British construction group, in an effort to build a major dam project in Malaysia. Edwards's opposite number in this other company, was taking the lead on putting together the finance to offer Malaysia, in order to win this project for Britain. But, at the vital time, he had decided to take an extended holiday abroad, and Edwards was asked to cover for him during the time that he was to be away. A meeting on this project was called by the Overseas Development Administration, which then administered the British Aid Budget, to decide the amount of the British grant that could be offered, in order to try and obtain this attractive construction contract for Britain.

In his colleague's absence, Edwards was asked to attend this meeting as the sole representative of the construction consortium. He found himself in a large meeting room at this Government Department, facing a numerous contingent of civil servants, including some from various other Government departments. The meeting was chaired by the third most senior official in the Overseas Development Administration, supported by several of his assistants. The discussions opened with a critical appraisal of why government support, including the aid money, was needed for this project. Edwards, because of his limited knowledge of the project, soon found himself getting out of his depth. The conversation then turned to the amount of aid money that was required to try and win this project for Britain. Then the senior civil servant, chairing the meeting, struck! Turning to Edwards he asked politely: "Do you know the level of Agency Fees that are included in the price of this contract please?"

Edwards knew immediately exactly what he was being asked. What was the level of payments, within the contract price, that had been included in order to win the contract? In other words, what was being demanded, as bribes, by the corrupt senior politicians and officials in Malaysia, to go into their own pockets, through secret bank accounts? It was a fact that such bribes were required, for them to award this construction project to the construction consortium, of which Edwards's company was a part. This was not abnormal; construction companies from all over the world knew that they had to make such payments in order to get work in Malaysia, and in many other countries. Fortunately, Edwards knew this figure. But he fixed the senior official with his gaze. "Could we talk about this privately please?" he asked.

The senior official indicated that they could talk outside, and they both left the meeting. They went to his private office and the official firmly shut his door. "Do you really need to know that figure?" asked Edwards, as soon as they had sat down. "You realise that it is very sensitive information!"

"Of course," replied the senior official. "But, if I am to help you with this, I will need to know honestly what the figure is."

"Very well," said Edwards and gave him the actual percentage needed, based on the total contract amount, that he had been told. He saw a look of slight shock cross the official's face, at the high level of the percentage. But then he nodded, and they returned to the main meeting room. Nothing more was then said about this matter in the meeting, and when his colleague in the other construction group returned from his holiday, Edwards asked to see him, to tell him exactly what had happened.

His colleague, in the other company, accepted what he was told. "Now that they know the truth, I can work with them properly, to see what they can really offer us," he had said. He had done that very effectively and within a few months, a compromise financing package had been worked out, which included an amount of British Government aid money, but only to be used to subsidise the interest rate on the loan that the British Government were supporting. As a result this major dam project was awarded to the British consortium, and then successfully completed.

Edwards did not like the need to provide hidden payments to corrupt foreign politicians and government officials, in many overseas countries. But he knew that construction companies, and major suppliers of goods and services, from every other country in the world, had to make such corrupt payments in order to get any work. The American Government had, of course, passed legislation some years before to stop such practises, but American companies still had to somehow get around this legislation if they were to win any contracts. They did this by working harder to much better hide such payments; usually they appointed a local company or representative, to make such corrupt payments within the country concerned, rather than be involved, in any direct way, themselves.

Totalitarian countries, like Russia and China, had no compunction about making such payments, sometimes in cash, if required, and they spread their largesse very widely. In fact, with the high rates of bribery that they offered, they often created a competition for companies from other countries, who then had to offer even higher percentage levels of bribes, in order to win any contracts that had been opened up to international competition.

Above all, Edwards was a patriot; he wanted his group of companies to succeed and for the British economy to get the benefit of major exports. But it was a continuing, and sometimes desperate battle. International trade was like a continuous war, fought between the major companies, which supplied the world with large construction projects, and with manufactured items such as aircraft and power stations. He knew that even international agreements to stop such corrupt practices, would never succeed; there would always be companies, and governments, who would break the rules. There would also always be corrupt politicians and officials who would demand bribes, either from international companies, or from their own people, in order to give them the simplest favour, or small contracts to supply local goods and services. That, unfortunately, was the real world, and the Human Condition!

Years later in the late 1990's, Edwards was now working within a Government department and employed as an expert on financial matters. Part of his job was to give answers to Parliamentary Questions. These were questions that were put verbally, or in writing, by Members of Parliament, to Ministers and Prime Ministers, in the House of Commons. They came as friendly questions, asked by members of their own party to enable the Minister or Prime Minister to make a statement about a certain matter, or as hostile questions from Opposition Parties. The general public seemed to think that such questions were answered by each Ministers themselves, from their own knowledge. The truth was that, if they had notice of the question, the answers were written for them by civil servants, who had a far greater knowledge of the situation, but had to put themselves in the "political shoes" of the answering Minister.

One day, as part of his new job, Edwards was asked to provide an answer to a hostile Parliamentary Question on the very dam project, in Malaysia, that he had worked on, many years before. The project had now become a contentious issue, and had been the subject of several government inquiries. Edwards asked to see the very senior official, to whom he directly reported. "I cannot answer this question," he had told him. "I know too much about this project and I find that I have a Conflict of Interest."

"I understand," had been the reply. "I will ask someone else to answer this particular Parliamentary Question instead of you!"

3

Before he had left the construction group, to enter Government as an adviser, Edwards had been asked by the Managing Director of one of the companies he looked after, to do some research for him. This man was a highly intelligent and capable individual, and he had noticed that, on his many visits to Malaysia, the name of one man kept being mentioned. He asked Edwards to investigate the background of this particular individual. His name was Anwar Ibrahim, and he was the current Minister of Education.

It seemed that many people in Malaysia trusted him more than any other of their politicians, and that he seemed, surprisingly, to be a reasonably honest man. Edwards did his research and produced a report on this individual. He had found that Anwar Ibrahim was a devout Muslim, had been a student radical in his university days, now led the Youth Wing of the ruling political party and had spoken out against the corruption and nepotism in Malaysia. Edwards had mentioned his report to a senior civil servant that he knew well, who immediately asked for a copy.

A few weeks later, the official had telephoned Edwards back. "Your report is very good." he had said. "We really know very little about this man. Do you mind if I distribute it to some of my colleagues who are interested in this kind of information?"

"Not at all," Edwards had replied, knowing full well that his work would now be passed on to the British intelligence services.

Over the following years, he had then watched the rapid rise, and then fall, of Anwar Ibrahim. The man had been promoted to Minister of Finance, and then to become Deputy Prime Minister of Malaysia. He seemed to be trusted by the long-serving Prime Minister, Doctor Mahathir Mohamed. But then, he had fallen out with Mahathir, when he had attempted to try and reform the corrupt Malaysian system. Shortly after that, he had been dismissed from his position, and had then been arrested and charged with trumped-up charges of corruption and sodomy! He had spent six years in prison, before being released. After his release, he had campaigned again to change the corrupt Malaysian system, and in 2008, he was again charged with sodomy. He was acquitted, but then the politically motivated, highest Court in Malaysia, overturned this verdict. He served another three years in prison before finally being pardoned, only because it then suited his senior political colleagues to do so!

Meanwhile, Edwards had now left his government work and had returned to the commercial world. It was now the early 2000's and he worked for an established property developer, a billionaire businessman, who wanted to extend his activities out of Britain, into the international world. He had employed Edwards to set up a new organisation to do this for him, and to establish a team of top people, who would specialise in getting business, in various parts of the world. In order to help him to carry out this task, a kind employee of the property company that he now worked for, had introduced Edwards to a lawyer that he knew. By chance, this young lawyer was from Malaysia, but he had received all his legal education at British universities, and was now working in London with a leading firm of solicitors. When he realised that Edwards knew a lot about his country, the young lawyer asked to meet Edwards privately and they became friends.

He soon talked openly about his background; he was a "Bumi Malaysian" belonging to the native group that were the original inhabitants of the Malaysia peninsula. Edwards knew that, as well as the "Bumiputras", which meant in English, "Sons of the Soil", during the time that Malaysia had been ruled by the British, many people from India and China had entered the then British Colony, and settled there. Because of this, the native Malaysians felt almost that they had become a minority in their own country, even though they still represented the majority of the population. One day, Edwards had invited his new friend, who used the English name Dennis, to his Club for lunch. Edwards was now a member of an exclusive Club, housed in an impressive building and situated close to Whitehall, the centre of British government power. It had a bar, a dining room that served simple British food, and a large sitting room, which Edwards used for a number of his business meetings.

After lunch, Edwards and Dennis sat down in comfort, with a supply of coffee, and Dennis revealed his real background. He was the son of a leading Malaysian Army General, and had been educated in an exclusive, preparatory school and then a secondary school, based upon the British Public School system, in Malaysia. Both of these schools were run and financed by the ruling Malaysian political party, the United Malays National Organisation, usually known by the acronym of UMNO. To be a member of this party, you usually had to be a "Bumi" Malaysian, and Dennis then explained at length, the tensions within Malaysia, between its various racial groups.

Dennis had confirmed the suspicions that Edwards already had, about his country. The native Malays ran the government and the civil service, but were very fearful of the other two races. The Chinese were the really successful business people, and many had made large amounts of money. The Malays were often jealous of them and anti-Chinese riots had broken out in the past, in which some Chinese had been killed. The Indians often provided the professional classes, such as the doctors and accountants, as well as acting as small traders, and the "middle men" importing and exporting essential consumer goods. The native Malays constantly feared that the other two races might get together, and overwhelm them! The native Malays were Muslim, while the Chinese and the Indians tended to be Confucian and Hindu respectively. Because of this background of racial, and also often religious, hatred and suspicions, Dennis admitted that he had been chosen, as a trusted Bumi Muslim from a good background, and had been helped with an excellent free education given by UMNO. This ruling political party had also freely contributed financially towards his university education in Britain.

Edwards found Dennis's explanation of how Malaysia really worked, most interesting. He mentioned the corruption endemic in Malaysia; Dennis immediately accepted that it existed. "The problem is that the ordinary Bumis fear the other two racial groups so much, that they are prepared normally to put up with it," he had said. "But things are changing at last, and there is a growing feeling that Doctor Mahathir has been in power for just too long." Then Dennis began to describe his other family members. "My Uncle is the Head of Intelligence," he suddenly said. "Our Prime Minister, Doctor Mahathir, takes him everywhere. He is his most senior Adviser. He is always with our Prime Minister when he meets other Heads of State."

Edwards began to realise the powerful connections that this young man really had. "I have been asked to go out to Malaysia within the next couple of months," Dennis had said. "Because of my family's status, and because I live abroad, many people want to hear what I think about the ongoing political situation there. Also, they want to know what I have heard about people's views over here, as I live and work in London. Would you like to come with me?" Edwards had asked his employer to fund the trip and, he had agreed, provided that Edwards examined the potential for him to get involved in some property development opportunities in Malaysia, while Edwards was visiting Kuala Lumpur.

4

Their week's trip to Malaysia had proved very educative. Despite the fact that Edwards had dealt with Malaysian projects for years, it was his first visit to Kuala Lumpur. He found the city rather green and pleasant, compared to other cities in South East Asia that he had already visited. While Dennis had disappeared, from time to time, to have private meetings, he had introduced Edwards to a number of interesting people. These included one of the sons of the Prime Minister, who ran a large insurance company. Another was a relatively young Malaysian, who was the Managing Director of a prestigious Malaysian merchant bank. They had dinner with this banker one evening. After dinner, over coffee and liquors, the banker had fixed Edwards with a knowing look. "Do you think that the Sultan of Brunei is rich?" he had suddenly asked Edwards.

Edwards thought that it was a trick question. He had smiled at the young banker and replied: "Well I suppose that he is really rather rich."

"Well, in that case, you should see the bank accounts of our Prime Minister!" the banker had immediately replied.

This reply had brought back to Edwards, the recollection of a story that he had been told about the current Malaysian Prime Minister. Doctor Mahathir was widely known as "Doctor ten per cent", because it was rumoured that he took ten per cent of the price, from every contract awarded by the Malaysian government, as a bribe. These kinds of payments were, of course, just added to their price by the contractors and suppliers obtaining contracts with Malaysia. So they became a "secret tax" paid for by the Malaysia population, imposed on them by their rulers and which ended up in their own personal bank accounts. Some years before, in an open Press Conference, the Malaysian Prime Minister had been asked, by a very brave foreign journalist, if this ten per cent figure was actually true? The Prime Minister's immediate reply had been, "No. I don't come that cheap!" But, of course, it did not stop there; taking their cue from the top, various other greedy Ministers and officials also demanded payments for themselves as well!

In some of the meetings that Edwards had attended between Dennis and senior Bumi Malaysians, in Kuala Lumpur, he sensed that Dennis was being probed for his political opinions. Although it was often asked in the Malay local language, Edwards was soon able to understand the main point of the question. It was "Who did Dennis favour to be appointed as the next Prime Minister, and how quickly should this change be made?" It became clear to Edwards that the level of resistance to the current Prime Minister was increasing; even the leading Bumi business people, academics and other leaders of the Bumi community, were becoming very concerned about the real, brazen and high levels of continuing political corruption practised by him and his cronies.

In Kuala Lumpur, Edwards had been pleased to be able to introduce Dennis, to one of his long-standing British friends, who was then resident there. Roger had started his career in the British Armed Forces and he had finished his period of military service, in Hereford, as part of the elite Special Air Service. He had then become a successful businessman, having successfully built up and then sold a number of businesses in both Britain and abroad. His current business had taken him to Malaysia, where he had established a company which profitably recycled old or defective computer components, including computer "chips". Roger was, as always, charming and had given them some of his time, to describe his local business activities and to give his views, as an expatriate British citizen, on running a business in Malaysia.

On the aeroplane, returning on the long, non-stop flight to London, Edwards had sat by Dennis, and had quietly asked him about some of the conversations that he had been involved with on their visit. "It is true," said Dennis. "The current Prime Minister, and some of his senior colleagues, are now recognised generally as being totally corrupt. Many people would like to do something about it. But people are also very frightened to do anything. They know how powerful he really is, and how he controls everything. They do not want to be arrested and sent to jail or even perhaps, if they are too open about their criticism, just disappear!" Edwards pressed Dennis about the real possibility of change? "It is the old racial fear again, of a takeover by non-Bumis," Dennis had replied. "Something really dramatic has to happen, before Mahathir could be displaced!"

5

About two years later, Doctor Mahathir was still the Prime Minister of Malaysia. Any internal efforts to unseat him seemed to have failed. One day, Edwards received a telephone call from Dennis; he wanted to meet with Edwards urgently and in private. Edwards met him at his Club, which provided a quiet and secure venue. He sensed that Dennis was very agitated. "My uncle has been in London recently, with our Prime Minister," he said. "As usual, the Prime Minister took my uncle to meet with your Prime Minister, Tony Blair, at 10 Downing Street. But then they went on to Washington. When it came to my

Prime Minister's meeting with President George W. Bush, at the White House, he refused to allow my uncle to go with him. My uncle protested strongly, but the Prime Minister still refused!"

"That is interesting news," replied Edwards. "But what do you want me to do?"

Dennis looked at him. "There is something wrong somewhere," he said. "I know that you have some powerful American friends. Can you find out for me, for us, what the President of the United States actually said to our Prime Minister please?"

Edwards was stunned; he asked Dennis what date the meeting with George W. Bush had taken place? Then he told Dennis that he would try and think how he might be able to help him, but that he could not guarantee any success.

Back at his home, Edwards reviewed his options. He did indeed know several well connected Americans; some of them still worked closely with the American intelligence services. Not only would he like to help his friend Dennis, but, he disliked how Mahathir had acted so corruptly all these years, and he too suspected that there was some reason behind the sudden exclusion of Dennis's uncle from this top-level meeting. At last, he selected one man that he would contact. His name was Mark and his background was in the sector of advanced defence technology.

Mark had served as the Technology Adviser to the White House under a previous President. He now owned his own consultancy company in a small town in Virginia, close to Washington. Edwards had visited his company several times; it was staffed with former intelligence officers. Mark still retained the highest level of Security Clearance in the United States and secretly advised the United States Department of Defence at the Pentagon, the Central Intelligence Agency at Langley in Virginia and the National Security Agency at Fort Meade in Maryland. The latter was the much bigger, American version of the British GCHQ at Cheltenham, responsible for global monitoring, and the collecting and processing of information and data, for foreign and domestic intelligence and counterintelligence purposes.

Edwards called Mark on his land line, knowing that mobile telephone calls were much more susceptible to being monitored. He quickly sketched out the background and mentioned the date of the meeting with his President at the White House. He then asked the question if Mark could help him, in any way?

Mark understood immediately; "I will get back to you as soon as I can," he had said.

Two days later Mark had called him back. "I have been able to obtain a short summary of the meeting between the President and the Prime Minister that you mentioned," he said. "The first part of the meeting went well; it was friendly and constructive.

But then my President strongly criticised his visitor for the level of corruption in his country. The Prime Minister of Malaysia seemed to take this criticism personally, and the President did not dissuade him from the fact that his comment was meant to be about him! The meeting ended very badly with a heated, angry exchange!"

Edwards thanked Mark profusely for the intelligence that he had provided. He had then called Dennis to arrange for another private meeting, where he could tell him quietly this news, for his onward transmission back to his senior contacts in Malaysia.

Just a week later, his friend Roger, whom Edwards and Dennis had met in Kuala Lumpur, had telephoned him. Roger was now back in London; Edwards knew that Roger was probably close to the British Secret Intelligence Service, known to the public as MI6. He asked Edwards for exactly the same help that Dennis has asked for. Edwards was pleased to be able to tell him, immediately, about the intelligence that he had received from Washington, and the background as to why he had asked his American friend to help.

A few months later, Doctor Mahathir Mohamad finally resigned as the Prime Minister of Malaysia. He had served in that office for over twenty-two years, but his political colleagues had now realised that he was a toxic, international pariah and was viewed as a disgrace to his country. Edwards hoped that, in his own small way, he had made some contribution, to the end of Mahathir's long and corrupt reign as Prime Minister of Malaysia.

6

By now, Edwards had concluded that Malaysia was an Established Serial Kleptocracy. Like many other countries around the world, racial, tribal and religious fear and tension, had served to turn a country into virtually a One Party State. Usually, in these states, there was one all-powerful political leader, who had been somehow successively elected, even, it was claimed democratically, and who then held on to power for decades, or even until they died. In Africa, these tensions were usually tribal, although in South Africa they were both tribal and racial. In the Middle East, these tensions that resulted in a form of Dictatorship, were tribal or often religious, even between different parts of the same Muslim religion. Clever politicians seemed always to be able to manipulate the divisions and fears in any society, to get "democratically" elected, and then continue to use those divisions and fears to maintain their power and serve their own corrupt ends.

In Malaysia, like in these other countries, successive generations of senior Malaysian politicians, had systematically plundered, for their own personal use, the riches of the country, which really belonged to the ordinary Malaysian people. This major theft had been largely ignored for years, and they had not been called to account because of the same racial, tribal and religious fears, that were also evident in so many other countries. Edwards continued to watch closely the political developments in Malaysia.

In October 2003, Mahathir was finally replaced as Prime Minister by Abdullah Ahmad Badawi, who had replaced Anwar Ibrahim as the Deputy Prime Minister, when the latter had been dismissed over the trumped-up sodomy charges against him. He served until April 2009, when he resigned, as he was considered to be responsible for the ruling UMNO party only being re-elected with a small majority. In fact, this political party was becoming increasingly unpopular with the ordinary Malays, because of the continuing high levels of corruption associated with it. He was then replaced by Najib Razak, the Deputy Prime Minister that Badawi had appointed. Najib was already considered, by many leading foreign exporting companies, to be the most personally greedy Minister of Defence in the world, when he had previously served in that role! He was already mired in corruption but, nevertheless, he had been promoted to Minister of Finance, and then to Deputy Prime Minister.

Najib continued his corrupt practices, and, indeed, seemed to intend to increase them. He was involved in heavy "Vote Buying" activities, to try to keep the ruling UMNO party in power. To do this, substantial amounts of money were needed; Najib teamed up with a strange fellow-conspirator, to accomplish this. He was a young Chinese businessman from the island of Penang, off the north-west coast of Malaysia. His name was Low Taek Jho, who soon became known around the world as "Jho Low". Low learned quickly how to set up offshore companies, and used very doubtful, creative accountancy practices. These practices were not spotted, by the major international accountancy firms that had been employed, on high fees, to audit these companies, until it was too late.

Low was helped in all this, by not only a network of accomplices in Malaysia itself, but also people in Singapore, Hong Kong, the Middle East, Switzerland, the United States of America and in other countries as well. With clever "sleight of hand", imaginary loans and investments were made, in ever growing amounts, using an increasingly larger network of offshore companies, bank accounts and corrupt people around the world. In all of this, this network was helped by the major international banks, who seemed "star struck" by the amounts of money flowing through the bank accounts involved. The total amount of theft was unimaginable and the main victim was a national development fund that had been set up by the Malaysian Government, to help in the economic development of Malaysia, and promote the prosperity of the Malaysian people.

This development fund was known as One Malaysian Development Berhad or just "1MDB". It was controlled by Najib who, as well as being Prime Minister, was now also Minister of Finance. Najib was certainly fed money, from this corruption, to buy votes for the ruling UMNO party, to try and keep it in power. But he, his wife, and his family, also benefited, with most of the stolen money going into expensive houses, jewellery and other luxury consumer items. As for Jho Low, he became the highest-spending and most well-known Playboy in the world. He threw the most lavish parties at unbelievable costs, mixing with world-class celebrities, film stars and political leaders, and gambled heavily in casinos around the world. He bought, or hired, several large, luxury yachts, on which to hold some of these wild parties, and he also bought several private jets. As a result of all his machinations, Low had managed to steal, and then spend from the Malaysian people, just from 1MDB alone, an estimated Seven to Eight Billion American dollars!

Despite growing pressure on him, Najib managed to survive as Prime Minister until 2018, with the application of fear and arrests and in one case at least, probably by murder. Then the equally corrupt former Prime Minister, now ninety-two years old, Doctor Mahathir Mohamad, managed to somehow oust him and become Prime Minister again. This he did by by forming his own new political party, and then working with other opposition parties against Najib. He claimed that, after all the years of his own corrupt dealings and leadership of the party that, in fact, UMNO was corrupt! To get re-elected he, of course, played to the fears of the native Malays, that they would otherwise lose control of their own country to other racial and religious groups. Najib was arrested and, at last, was brought to trial for corruption. Jho Low literally disappeared, with the remainder of the money that he had stolen, and, despite great efforts, could not be found. It was suspected that he had fled, with the rest of the money that he had stolen, to China.

To become Prime Minister, as a political concession, Mahathir made the wife of Anwar Ibrahim his Deputy, and promised that Anwar, himself, would most certainly succeed him as Prime Minister by April 2020. On this promise he, of course, reneged. In February 2020, a number of opposition parties held meetings to try and form a coalition between them, and then form a new government. This situation was supported by Anwar Ibrahim, who expected to take power, but he then failed in his attempt to become Prime Minister. Although Mahathir finally resigned, for the second time, he then failed to support Anwar to become the new Prime Minister, as he had promised. Anwar had made the mistakes of appearing to be too honest, and of trying to reconcile the three racial and religious groups in Malaysia.

Instead, Muhyiddin Yassin was appointed. He was another UMNO politician, who had been appointed as Deputy Prime Minister, by the totally corrupt Najib Razak in 2009. He was recognised as a right-wing, "Put Malays First," politician, and a strong supporter of Mahathir, against the growing number of people who had opposed him. But soon there were new accusations of corruption raised against him and a replacement inevitably became necessary. Of course, it was unacceptable to the native Malaysians for power to be handed to a member of the other minority racial groups in the country. So, the Corrupt Political Game of "Musical Chairs" continued in Malaysia; a result of the strong racial and religious intolerance and the continuing fears of the native "Bumi" population, within this unfortunate and divided country.

Finally, in November 2022, Anwar Ibrahim, after a long personal struggle, was appointed Prime Minister of Malaysia. He managed to form a working coalition of his own and other parties, not including UMNO, which had been in power for so many years! The complex negotiations to achieve this political upset had been long and hard, but Anwar then introduced a more right-wing form of Islam, promoting religious teaching and the teaching of Malay history and culture into schools. For Edwards, it was interesting to see the final success of this man who he had first identified and studied nearly forty years before. He was still not convinced that Anwar would provide the best solution for Malaysia's many problems, but, he had recognised that there was still an element of "religious idealism" about this man. Perhaps his strong Islamic beliefs would help guide him to begin to try and change Malaysian society and, hopefully, to begin to erode the decades of serial corruption and theft, at the highest levels, that had long been Malaysia's tragic fate.

CLUB TALK

"Injustice anywhere is a threat to Justice everywhere" –
Dr Martin Luther King Jr.

In Memory of D.L. – a Brave and Loyal Friend.

1

It was a strange scene. It took place in the small Bar of a very exclusive, gentleman's Club in Saint James's in London. The Club had a long history; it had been been founded in 1762 by the Earl of Shelburne, a member of the British aristocracy and a future Prime Minister of Great Britain. It was considered to be one of the most prestigious Clubs in the world, and its membership list had always included members of the aristocracy, senior politicians, leading judges and barristers, and the "Captains" of British industry, commerce and finance of the day.

Edwards had just ushered into the Bar a very short man, with a round, jovial face. Already standing at the Bar was Edward's long-standing friend Daniel and a tall, thin man, who was the then current Chairman of this Club. The Chairman stood aside; behind him there was standing another tall man who, like them all, was impeccably dressed in a smart business suit, sober shirt and tie, as was required by the strict rules of this Club. Up to then he had been crouching down behind the Chairman, so as not to be seen, but now he had stood up. The short man's jaw dropped open and he let out a loud gasp. He marched forward, went down on his knees, and kissed the right, burnished, black leather toe cap of the shoe of the second tall man standing at the Bar!

Looks are very often deceptive; nobody in the street would have given this short little man a second glance. But he was a War Hero; he was the last British naval commander to lose his ship in a war, as a result of enemy action. Rear Admiral Sam Salt held the order of the Companion of the Bath, which was only awarded for service to your country of the highest calibre. As commander of the warship H.M.S. Sheffield, he had seen action in the Falkland Islands, in the undeclared war against the Argentinians in 1982. On 10 May that year, the Sheffield had been hit by an Argentine, sea-skimming Exocet missile. The warhead of the missile exploded and had started a major fire, which had killed twenty of her crew. Sam Salt had ordered the crew to abandon ship. The vessel was left to burn for several days, before being taken in tow. But, under tow, the burnt-out hulk filled with water, and had then sunk.

Several official Inquiries had concluded that Sam Salt was not to blame; he had been on the ship's bridge for three consecutive days and nights, with only short rests, to keep him going. He had retired to his cabin for a well-earned sleep and had left his second-in- command in charge. These Naval Inquiries had found that the second-in command was inexperienced in naval warfare and had, somehow, left the bridge and was unable to be contacted when the incoming missile was spotted. Two other vital warfare officers were also missing from their posts in the vessel's control room at the time, and the rest of the crew failed to take any evasive action. Subsequently, two of these officers were promoted, and continued to serve in the Royal Navy. Sam Salt was also promoted, but his tragic experience was used to improve ship design and tactics against such sea-skimming missile attacks. He then served at the N.A.T.O. Allied Maritime Command Headquarters at Northwood, in north-west London, which also acted as the Command Operations Centre for the whole of the Royal Navy.

One of the legendary stories about Sam was that, one day, he was giving a presentation to the then Prime Minister Margaret Thatcher, at the Northwood Headquarters. She had interrupted him with a complicated question. Sam drew himself up to his full height; just over five foot tall. "I would like to take any questions at the end of my presentation, please, Prime Minister," he had said. The Prime Minister did not interrupt again! From that time, Sam was known as the only man, besides perhaps her husband, who had ever silenced Margaret Thatcher. It was a dangerous distinction to have, but she probably respected his War Record too much, to take any action against him.

The man standing at the bar, to whom Sam Salt had just paid this strange, but amusing, homage, was Admiral Sir John "Sandy" Woodward, who had commanded the whole of the British Naval Task Force in the South Atlantic during the Falklands War. They had not seen each other since that war had ended, and Edwards was very happy, along with Daniel, to have arranged this surprise reunion between the two of them. Edwards now worked with Sam Salt in a London-based company, which specialised in engineering, defence and security products. He had been happy to arrange for Sam to join him there, on a part-time basis, after Sam had finally retired from the Royal Navy.

Sam Salt and Edwards used to lunch together, several days a week, and Sam told him some of the stories that had happened in his life. It was now the late 1990s, and the "Cold War" between the former Communist Russia, and its satellite countries in the Warsaw Pact, against the opposing Western military alliance of the North Atlantic Treaty Organisation, was now over. Sam told Edwards the story of his visit to Moscow, just before he had left the Royal Navy.

"I was invited by one of their senior Admirals to visit the Russian Navy Command Headquarters," he told Edwards. "Like our concrete bunker, buried deep underground, it was a large buried bunker, just outside Moscow. It was a most interesting visit. They showed me everything. In front of me was a large map. It showed the current position of every Russian submarine, including their boats that carried their nuclear missiles! It was incredible; only a few years before we were working ceaselessly, and spending a fortune, on trying to track these vessels. Now, here was the position of every one of them, all laid out in front of me!"

2

Edwards had left that particular company, and he was now advising a major technology group, but he had maintained his contact with his friend Daniel. They had known each other for many years, and introduced each other to their various contacts, if they thought that this might be useful. They now lunched occasionally at the same exclusive Club; the Chairman of the Club invited them and used to join them for lunch. Indeed, he kindly paid for their lunch on several occasions. The Chairman was a charming man; the product of a leading Public School, and Cambridge University. He owned his own flat in London and a house in the country, where his wife and children lived. At his country home, he was the Chairman of the Bench of his local Magistrates Court. He was also the Managing Director of his successful family company, founded over seventy years before, and he seemed to spend lavishly. Daniel had thought about becoming a member of this Club, but he was just a Grammar School boy, and had never gone to university. Nevertheless, he had worked hard for a professional qualification, and he was a success in what he was doing, working within the construction industry.

Then, one day, Daniel told Edwards some astonishing news; the Chairman of the Club had been arrested and charged with fraud! The Chairman had been accused of stealing funds from his family company, and even more money from his elderly mother, who was eighty-nine years old. He had also tried to persuade her to sign her house over to him, so that he could then have sold it over her head. He had himself borrowed up to the hilt, with his family home as security. He had used up all this money it seemed, on a very lavish lifestyle for himself. He had not taken his wife and children away, on holiday, for years, and neither had he ever given any money to his wife for the family expenses. Instead, for all this time, she had had to keep herself and their children from her own funds. As a result, she had suffered from illness and depression. In all, he was accused of stealing up to four million pounds from his family firm and from his family, but the total amount that he could have taken was up to nearly eight million pounds!

Fortunately for him, he was quickly released after he had been arrested and questioned, so that he did not have to spend any time in prison on remand. He was found guilty of his crimes, but, of course, he had attended the right kind of school and gone to the right kind of university. He was even the Chairman of his local Magistrates! As a result, he was sentenced, by a friendly judge, to just two years imprisonment. With time off for good behaviour, he ended up spending only nine months in a comfortable open prison! Either the judge was overawed by this man's upper-class background or, maybe, the judge had just accepted a bribe, to give him just this short prison sentence? Ordinary prisoners first had to spend part of their sentence in a closed prison, before being transferred to an open prison for the rest of their sentence. But this did not seem to apply to this special category of upper-class prisoner, who spent just one night in the hospital of a London closed prison, before being immediately transferred to his comfortable open prison for the rest of his time "inside!"

Unfortunately, of course, he had to give up the Chairmanship of the exclusive Club, as it was not possible to carry out this role from jail! Shortly after this disgracefully light sentence, Daniel had met with Edwards to discuss this man's fate, and their mutual disbelief, that he could really have done the things for which he had been found guilty.

"We really must go and visit him in prison," said Daniel.

Edwards was amazed at his friend's attitude. "That man is now a convicted criminal. He stole money from his own family, he has now bankrupted his family firm, and he even stole money from his own elderly mother," retorted Edwards. "He then spent it all on himself. He is a disgusting creature, and I never want to see him again!"

3

Daniel had recently suffered the results of an unfair divorce settlement; although it was his wife that was having an affair with another man. She was a joint British and Austrian citizen and, as an Austrian citizen, she was able to keep the lovely house that Daniel had funded to be built, half way up a mountain, close to Salzburg. Daniel had also to pay her some money, but managed to still pay the rent on the small, London flat, that they had lived in for many years, so that he could remain living there. Fed up, he had retired early from his current employer. He had travelled widely in his job, and had now made the decision to go and live in South East Asia, where the cost of living was lower than Britain, and where his reduced income would still be sufficient to keep him. So he left London; but he and Edwards still kept in regular contact.

Daniel first went to live in another South East Asian country for some years, but then settled in Bangkok, the capital city of Thailand. Because of his long experience in international business, he managed to find things to do to try and earn a living there. He quickly developed, in a number of South East Asian countries, contacts at the highest level in the government and in the commercial life of the country. The inevitable then happened; he met a beautiful Thai girl, who came from a prominent Thai family, and they married. Soon she had given birth to twin children, a boy and a girl.

On one of his visits back to London, Daniel showed Edwards photographs of his new wife and family, out in Bangkok. Edwards also visited Thailand, on a business trip, to examine a potential project that Daniel had introduced to him, for the Royal Thai Armed Forces. While he was there, Danial gave Edwards the benefit of a "Night Time Tour" of Bangkok. Edwards grew a little worried that his old friend was becoming a little dissipated but, he was assured by Daniel, that this was part of the business culture of Thailand, and such a tour was expected by the senior Thais with whom he dealt. There was no doubt, however, that Daniel had established very good contacts with senior politicians, military officers and businessmen in that country. He seemed to "have a knack" of quickly getting to the top of any society in which he lived, and understand the intimate ways that any foreign country worked.

But then things began to turn sour for Daniel; his Thai wife began to develop a jealous streak to her character. She protested that Daniel was spending too much time with his senior contacts, particularly in the evenings. One night, she had even stabbed him with a small knife, and he had to go to hospital to have the wound stitched up! In another incident, she had ripped up his British Passport, with his Thai Residents Visa within it, and also destroyed some of his business papers. Eventually, she threw him out of the house, which belonged to her, and Daniel was now forced to live in a series of cheap Bangkok hotels. All of this news, Daniel had told Edwards either in emails or in telephone calls. But, it was about this time, that Edwards began to hear some stories about Daniel's other business activities.

One day a successful London businessman telephoned Edwards; years before, Daniel had introduced him to Edwards, and they had then jointly met with him over the years, while Daniel was still in London. This man wanted some help with a project that he was working on, and Edwards willingly went to meet him. The project was large and required financing, and he asked Edwards, who had a long experience in the financial sector, if he could put the finance together for him. Edwards agreed, but only under certain conditions that had to be met. As an aside, the businessman mentioned to Edwards that he was doing some business with Daniel in Thailand.

"Can you tell me what kind of business you are doing with him?" asked Edwards.

"Of course," was the reply. "I have invested some money in a deal that Daniel has brought to me. This is a trade deal with a West African country and it is about releasing some foreign currency funds that are held in that country."

Edwards was always very doubtful about doing deals with particular African countries; it seemed to be the home of so many of the Confidence Tricksters in the world! But he knew that Daniel, in his younger days, had lived and worked in Nigeria for many years, so he should know something about doing business with that part of Africa. He was also concerned that he had heard nothing at all from Daniel about this particular deal that he had brought to this man.

But then the businessman went on. "I also introduced Daniel's deal to a friend of mine and he has invested some more money into it. Between us, we put in just over one hundred thousand pounds. Unfortunately, my friend died a few months ago, and his son has now reported this deal to the Metropolitan Police, as he thinks that it is a fraud. I have now been contacted by Scotland Yard; they want me to meet some of their officers, who want to question me about it. I think that this is not right; both my friend and I went into this deal with our eyes open. After all, we were both experienced business people. But the Police seem to be accepting totally what my late friend's son is saying. He has, after all, inherited his father's building business and is now running it. Of course, his father paid for him to go to a leading Public School and then to Oxford University; I suppose that the Police are a bit overawed by him!"

Edwards enquired about the name of the other person who had invested in this West African deal; he was then told the name of the second businessman which Edwards recognised as the name of the owner of a well-known, medium-sized, construction company.

4

It was about two months later when Edwards met the businessman again; they had lunch together at a restaurant in the large Barbican residential development that had been built in the financial centre of the City of London, where this man lived.

"I have now met with Scotland Yard," he was told. "But they do not want me to talk about this case with anyone else," the businessman continued. "They seem to believe that this deal is a fraud and that Daniel is the person responsible."

"But what are they going to do?" asked Edwards.

"I think that they are now going to ask the Thai Police to try and find Daniel," was the reply. "The son of my late friend seems absolutely determined to pursue this matter. I do not feel so strongly about it. After all, I invested in it with my eyes open."

The next time that Edwards heard from Daniel was by a short letter posted from Bangkok. It told him that Daniel had been found by the Thai Police, living in a cheap, run-down hotel, in Bangkok. They had asked to see his Thai Visa but, of course, that was in his British Passport that had been destroyed by his wife, and he had not had the money to replace it. He had promptly been arrested as an illegal immigrant, and detained in the main Bangkok Prison, until the Thai authorities had decided what to do with him. He was in a not very large cell with thirty other men; some Thais and some other foreigners. Conditions were terrible; they were made to sleep on the hard, concrete floor, wrapped only in dirty blankets. Daniel had tried to contact some of the well-placed people that he knew in Thailand, but nobody seemed to want to know him, now that he had been arrested, and had been declared an illegal resident in their country.

The next letter from Daniel, told Edwards that the Metropolitan Police had now applied to the Thai authorities, for him to be deported from Thailand, back to Britain. He expected to appear before a Thai Court the following week, and for them to agree to his immediate deportation. Could Edwards please help him? Once Daniel arrived back in the United Kingdom, he expected to be arrested and charged with fraud. He would need to get a good London lawyer to help him! Fortunately, Edwards had some good contacts in the legal profession; through them he managed to find what he hoped was the right legal firm of Solicitors, specialising in criminal law, to help Daniel. Edwards then called the prison in Thailand, and made sure that the name and contact details of one of the Partners in this legal firm, was communicated to Daniel.

A few weeks later, Daniel was deported from Thailand, back to Britain. A few days after Daniel had arrived at Heathrow Airport, he called Edwards from a friend's flat, where he was staying. They arranged to meet up at a bar that they both knew. Edwards did not know what to expect, but was not prepared for the state that his friend was now in; while he was smartly dressed, he had lost a lot of weight, and his clothes hung off him, as if he was a skeleton!

"These are some old clothes that I had left in storage in London," he explained. "I left Thailand only with the clothes that I had when they arrested me. Everything else was stolen by the Thai Police. I was put on a non-stop Thai Airways flight to London. I was only in the back of the aircraft, but the food they gave me was wonderful!"

"But, you have lost so much weight, and you are so pale," said Edwards.

"You try living in a small cell with thirty other guys for nearly a year," said Daniel. "There was one hole in the floor for a toilet. We were lucky if they let us out twice a week for some exercise in the prison yard. And the food was terrible!"

"So what happened when you got back?" asked Edwards.

"When my aircraft landed at Heathrow," answered Daniel, "four heavily armed policemen boarded the plane, arrested me, and took me off it. I was terrified, and so were all the other passengers. They must have thought that I was a dangerous terrorist and I might have been carrying a bomb!" Edwards winced for his friend!

"But then they were very nice to me," continued Daniel. "They took away the temporary travel document that the British Embassy in Bangkok had issued to me. Then they took me to the small Police Station at Heathrow Airport. There they put me into a cell. It was like a luxury hotel room after the jail in Bangkok! Then they asked me what I wanted to eat for dinner? I said a pizza, please, which they brought me. The next morning they asked me if I would like a full English breakfast? I said, Yes, please! Then they took me out of the cell, as two detectives had come from Scotland Yard to question me. That's when a solicitor, from the legal firm whose name you gave me, first appeared. They then formally charged me with fraud. Then I was finally released on Police Bail."

Edwards could not help himself; he had started laughing at his friend's account!

"It gets better," continued Daniel. "I told them that I did not have any money to get into central London. They said not to worry. They had a police car going into London, in half an hour's time, and I could get a lift in that. They even kindly dropped me, just outside my friend's front door, where I was going to stay. I realised then, what a civilised country Britain actually is!" he ended.

Edwards fixed him in the eye. "You can tell me honestly," he said, "did you steal that money that they claim you did?"

"Absolutely not," replied Daniel. "It was all sent directly to my contact in West Africa. I was, of course, due to be paid an introductory fee if the transaction went ahead, and those two guys would have been repaid the amounts they put in, plus some more. But, after the money was sent, nothing happened. Do you think that, after my wife threw me out of her house, I would have been staying in such cheap and nasty Bangkok hotels, if I had been given even just a small part of that money?" Edwards looked at him carefully; he felt that he had to believe him.

5

Edwards tried to see Daniel, as regularly as he could. First, his friend was asked to report regularly, at the local police station, where he was staying. One morning, he was told to report at a different police station, two days later. There, he was rearrested, questioned again and then kept overnight in a cell, ready to appear in Court the following morning. Daniel had, meanwhile, been meeting regularly with his solicitor. He had been advised that it would probably be best to plead guilty to a lesser charge of receiving monies illegally, although he claimed to have never kept anything. But the police said that they had clear evidence that the money had been sent to him in Thailand.

At this first Court hearing, he had pleaded guilty to this lesser charge, as he had been advised. But no date had been set for his trial and the prosecution was determined to bring the greater charge of fraud against him as, they said, that he had kept all the money for himself. Daniel claimed that the money had been sent to his West African contact but, unfortunately, he had no written proof, since his wife had destroyed all of his relevant business papers in Bangkok. He said that he had not benefitted, in any way, from the money that had been sent. Once the money had been sent to his contact in West Africa, to carry out the supposed deal, he had never heard from the man again. Why had he been living in cheap Bangkok hotels, frequented by back-packers, if he had received any of this money to spend on himself?

The judge, at this first Court hearing, seemed to favour the prosecution, and said that there was still this greater charge to answer. But then, the Judge determined that this fraud case was far too complicated for a jury to hear. Instead, Daniel's trial would be held as a "Newton Hearing", without a jury, in front of this same judge, sitting alone, who would decide his fate. In this way Daniel was deprived of his right to be tried before a jury. Meanwhile, as he had pleaded guilty to the lesser charge, Daniel would be held in custody on remand, in a closed prison, until the time that his trial could be held.

His new home had been built in 1851, in the reign of Queen Victoria, and he was to be held there for nearly twelve months, until a date for his trial was finally set. Daniel's solicitor did not seem to have defended his client very well, against this travesty of justice! Edwards had followed these legal proceedings, and was determined to help Daniel, in any way that he could. Edwards knew something about Daniel that only a very few other people knew. So, he asked Daniel's solicitor if he could appear as a character witness in Court, and he gave him a written statement of what he would say.

Edwards received regular letters from Daniel, about the dreadful conditions inside one of the most notorious London prisons, in which he was now incarcerated. Deep depression and suicides were common amongst the prisoners, as well as regular violence between them, coupled with widespread drug taking. They all seemed to be imprisoned there, to seemingly exert punishment and retribution, with absolutely no attempt at any kind of rehabilitation. Daniel wrote to Edwards, that he had even had to share a cell with a convicted murderer for a while. The months went by, while the inefficient British legal system tried to find a day and a place to finally try him. The date for his trial was postponed several times, but, finally a date and a place were determined.

Unfortunately, during this period of Daniel's detention on remand, his friend who he had once introduced to Edwards and who had invested in the West African deal, had passed away. He was the last person, other than Edwards, who might have been able to give some evidence in favour of Daniel. When the day eventually came, Edwards had to make his way to a Crown Court building, in a southern London suburb, to attend the hearing that would determine Daniel's final fate.

In a break in the hearing, before he gave his evidence, Edwards met with Daniel's legal representative, who was a qualified criminal barrister, and had been appointed to try and defend Daniel, before this Crown Court. They met in a small, hot and stuffy meeting room; it was a very warm summer's day outside. The barrister seemed to be doing his best to try and save Daniel.

"The problem is," he said to Edwards, "we have a very hard-nosed judge here, who just seems determined to find him guilty and to punish him, as hard as he can! I hope that your character reference will result, at least, in a shorter jail sentence. By the way, you are the only one of his so-called friends and contacts, who have decided to take the trouble to appear, and give any evidence in his defence."

Edwards did not comment, but he had his own thoughts about the situation. Unfortunately, Daniel had not gone to the right kind of school, nor to the right kind of university. Furthermore, he was not the Chairman of an exclusive Club, or of his local Magistrates Court! People were not equal before the Law; if you were from the right background, but still a criminal, you were treated like an erring gentleman. If you were not from this entitled background, but, nevertheless, you were a gentleman, you were treated by the Law as a ruffian! But Edwards ignored his personal views for the moment; instead he wanted to do his very best for Daniel. So he carefully rehearsed, with Daniel's lawyer, what evidence he was going to give.

"I have never had to ask questions like this from a witness before!" said the barrister excitedly, as they went through the questions that he would ask Edwards in the Court.

6

Edwards was sitting outside the right Courtroom, in which Daniel's case was being heard, when the Clerk to the Court opened the door and called him in, to give his evidence. It was a modern Courtroom, with all the furnishings made from a light brown wood. Immediately, Edwards's eyes fixed on the Judge; he was sitting on his raised seat, resplendent in his robes and an antiquated wig! He looked to be an elderly, stern and impassive man; Edwards made the decision that, although he was a non-believer, he would take the oath on the Bible, if only to impress the Judge!

He climbed the few steps into the Witness Box. In front of him, he could see Daniel, imprisoned, like an animal, in the large glass case, that was the Dock. Behind him sat a Prison Guard in uniform. Daniel was dressed in a white shirt, with no jacket, as it was a hot day. He appeared to be taking a great interest in the proceedings. But, to Edwards, he looked tense and his face had aged considerably. He face was also totally white; the so-called "Prison Pallor," that happens as a result of a long period of imprisonment indoors.

Edwards took the oath, holding the Bible, and each time emphasised the word "truth," as he read from the card, held by the Clerk, in front of him. Daniel's barrister, now wearing his black robe and wig, stood up to question him.

"For how long have you known my Client?" he asked.

Edwards calculated quickly. "For just over thirty years," he replied.

"How well do you know him?" was the next question.

"Very well," replied Edwards. "We have met regularly over that period, we have worked together on various projects, and we have travelled together to various overseas countries."

"From your knowledge of my Client," continued the barrister, "do you consider him to be a man of good character?"

"Yes, I believe him to be an honest man," replied Edwards. "He is of good character." Then, just to try to help Daniel in his case, he added; "But sometimes I have found him, despite his experience, to be a little naïve."

"For how long have you been active in international business?" was the barrister's next question. Then he added; "I understand that you have a banking background and are an expert on financing projects, particularly overseas. Is that correct?"

"I have been active in international business and finance for over forty years," replied Edwards. "And, yes, my main skill is in financing overseas trade and projects."

The barrister was now warming to his theme. "As a result of your experience, were you employed as an Advisor to Government?" he asked.

Edwards looked around the court. The public seating in the Court was empty; there were no members of the public or journalists present, as there were entitled to be. Edwards now felt more relaxed about giving all the evidence that he wanted to give. He answered the barrister's last question in the affirmative, and gave the Court short details of the government organisation that he had worked for, and the dates between which he had worked for them.

Daniel's barrister drew himself up to his full height. "Is it the case," he asked, "that while you were there, you worked closely with a senior, serving intelligence officer?"

"Yes," replied Edwards. "We worked very closely together on matters that I cannot talk about."

The barrister's next question was the important one. "Is it the case," he asked slowly, "that you arranged, together with your colleague, for my Client to meet and be recruited by the Secret Intelligence Service as an agent?" He glanced around the Court, in case anyone did not understand the question. "Otherwise known by the public as M.I.6." he added.

"That is correct," was Edwards's short reply.

"Can I ask you, did my Client perform well as a Secret Agent of the British Government?" asked Daniel's barrister.

"I believe so," replied Edwards. "Obviously, I was given no details of his actual operational arrangements. But I understand that he performed very well, and provided excellent intelligence about at least two South East Asian countries over a number of years. S.I.S., as we call that organisation, were apparently very pleased with him."

The barrister appeared pleased. His next question was obvious. "And during his covert duties, did my Client put himself in any danger in the service of this country?" he asked.

"Yes, he would have done," replied Edwards. "It is in the nature of this kind of work as an agent, that you are not protected by Diplomatic Immunity. Unlike an Intelligence Officer, working undercover at a British Embassy, as a British Diplomat, who would be so protected. If he had been discovered, at any time, by the foreign government concerned, providing this kind of secret information, he could have been arrested, perhaps tortured, and then possibly secretly killed. Or he could have been tried, under their laws and in their courts. He could then, in certain countries, have been executed or face being imprisoned for a very long time."

Daniel's barrister sat down; he seemed satisfied that he had done his best. The prosecuting barrister then stood up. "Can you give me the name of the Intelligence Officer, who you worked with, and who, with you, introduced the Accused to M.I.6?" he asked.

Edwards shook his head. "I am afraid that I cannot give you that," he answered. "The Official Secrets Act would prevent me from giving that kind of information."

The prosecuting barrister sat down. Then the Judge cleared his throat and asked a question of Edwards. "Am I to understand," he said, "that you and your colleague arranged for the Accused to be recruited as a Secret Agent to spy for Britain?"

Edwards turned towards the Judge. "That is correct, sir" he replied.

His evidence over, Edwards left the Witness Box, and went to sit on a chair in the public seating area. But he was not there for long. The Judge asked Daniel's barrister if that was the end of the evidence that he would present. When the man replied that this was the case, the Judge announced that he would now call a recess, to consider his verdict and, ominously, the sentence that he would apply! Edwards could not wait any longer, but he first waited for Daniel's barrister outside the Court. "Did that go well?" he asked him. Then he added, "I have to leave now."

"I thought that it went very well," the barrister replied. "But now, we will have to await the verdict and the sentence. That should be delivered later today. I suggest that, in a few days, you call Daniel's solicitor, and he can then give you the result."

7

So a few days later, Edwards did make that telephone call. He spoke to Daniel's solicitor, and asked what had happened, in the Court, after he had left?

"The Judge found him guilty of the greater charge of fraud, as we had expected him to do," replied the solicitor. "Then he sentenced Daniel to four years and four months in prison."

"What?" gasped Edwards. "But did my evidence help at all in his defence?"

"I think so," replied the lawyer. "Otherwise that Judge would have sentenced him to five or six years in prison! But, don't worry, the time he has already spent in jail on remand will be deducted from that sentence."

Edwards had now recovered a little, from his shock at the severity of Daniel's punishment. "When could he be released?" he asked the solicitor.

"Well, with good behaviour, he may only have to serve half his sentence," came the reply. Hopefully, when he is judged to be, say, twelve months from his release, we can apply for him to be transferred to an open prison."

"But I know of a man who stole many, many times more than Daniel, from his own family. Even from his aged mother!" Edwards retorted, angrily. "And he got a two year sentence, reduced to under one year for good behaviour. He served his sentence completely in an open prison."

There was silence at the other end of the line. The solicitor seemed not to want to explain the finer workings of the British legal system to a "Mere Mortal" like Edwards. Instead, he went on to crack a joke. "Both Daniel's barrister and the prosecuting barrister were very excited, after your evidence. They said that they had never known two spooks, or spies, in the same court before, on the same day!"

Daniel continued to write to Edwards about his long and difficult journey, through the British prison system. He was kept in the same closed London prison, under the severe conditions that he had described, for another fifteen months, after his sentencing. His solicitor petitioned, several times, for him to be moved to an open prison. But, it seemed, almost as an afterthought that, at last, the prison system transferred Daniel to an open prison, on the South Coast of England.

"It is like a luxury hotel here, after the last place," Daniel wrote to Edwards. Then he went on, "So many of the men that I met in that previous, dreadful place were there because the state education system had just failed them. They could neither read nor write! So they could not get a job; no wonder that they had to turn to crime to feed themselves and their families. I taught some of them there to read and write; there was one old guy, who had never written a letter in his life before. I helped him to write the first letter that he had ever written, to his son. He was so proud of his achievement! It really brought tears to my eyes."

Daniel went on to do much more voluntary work in his new open prison; it was full of men who had been transferred there, towards the end of their often long sentences, and it therefore gave them some kind of opportunity for rehabilitation before release. But, the prison system actually provided very little of this kind of support to help them. Instead, Daniel worked closely with the Prison Governor on this aspect; with his encouragement and approval, he had set up some reading and writing classes, for some of the inmates that really needed them. With his experience of the business world, he also set up some discussion groups, with the inmates who were shortly going to be released. These were mainly about how they could integrate back into the world of work. Daniel also organised, in conjunction with the Prison Chaplain, some interesting talks for the prisoners on a number of subjects, about which he was knowledgeable.

After a while, the Prison Governor realised that his work was invaluable, and gave him a desk of his own in the Prison's administrative area. "The Governor was quite sorry to see me leave," Daniel told Edwards, after he had been finally released, and they had met for a celebratory lunch. "The day before I was due to be released, he met with me, to thank me for all that I had done. He said that he did not know how he was going to cope without me! It was funny, many of the prisoners had taken to calling me "Sir", and some of them actually thought that I was part of the prison staff!"

Despite this, Daniel's application to be released had somehow been lost, and he had had to stay on in the open prison, for some months past the date that he should have been released! To add insult to this injury, the Proceeds of Crime Unit of the Crown Prosecution Service, had also intervened in Daniel's case. They saw it as their job to harass Daniel further. All his British assets had been seized and sold, including his clothes, books and other belongings. His private pension, that he had contributed to for many years, was also seized and disappeared into the Proceeds of Crime Unit's funds. Two senior police officers from Scotland Yard, no doubt not seated in the back of the aircraft, flew at the British taxpayer's expense, to Bangkok, to stay in a luxury hotel, to try and find the supposed funds that Daniel had somehow hidden there. They came back with nothing!

On his release, Daniel was lucky to find a small flat to rent, which now had to be paid for by the British taxpayer, since his private pension had been confiscated. The Social Services also had to give him a grant, to buy some new clothes and then a regular income to be able to live! All the activity to try and find his "ill-gotten gains" resulted in not one pound being returned to the supposed victims; instead, everything confiscated from Daniel, was used to help run the Proceeds of Crime Unit!

But Daniel was still not a free man. He had been released early from prison under licence. He still had to register his address with the local police station and with the Probation Officer who had been appointed to keep a check on him during the rest of his sentence. He was not allowed to leave the country or to leave his registered address without permission. Every week he had to meet with his Probation Officer and even the smallest misdemeanour, or a failure to comply with these strict rules, would quickly result in his being re-arrested and placed back into a closed prison, to serve the rest of his sentence.

One day, Edwards met his friend again for lunch. "How are you getting on with things?" he asked Daniel.

"Not bad," was the reply. "My defence solicitors now want to put some paid work my way. They have recognised that I am an expert on construction, and they have a number of complex, international cases arising from disputes in the construction sector. They have asked me to advise them. I will be paid very well for each day's work that I will do. Once the period that I am out of prison on licence expires next year, I will be allowed to leave the country again. Then I might even be doing some travelling, first class of course, around the world and staying in the best hotels, like I used to do. All expenses paid by them, of course." A big smile came over his face, at that rosy prospect!

"Oh, and by the way," Daniel went on. "My new employers now think that I have a case to mount against my original fraud conviction and my long prison sentence. They are beginning to prepare the necessary papers and they are looking forward to getting their fees, paid for by the Government of course. They will then appoint a leading civil rights barrister, who will also claim his fees. If they and I are successful, then I will get a large compensation payment from the taxpayer. That means you!" he said, grinning broadly.

THE JOURNALIST

"There is no doubt fiction makes a better job of the truth." – Doris May Lessing.

1

It had all been so easy! It was a warm spring day in 1999 and he had waited patiently, just across the road, for her to return to her home in West London. Currently, she was staying with her new fiancée in another London suburb. He had already reconnoitred her movements carefully and knew that she had the habit of returning to this house, which she was in the process of selling, to collect her post, every Monday at around this time. It was in a very quiet street and suited his purpose well. When she arrived, he quickly and silently crossed the street. As she opened her handbag to get out her keys, he came up behind her. With his right arm, he grabbed her around the neck and forced her to the ground, onto her own doorstep. In his left hand, his replica automatic was ready. To avoid any blood splatter and the sound of the gunshot, he pressed the reactivated gun, which he had bought for cash in the East End of London, to her left temple, and fired a single shot. The specially made bullet with a reduced charge, to reduce the noise of the shot, exited from the right-hand side of her head. She died instantly. The gunshot had sounded only like a bottle of champagne being opened, he thought grimly.

Fully satisfied with his work, the professional assassin calmly and slowly returned to the street and walked away. He had been very well trained; he had had plenty of practice of killing and knew never to run away, as this merely drew attention to yourself. He was a member of a close-knit team, but had been living alone, under cover in London, for some months. London was somewhere you could hide in easily, but it was close enough to Europe to provide a good base. He had begun to get bored, just waiting for orders to carry out another assignment. Only three weeks before, one of his colleagues had carried out a similar task in their home city of Belgrade. Afterwards, some people would believe that the two professional killings were carried out by the same man. They failed to understand that over the years, a small, elite team had been created, and had been highly trained to carry out such tasks, against their country's enemies.

He arrived at his rather battered second-hand car, that he had bought with a wad of cash and then had registered it to a fictitious name and address, without any questions being asked. He had parked it carefully, some streets away. Then he drove it back to his small rented room, being careful not to exceed any of the speed limits. Now it would be necessary to give that room up and to abandon his car well away from where he lived. Then he would take a train to Dover, followed by a ferry to Calais. Flying involved airport security, and he wanted to carry the gun that he had gone to a lot of trouble and expense to purchase, in the false bottom of his suitcase. He would then only take trains, to carry out the several other necessary killings, in several major European cities, that had now been assigned to him.

As he drove back to where he lived, he considered the wider implications of what he had just done. "These damn Western journalists," he thought. "They are always causing trouble, with their criticism of my country. I am so pleased to be able to dispatch them but, of course, humanely." His latest victim had never realised what was about to happen to her. Using her fame as a television presenter, she had been rattling on for months about helping the refugees that had been created by the legitimate actions used by his government, to defend their own people. Her employers had been warned several times, by telephone calls, that this would not go unpunished and he had been detailed to fly to London and begin to reconnoitre her movements.

Then, just three days before, Western aircraft had attacked their national television station and sixteen of his countrymen had been killed. It had been decided, at the highest level, that since their television service had been attacked and its staff killed, then immediate retribution should be taken. He had received the agreed coded phrase to carry out this killing just two days ago; he was already well prepared to carry it out. Then he had been ordered to move on to another European city, where he would receive more orders as to when, and where, to eliminate another annoying journalist.

2

The Metropolitan Police investigated the crime; because of her standing and popularity, they were under intense pressure and scrutiny to find the perpetrator immediately. But six months later, after they had spoken to several thousand people and taken over a thousand statements, they were no further forward. Theory after theory was put forward; had it been a "gangland killing," since she was closely involved with a television programme that tried to get the help of the public to solve serious crimes? Had it been a previous lover or, perhaps, a deranged fan whose advances she had rejected? Was it a case of mistaken identity, and the wrong person had actually been killed? Had a rival journalist engaged a professional killer, so that they could benefit in some way from her death? The police seemed to be getting nowhere and the pressure on them was increasing. Although the possible theory that she had been killed for political reasons, had to be examined, that never proved popular with the police's political masters. Not only did it have international consequences, but it also showed the inability of the government to even protect its own celebrity citizens, against foreign agents, tasked to kill them. Also, it was very difficult to detain a foreign contract killer, who had probably already fled the country, and whose government would protect them against any attempt to extradite them back to face British justice.

After twelve months had elapsed, and after increasing pressure on the police, a suspect was at last found. He was really an ideal suspect: an epileptic who also, as a child, had suffered from emotional and behavioural difficulties. He had left school without any qualifications and while there, in his unhappy state of mind, had used several pseudonyms to try and give himself some status. He wanted to join the Metropolitan Police, but failed in his attempt to do so. He then obtained several forged Warrant Cards and posed as a policeman. As a result, he acquired his first criminal record. Haunted by various celebrities, he tried to assume their personas, but was always found out. He even pretended to be a member of the Special Forces to give himself some status. He was then convicted of a number of sexual assaults against women and served time in prison. His IQ was well below average and he was diagnosed with several different personality disorders, and with Asperger's Syndrome.

He was charged with the murder and brought to trial. The only real evidence, that seemed to convict him, was that he was a local man and had been seen in the street, where the murder had been committed, some hours before the murder took place. The only forensic evidence was a tiny particle of a firearm discharge found, a year after the murder, in his overcoat pocket. He was found guilty by a majority verdict and sentenced to life imprisonment. Over six years later, an Appeal was at last allowed, and his conviction was quashed.

A retrial was then ordered, but he was still kept in prison for another nine months, until his retrial could be heard. A lot was made by the prosecution of his bad character at the retrial, but the evidence of the firearm discharge was not allowed, as considerable doubt had, by then, been placed upon it. It could easily have been an innocent contamination, as his overcoat had been kept with other evidence. New witnesses were brought forward, who testified that he could not have committed the murder, as he was with them, in another part of London, at the time. There was also new evidence that other witnesses, who may have seen the real murderer, had failed to identify him. As a result, he was at last acquitted and released from prison, after serving over seven years in jail. He was, for some spurious reason, never awarded any compensation for his long, false imprisonment.

3

Edwards sat with his friend Tim in Tim's new plush offices near to Hyde Park. Tim was the part-owner and Managing Director of a company that specialised in making discrete enquiries for private clients, giving training courses for foreign police, and Customs and Excise services, and it also helped major companies battle against the people who made large amounts of money, by counterfeiting their branded goods. Tim's background was as a senior British Customs and Excise Officer; he had founded this company with a former Metropolitan Police officer some years before. Edwards had tried to help Tim by introducing potential new business to him, and advising him on international matters.

Edwards was fascinated by the techniques that Tim and his team used to try and defeat counterfeiting, which had grown substantially over the last few years. In particular, they used "Pretext Techniques" that involved pretending to be potential buyers of certain goods that, they knew, had been counterfeited. They used various methods, once they had been employed by the company, whose goods were being counterfeited. These included having a network of paid informers in the underworld, finding out and contacting those people who were selling counterfeited goods, using the search powers of the Internet, and even placing carefully worded newspaper advertisements. Edwards had once been admitted into the area, on the top floor of the office block, where this clandestine activity took place. It was behind a heavy door which, for security purposes, was always kept locked, and only people who worked there were normally admitted.

He was shown a row of telephone booths; each telephone was connected to a different number and represented either an individual, using a false name, or a company, recently set up for just this purpose, who had expressed an interest in buying particular counterfeited goods. In the middle of the room was a large table and on it were exhibited examples of counterfeit goods which the company had acquired. There were packs of cigarettes, pairs of sports trainers, handbags, clothing, bottles of perfume and even bottles of spirits, which you would not want to drink. All of them bore the well- known names of certain suppliers. Tim employed a number of intelligent young women, to do this type of work. He believed that females were often far better at putting up a "false façade" than men, and that hardened criminals would be less suspicious of them.

When the telephone rang in one of the booths, the relevant young woman left her desk to answer the telephone, and had to remember who she was pretending to be. The final aim was always to track back the counterfeited goods to their source of manufacturer and, if they could, then to shut down this source of counterfeited goods. It was during one of those operations, paid for by a leading tobacco company, that Tim had flown to the Balkans and found himself in Serbia. He had told Edwards the story of what had happened and what he had found there.

This particular "Pretext Operation", for a major tobacco company, had identified a possible source of poor quality cigarettes, but packed in perfectly counterfeited packets, in Serbia. Tim had flown to Belgrade to meet with the man, who had finally contacted them, with an offer of supplying them with large amounts of these fake cigarettes. He was an unpleasant character and seemed to be an underworld criminal type. Tim already knew the supply route from Serbia; by road to one of the smaller ports on the Adriatic, then in a very powerful speed boat across to a landing place on an Italian beach. These boats were so fast, that the poorer quality speed boats, supplied to the Italian Customs, could never catch up with them. From there, the counterfeit cigarettes could be distributed by road, across Europe, and then on to Britain. Tim played the role of a major potential buyer for the British market and demanded to see where the cigarettes were actually made.

The counterfeiter identified a factory, on the outskirts of a rural Serbian town, which was making the poor quality cigarettes very cheaply, and also supplying the perfect copies of the packaging, which was used by Tim's client. Tim took the opportunity offered to visit this factory, to try and ascertain the full scope of this criminal operation. Serbia had really started the major Balkan Wars in 1991, after the collapse of the former Yugoslavia, in an attempt to protect the Serbian population in Croatia. The war then escalated into Bosnia, where the Serbs found themselves fighting against its Muslim majority. Various major atrocities were committed by the Serbs, and many innocent Muslims were killed by them. The Western countries eventually came into the war, against the Serbs, and Serbia was at last defeated. When Tim had visited, Serbia was still in some disarray, after it had finally lost to the power of the N.A.T.O allies, who had mainly used their modern, well-equipped Air Forces to defeat Serbia, some years before.

Like in many countries, in a similar condition of poverty and dislocation, some of its population had turned to crime to support themselves. Tim found the factory and managed to gain a lot more information about the whole counterfeiting operation, by talking to the factory manager, who could just about make himself understood, in his broken English. The factory making the fake cigarettes was efficient, with modern equipment, and he also was shown the machines that produced the counterfeit packaging, that enabled this criminal gang to make substantial profits. The next stage of the operation was to smuggle out these cigarettes, in very large numbers, to European countries. There, many people were willing to buy them, at low prices, and then to sell them on, albeit still at discounted prices, to members of the public, duped by this well produced counterfeit product.

4

As had been agreed, Tim then returned to Belgrade, to meet again with the Serbian mastermind of this counterfeiting operation. He had now learnt a lot more about how and where it manufactured its illegal products. This time, he wisely decided to take some protection with him. Using a contact he had with a senior police officer in Belgrade, he employed a bodyguard who he was going to introduce as their local representative, who would make all the arrangements for shipping the counterfeit cigarettes on his behalf. Tim knew that, at some stage in this meeting, once he had discovered as much as he could about how this unpleasant man operated, he would have to tell him the truth about who he really represented!

It would be both difficult and perhaps dangerous, but he would have to tell him that what he had being doing had been discovered, and to try and persuade him to wind-down all his illegal activities. He would have to do this, as he was very uncertain if the still fragile Serbian government were really capable of shutting down this illegal enterprise, even if he now reported it all to them.

Tim looked at Edwards across his desk. "I first told him how good his counterfeiting operation was and that I was interested in buying from him," he said. "He took this as my sign of approval, and started bragging about how good he was. He told me a little about his background and how he had been in the Serbian forces, but had then been selected as a member of a small, highly trained elite team, to carry out special operations abroad."

Edwards had now become fascinated by what Tim was telling him. "What special operations did he carry out?" he asked.

"I was coming on to that," replied Tim. "He said to me that, as I was an Englishman, I would be interested in how he had personally carried out, on the direct orders of their then President Slobodan Milosevic, a contract killing in London in April,

1999. His victim was a journalist and television presenter called Jill Dando."

Edwards gasped. He well remembered this popular television personality, who used to present the B.B.C. Crime Watch program and who was brutally murdered on her own doorstep in Fulham, West London. He also knew that this crime was still really unsolved. The police had, some twelve months after this terrible event, arrested a local man called Barry George. He had been tried, convicted and sentenced to life imprisonment, but had always protested that he was innocent. Now, there were some real, serious doubts about his guilt, and an appeal against his conviction was pending.

"But Tim," he asked, "was he just boasting? Did you believe him?"

"Yes I did believe him," replied Tim. "I judged that he was telling me the truth. He also supplied me with some real details that, I think, only her killer would know."

"You must really report this to the police here," said Edwards.

Tim shook his head. "I am not going to do that," he replied. "It gets a lot worse and more complicated than that. This man then told me that he went on to murder three other journalists in Paris, Frankfurt and Madrid. It was all done because all these four journalists had spoken out strongly against what the Serbs were doing to their Muslim neighbours. The Serbs had justified their terrible acts of Ethnic Cleansing, by saying that they were protecting the Serb minorities in these other countries, which had once formed part of the united Yugoslavia. This man is a crazy Serb Nationalist and he was actually proud of what he had done!"

"But what about that poor guy, called Barry George, who is still in prison?" asked Edwards.

"I have looked into that," said Tim "And I think that, on appeal, he is going to get off."

"But you can't be sure of that," replied Edwards. But Tim was not interested; he was more interested in telling Edwards what had happened next.

"I humoured him a bit," continued Tim. "I tried to find out more about his counterfeiting operation. Then, when I became convinced that I had got out of him all the information that I needed, I switched the whole thing around. I told him who I really represented and that he was just a criminal, who should now give up on this illegal activity. That's when it happened!"

"What happened?" asked Edwards quickly.

"He drew a gun! But, fortunately, the guy that I had employed was quicker on the draw. He drew out his gun faster and shot him in the arm. The bastard dropped his gun, but he got one shot off first. I felt the bullet as it whistled past my ear!"

"Good God!" responded Edwards. "He could have killed you!"

"That was his general idea," replied Tim calmly. "But by now he was squealing like an injured pig. I took his gun and left him to be looked after by my bodyguard. I reported the whole situation to my police contact there and gave him the gun, before flying back home. I also told him what this bastard had told me, about what he had done. Now, I am still waiting to see if the Serbian government will close down the whole counterfeiting operation. But, at least, I have now identified the source of the counterfeit cigarettes, which I had been asked to do by our client. It is now up to them to use their lawyers, and to exert any political pressure that they can, to try and stop this criminal activity."

Back in his home, Edwards thought about his conversation with Tim. He was surprised that Tim had refused to report what he had been told in Belgrade, to the Metropolitan Police. He could not understand why Tim could not try and help what appeared to be an innocent man, who had been wrongly imprisoned. He decided that, therefore, he must do something himself. He looked up the email address of the Pressure Group that was trying to prove that Barry George was innocent. He then drafted up a long, carefully worded and confidential email to them, telling them what he had been told but, of course, leaving Tim's name out of it. Then he had sent them his long email, signing it with his full name.

He received no response to his long communication, and he would never know if this email had any effect on the final outcome. But, a few months later, Barry George's appeal against his conviction, was finally accepted. He was then released from his long imprisonment, for a terrible crime that he had never committed.

A WALK IN THE WOODS

"How easy it is, Treachery. You just slide into it"
– Margaret Atwood.

1

Edwards listened carefully to Michael, his friend and old colleague. Edwards had used his land line to call Michael's land line, for reasons of security. Both men knew that, in this day and age, the modern mobile telephone was the main instrument used for advanced personal surveillance by both governments, and by the commercial sector, and that mobile telephone calls could be easily intercepted and listened to.

"Whatever you do," said the familiar voice on the other end of the line, "do not go for a walk in the woods!"

Edwards had called him because of the sad news; he remembered well the man who had just died. He had met him several times at the Ministry's social events. Edwards had thought him rather quiet and reserved; in many ways just the rather shy, mild-mannered, academic scientist that he actually was. Michael, a colleague of Edwards at the time, had introduced them before going off to speak to some other people at the party and leaving them to talk together for a while. The party was being held in an astonishing venue; somewhere where normal members of the public were never allowed to enter. Besides the staff serving in the massive Main Building upstairs, and some others in nearby outposts, the only other people ever to be taken down there, under close escort, were very senior foreign dignitaries who were visiting Britain.

Around them now were the red brick walls of a sixteenth century cellar, which had once been part of the largest palace in Europe. Most of this vast building had been destroyed in a major fire in 1698, but this part remained. To reach this cellar, you had to descend endless flights of stairs, past many mysterious basements and sub-basements. It was now hidden deep in the bowels of the more modern building above. As you descended the last staircase, you came to a heavy door; beyond that was a surreal sight. In the middle of a huge room stood these almost intact Tudor remains of what was once a great building. They were just as they would have been over four hundred years ago, when they had stored the large stocks of wine and the other alcoholic drinks that had then belonged to the Kings and Queens of England.

Edwards was shocked by what his friend had just said and the tone that he had used. He was being very serious. It meant only one thing. The late scientist, whose body had been found in woods near his home in Oxfordshire, had not committed suicide, as had been announced. He could have been murdered!

Edwards knew that his friend Michael had worked very closely with this man, to jointly provide the definitive study on the chemical and biological weapons capability of the Iraqi regime. That was his job, as he had a senior role in the secretive intelligence organisation that was never talked about, and was rarely even called by its real name.

The public now thought that they knew quite a lot about the two organisations that dealt with internal, and external intelligence, but they really knew very little about the activities of this even more vital organisation. Its main role was to very carefully assess the aggressive and defensive military capabilities of Britain's potential enemies, and its friends. With some people, where he knew it would go no further, Edwards often amused himself by asking them this question: "We have M.I. Five and M.I. Six, but what do you think has happened with M.I. One through to M.I. Four?"

He knew that this organisation was the answer, and he would then remind those that he was speaking to, that the term "M.I." went back to a period before the First World War, and actually meant "Military Intelligence." Although both "5 and 6" had little connection these days, with that area of activity, this branch of the British intelligence services had everything to do with it. Staffed, as it was, with a mix of serving senior military officers, and civilian specialist experts in weapons, military technology and tactics, planning, training and military deployments of all kinds, it provided a constant and updated picture of the most serious threats facing Britain.

When he had worked closely with his friend and his colleagues, some years before, he had been asked to assist in the analysis of certain information that had been gleaned secretly from around the world. Edwards was an expert in international finance and those around him had little knowledge of these matters. Usually he was given a report on the activity of certain overseas companies; many of these were located in countries far away, or in overseas territories that were deemed to be "Tax Havens." In these territories, the local authorities were really little concerned about the actual ownership of these companies, or their activities.

The reported activity of these companies usually involved the purchase and shipment of certain specific, sensitive items, that could deemed to be useful in the manufacture of certain types of weapons. Usually these were to be shipped to some third country but then, of course, they would be diverted at sea, or just shipped on, to their ultimate destination. It was on the method and source of payment that he was usually asked to give his views, and he was happy to help in this work. He quickly realised that this was of vital national and international importance and helped, in some way, to prevent the international proliferation of nuclear, chemical and biological weapons. The collective term for these was the so-called "Weapons of Mass Destruction."

2

In 1916, with the impending collapse of the Ottoman Empire during the First World War, a secret agreement was signed between Britain and France. It was later to be known as the Sykes-Picot Agreement, after the two diplomats who had negotiated it. This agreement split the Middle East, then controlled by the Ottomans, into two agreed spheres of influence, between Britain and France. Straight lines were often drawn, using a ruler, on a map of the Middle East, without having much regard to political precedent, the ancient history of the region, religious beliefs, or the strong tribal nature of the peoples contained within these straight lines. Britain acquired the right to control the territory which would later be combined into the country to be called Iraq. This had been previously been ruled, for some four hundred years, by the Ottomans, who had wisely split this area into three autonomous provinces containing the Arab Shia Muslim majority, the Arab Sunni Muslim minority, and the non-Arab Kurds.

The Sunni and Shia sects of Islam had been in dispute ever since the clear emergence of the Shia sect in the seventh century. This schism had been caused by a dispute over who should inherit the religious leadership of Islam, from the various family branches of the descendants of the Prophet Muhammad. This dispute was both long-standing, and current; and so the scene was set, by the action of the Western Powers, in their ignorance and their arrogance, for an unstable future for the Middle East, and for decades of Western meddling in that region.

In 1921, the British established the new country of Iraq as a monarchy, with a King chosen by the British from the Hashemite Royal Family from Jordan. The British also made use of the minority Sunni Arab elite, appointing them to local ministries and as administrators, against the wishes of the Shia Arab majority. This new country gained independence from Britain in 1932, but was never politically stable. During the Second World War, the Western Allies invaded and again controlled Iraq, in an effort to keep its oil wealth away from the Germans. In 1958, the monarchy was overthrown by a military coup, the Royal Family were killed and the Republic of Iraq was created. Further military coups then followed, and the country descended into a state of complete instability.

In 1968, the then ruling military dictator was overthrown by representatives of the powerful political Socialist Ba'ath Party, which had been founded in 1951. The Americans became very concerned about the Socialist nature of the Ba'ath Party, and feared that it might take Iraq, with its vast oil reserves, into the Soviet Union sphere of influence. In 1979, after years of American effort to control the Socialist inclination of the Ba'ath Party, a probable agent working for the American Central Intelligence Agency, called Saddam Hussein, seized power and became President of Iraq.

Also in 1979, the Iranian Islamic Revolution had taken place; the new Iranian government overthrew the pro-American ruler, the Shah of Iran. It was anti-Western and took fifty-two American citizens hostage when the American Embassy in Tehran was stormed by a mob in November of that year. Iran had always been a majority Shia country and, in retaliation, Saddam Hussein, the new Iraqi President, was encouraged by the Americans to invade Iran, which he did in September 1980. This initiated the Iran-Iraq War that continued until 1988. Hundreds of thousands of troops and civilians were killed on both sides and, for the first time, chemical weapons, with the components supplied by the West, were used by Iraq. Despite continuing, heavy support from Western countries, Saddam Hussein failed to secure the major victory over the Iranians that his Western backers had expected. The West continued consistently to support him and the Iraq military, against the Iranians, until it became very clear that the two sides had fought themselves to a standstill, and that the war could not go on.

On the 3 July 1988 Iran Air Flight 655, flying between the Iranian port of Bandar Abbas and Dubai, was mistakenly shot down by an anti-aircraft missile fired by the American Navy ship U.S.S. Vincennes, with a loss of 290 lives. It is now becoming clear that in retaliation, Pan Am Flight 103 was brought down by the Iranians, over Lockerbie in Scotland on 21 December 1988, by means of a bomb in the luggage hold, with a loss of 259 lives. This revenge attack was carried out on the direct orders of the Iranian leader Grand Ayatollah Khomeini. The bag containing the bomb had been put on the aircraft when it had stopped in Frankfurt. It had been transferred, without proper inspection, from a flight from Malta, as onward baggage.

Despite the obvious connection, the West refused to blame the Iranians. It would have been embarrassing to do so at that time, because the Iranian government had so recently agreed to end the disastrous Iran-Iraq War. Instead, the blame had to be placed on another country, whose borders had also been drawn by the West using a straight ruler. Instead of Iran, Libya and its strongman ruler Colonel Muammar Gaddafi were allocated the blame. He, like Saddam Hussein, was also struggling to keep his artificial country, again created by the West, together. Originally Libya had consisted of three autonomous territories. After the Second World War, these had been forced together, by the West, into one country, ruled by a puppet King. In 1969, a military coup had forced the King out and its leader, Gaddafi, had seized power.

3

Edwards sat with his American friend, having breakfast in the dining room of the first-class London hotel where the American was staying. Under the American social code, his rank as a former American Ambassador was still recognised, and his business card still carried that title, even though he had retired from the American Foreign Service some years before. He had been born in Connecticut, but had spent many years in California, where he had attended the University of California at Santa Barbara. He had become fluent in French and, when he joined the American Foreign Service, he had been first posted to a number of French-speaking African countries. He had finished off his diplomatic career as the American Ambassador to several of these same French-speaking countries. Between 1988 and 1991 however, he was the Deputy Head of Mission in Baghdad, and he was there when Saddam Hussein had decided to invade Kuwait in 1990.

The female American Ambassador had been ordered back to Washington, so he had become the acting Ambassador. As such, he was the last American diplomat to meet with, and to try and negotiate with, Saddam Hussein. In this role, he had been highly successful; he personally negotiated with the Iraqi President for the safe release and removal from Iraq of several thousand foreigners, including both Americans, and many other nationalities. Each time that these people were leaving, he went to Baghdad Airport and personally supervised their exit from the country, in order to ensure that there was no Iraqi last-minute attempt to block their final departure. His fear was that these foreigners would be taken as hostages by the Iraqi regime, once the Western countries themselves invaded Kuwait, in order to free it from its Iraqi captors. When he finally safely returned to the United States, President George H. W. Bush had hailed him, Acting Ambassador Joseph C. Wilson, as "a true American hero."

Edwards was interested in his friend's stories about the time that he had spent in Baghdad, particularly in his interaction with Saddam Hussein. When Hussein had sent a note to all the Embassies in Baghdad, threatening to execute anyone sheltering foreigners, Joe Wilson had appeared at a Presidential Press Conference, with a homemade noose around his neck. He had then publically told Saddam Hussein that, "If the choice is to allow American citizens to be taken hostage or to be executed, I will bring my own fucking rope." This act of sheer bravery seems to have endeared him to the Iraqi dictator; they had met many times afterwards in a friendly and co-operative atmosphere.

"Saddam liked large cigars," his friend had told Edwards. "Whenever we met, just the two of us, in his private office, where he kept a large box of them on his desk, he would offer me one and then take one himself. Then we both lit them up, and smoked them together, as we talked. Whenever he objected to what I wanted to do, I would blow my cigar smoke directly into his face. Then he would do the same to me. Then we would both burst out laughing. After that amusing routine, he would agree to all that I wanted!"

Whenever this American friend visited London, they would meet. Edwards enjoyed these occasions; his friend had a quick and erudite mind. The conversations between Edwards and his American friend, Joe, always covered many topics. Joe Wilson was fast talking and very knowledgeable about many parts of the world. When they met, they compared extensive notes on a number of different topics and countries. In one of those meetings he had told Edwards of his fears about the growing Republican Neo-Conservative element, within American politics.

"These people think that the rest of the world is just like the United States," he had said. "They think that they can easily impose American ideas and political systems on other countries."

Edwards now knew exactly what he had meant. The next few years had proved to be traumatic; the son of the former American President, George W. Bush, had now been elected to the same post as his father. Just eight months after taking office, the new President had to deal with the horrific events of 11 September 2001. The American invasion of Afghanistan quickly followed. But this was not enough for the secret coterie of "Neo-Cons", which now controlled the new Bush American administration. They decided for no apparent reason, that Saddam Hussein had been responsible for, or had assisted in terrorist acts, despite the fact that he was, as a secular ruler, totally opposed to Muslim extremism and to Al-Qaeda, who had carried out the attack on the "Twin Towers" in New York. It was also claimed that he was creating an increasing stockpile of chemical and biological weapons and, at the same time, seeking to develop nuclear weapons. As such, he was a serious threat to the West and had to be removed.

In February 2002, Ambassador Joseph Wilson was sent by the American Central Intelligence Agency, because of his experience of the area, to the French-speaking African country of Niger. He had been asked to investigate reports that Saddam Hussein had bought substantial quantities of "yellowcake uranium," which was mined in this country, in order that he could make nuclear weapons. Using his many high-level contacts in Niger, Edwards's friend had found absolutely no evidence of this claim, and reported back to Washington the truth as he had found it. Despite these facts, President George W. Bush, in his 2003 State of the Union Address, again raised this allegation against Saddam Hussein. This allegation, and further allegations, that the Iraqis possessed chemical and biological "Weapons of Mass Destruction," were then used to justify the start of the Second Gulf War in March 2003, and the subsequent invasion of Iraq.

In response to this failure to accept his true findings in Niger, Edwards's friend wrote an article for a New York newspaper, repeating that he had found nothing in Niger to justify these American government claims. He wrote that the facts, and all the intelligence reports, had been twisted to justify the war and the invasion of Iraq.

Edwards had also met his American friend's current wife, Valerie Plame; he had been introduced to her, and the three of them had lunched together at their London hotel. His suspicions about her actual job were confirmed when, one week after her husband's newspaper article, she was illegally revealed, by an aid to the American Secretary of Defence, as a senior undercover agent of the American Central Intelligence Agency. Her speciality was in the area of preventing the proliferation of "Weapons of Mass Destruction" and, as such, she was clearly in a position to advise her husband on his views about his visit to Niger. As a result she had to leave her secret position; the government adviser was eventually found guilty of the criminal offence of "outing" an American intelligence officer, but his jail sentence was commuted by President George W. Bush.

The couple never recovered from the stress of this attempt to discredit them by illegally revealing her secret, and very sensitive role. This had been done by the then American government, clearly in revenge, for the reasoned and sincere opposition of her husband, to what they had decided, despite the facts, to do in Iraq. Over the following few years, this continued government persecution had put a considerable strain upon them and their family, and they had eventually left Washington, with their two small children, to live in New Mexico.

What became clear were the reasons for this twisting of the facts to justify, what many people still believed, was an illegal war. It was not, as some believed, to gain control of the Iraqi oil reserves. The Second Gulf War was the first "fully privatised" war; many of the goods and services required to fight it, which were previously provided by the military themselves, were now bought, at an inflated cost with high profit margins, from the private sector. Along with this, all the weapons and military equipment were also provided by the American defence industry. At a total estimated direct cost of 1.7 trillion Dollars, this proved to be the largest ever transfer of funds from the American taxpayer to the private sector. Many major American companies made huge profits and those clever investors, some of whom no doubt had prior notice of the war, and had bought shares in these American companies, made personal fortunes. For these kinds of people, a mere 4,400 American military dead, no doubt seemed a very cheap price to pay for their vast profits. But the nearly eight years of war and the communal strife that followed it, also resulted in nearly one million Iraqi dead, and many more dead from the forces of the other countries, who foolishly had decided to contribute as military allies to the Americans.

Edwards learned from this story; loyal, brave, but perhaps too honest public servants could so easily fall out with the current political regime. In the world of high politics, how easy it was to move from being hailed a "hero," to being clearly identified as a "villain!" These kinds of people could easily become embarrassing and inconvenient to their political masters, particularly if they failed to comply, or stood out against their current political thinking and desires. As a result they could suffer continued harassment, lose their positions and be publically eliminated, so that their voices, which spoke against the then political orthodoxy, could be drowned out. This total public elimination could also serve as a lesson to others, who might themselves be inclined to criticise the current political regime for the decisions that they had made. Edwards began to look for other such examples, perhaps nearer to home?

4

On both side of the Atlantic Ocean, those that confronted the government propaganda to justify this war, with the simple truth, were made to suffer. In Britain, the facts were twisted to justify the decision to support the Americans. A technical Dossier, to be considered by senior levels of the British government, was carefully prepared by Edwards's friend and former colleague, Michael, and parts of it were provided by Doctor David Kelly, the highly experienced Weapons Inspector who had visited Iraq many times. It was finally published in September 2002, to justify Britain joining the Americans to remove Saddam Hussein by force of arms. David Kelly was an authority on biological warfare; he was seconded to the British Ministry of Defence, and was a much-admired Weapons Inspector with the United Nations Special Commission for Iraq. This Commission was centred on the area of counter-proliferation of "Weapons of Mass Destruction," and was slowly removing the Iraqi advanced weapons capability, as agreed with Iraq, after the Iraqi defeat in the First Gulf War that had followed their invasion of Kuwait.

But the views of others had then been added to this objectively prepared dossier, including the claims of a long-standing paid Iraqi agent, who now resided in Germany. The intelligence provided by this man proved unreliable as, like many paid agents, he often provided intelligence that he thought that his spymasters would like to hear, and pay him well for. David Kelly was interviewed, in confidence, by a British journalist, and expressed his serious doubts about the current form of the dossier which he had originally helped to write. By now, it had been very much altered by the Prime Minister's office, to include a spurious claim that the Iraqi's were capable of firing battlefield biological and chemical weapons within 45 minutes of the order to use them. This false claim, within the dossier, led to some British newspapers, no doubt prompted by the government's propaganda machine, to publish the ludicrous claim "that Britain was 45 minutes away from an attack by Iraq's Weapons of Mass Destruction!"

In the same way as the wife of Edwards's American friend Joseph Wilson, David Kelly was then purposely "outed" by the British government as the scientist who had raised serious doubts, with a journalist, about the false claims contained in what later became known as the "Dodgy Dossier." He was very well qualified to raise these doubts, having inspected numerous so-called chemical and biological weapon facilities in Iraq, over many years, and having found out that all the claims about these dangerous developments, that had previously been put forward, had been totally false.

David Kelly was called before the House of Commons Foreign Affairs Select Committee on 15 July 2003. His questioning by the Members of Parliament present seemed quite aggressive, and it was assumed that this had put him under some stress, although afterwards he seemed very relaxed and had even joked with some of his colleagues about the questioning that he had faced. Despite the government's claim that he was the "source" of the doubts expressed, the Committee decided that Kelly was not the main source that had been used by the journalist. The following day, he was questioned, behind closed doors, by the House of Commons Intelligence and Security Committee; again he did not seem to have had a particularly stressful time. He told them simply that he was part of the United Nations inspection team in Iraq that ensured that all "Weapons of Mass Destruction" had been destroyed, following the First Gulf War in 1991. As such he was a regular visitor to Iraq and was well known to the Iraqi authorities.

Around the same time as these Committee Meetings, a former American military intelligence officer had revealed that David Kelly was a vital part of the secret "Operation Rockingham"; a long-term joint American-British effort to amass evidence against Iraq of their unconventional weapons activity, despite the fact that it appeared that the Iraqis were now really doing very little of this kind of advanced development. The timing of this revelation seemed to be surprisingly convenient for the British government, as it seemed to increase the stress on David Kelly, and led to the conclusion that, as a result, he had taken his own life. David Kelly was obviously worried about his work in Iraq; in February 2003 he had told a British diplomat in Geneva that, if Iraq was invaded, he "would probably be found dead in the woods!" At the time, the British diplomat took this as a reference to the fact that the Iraqis would try and kill him for what he had done.

On the morning of 17 July 2003 David Kelly was working normally at his home in Oxfordshire; he appeared optimistic to the people who telephoned him, and grateful for the many messages of support that he was getting. In the afternoon he went out for his regular walk, which usually took just thirty minutes. He was seen and spoken to by someone who knew him well: he was in good spirits and walking back towards his home. It was not until just before midnight that his daughter reported him missing; a full police search was immediately put into place, including the use of a helicopter with heat-detecting technology. Early the following morning, he was found dead in woodland on Harrowdown Hill, about a mile from his home, but in completely the opposite direction from that he was last seen walking in, by the last person who has admitted to seeing him alive. He was only fifty-nine years old and, according to his regular medical examinations, fit and healthy. It was immediately claimed that he had committed suicide, despite no proper inquest having being carried out. He was said to have swallowed nearly 30 painkiller tablets and have cut his left wrist with a knife, which he had owned since his youth. But, just a few years before, David Kelly had converted to the Baha'i Faith which, like many other faiths, teaches that suicide is a mortal sin against God.

5

The news that David Kelly's body had been found, was deemed to be so important that the most senior legal official, the Lord Chancellor Charles Falconer, was quickly informed, and he immediately telephoned the Prime Minister, Tony Blair. At the time, the Prime Minister was 35,000 feet above the Pacific Ocean, flying between major international meetings in Washington, and Tokyo. Blair was told that David Kelly "had been found dead as a result of suspected suicide." Blair immediately told Falconer, his friend and former flat-mate, to appoint a Public Inquiry "into the events leading up to David Kelly's death." Both Blair and Falconer were qualified barristers and therefore knew the law well. Within hours, Falconer had appointed his trusted contact, Lord Hutton, to carry out this Inquiry, even though Hutton had no experience whatever of such Inquiries, or of the law surrounding the type of inquests that are normally always carried out in the case of a suspicious death. The form of

Public Inquiry chosen was also deficient as, unlike a Coroner's Court, it had no legal right to call witnesses and demand that they give evidence under oath.

The Hutton Inquiry was then used to cleverly supersede the tried and tested procedure of a public Coroner's Inquest. From the outset, it was assumed that David Kelly had committed suicide, and the Inquiry carried out none of the proper questioning that a Coroner's Inquest would have done, to determine the true causes and circumstances of the death. Many witnesses were not called who could have contributed vital evidence, and the proceedings were clearly slanted so that, in January 2004, the Inquiry concluded that David Kelly had indeed committed suicide as had been first presumed. But Lord Hutton then took an unprecedented step; so that his conclusions could never be examined, he locked away all the papers and the medical evidence from public scrutiny for seventy years!

Nevertheless, various medical opinions were then voiced for, or against, the Inquiry result. The civilian searchers, who had found the body, reported that the scene of death looked "almost like a film set." The paramedics, who had then attended the scene, reported that there was virtually no blood loss from the body, and also felt that the scene looked contrived. Both teams reported that the body was initially in a different position from that shown by the official police photographs, taken shortly afterwards. Even this fact was ignored by the Hutton Inquiry!

Some doctors claimed that the dosage of tablets that David Kelly had taken, were insufficient to cause his death. Because his right arm had not been properly repaired after a riding accident some years before, a witness who knew him well but was never called as a witness, said that it would have been impossible for him to inflict the wounds found on his left wrist, because of this past injury.

Other doctors then claimed that that this was a failed suicide attempt but, because of the severe narrowing of the arteries that he suffered from, and the stress that he had been under, he had died of a heart attack. But this heart problem had never been diagnosed during his regular medical examinations by Ministry of Defence doctors over many years. Furthermore, the Post Mortem had been carried out in the very early morning, the day after the body had been found, and it appeared slipshod. This was because the height and weight of the body given was inconsistent with the same measurements, taken over time, at the regular, thorough medical examinations that David Kelly had attended. The last such regular medical examination that he had been given, had taken place only ten days before his death!

There were calls for his body to be exhumed, for a second Post Mortem to be carried out, and then a proper formal Inquest to be held. But his body was then quietly removed from its grave and cremated at the request, so it was later reported, of his family. But there were too many other uncertainties and anomalies in the circumstances surrounding his death, and the events leading up to it. One person, who knew him well, reported that he had great difficulty in taking tablets, and for him to have swallowed nearly thirty tablets would have been impossible. Further to that, the bottle of water, that he had not taken from home, and had mysteriously been found with him, was still nearly full. Insufficient water had been drunk from it to swallow the large number of tablets that it was claimed that he had taken. The contents of his stomach showed the presence of just a small number of tablets, so where had all the other tablets gone? During its aerial search, the helicopter had flown over the exact spot where the body was found, but its advanced heat-seeking equipment had failed to detect it, even though it would have still been warm enough at this time, to have been picked up by this equipment.

Most telling of all was the result of a Freedom of Information Request made in October 2007. It had been a warm July day and David Kelly had not been wearing gloves. But the answer to this Request revealed that no fingerprints, of any kind, were found on David Kelly's mobile phone, on the blister packs for the tablets that he was supposed to have swallowed, on the bottle of water he was thought to have used, or on the knife that he had supposedly used to cut his wrist. All these items must have been carefully wiped clean of any fingerprints! Either David Kelly had done this himself, before he had died, or any fingerprints had been carefully wiped off before these items were taken by the police as evidence, and then closely examined. The conclusion seemed clear; some unknown person or persons must have been present at his death and had then arranged his body to look like suicide. They had touched these items, and had then carefully wiped them clean to hide their presence. How else could this have happened?

6

So what had really happed to David Kelly? It seems, on the balance of the evidence, that he had either conveniently died of natural causes or had been murdered and then the unconvincing signs of his suicide had been faked. He was well known to the Iraqis and, despite the doubts he had expressed about the Dossier, he had been identified by them as the man who had carried out numerous sensitive weapon inspections over many years. He had just been "outed" as being an important part of "Operation Rockingham" which, the Iraqis would have thought, was designed to provide false evidence against them. The Iraqi Secret Service operated in Britain and they appeared to have carried out at least one murder in the past, which had not been reported as such.

David Kelly was a man of regular habits; when he was at home he always took the same short walk, at the same time of day. How easy it would have been to intercept him in a quiet street and then take him to an isolated wood? If the pills or the knife had failed to work, a clean plastic bag held over the head would induce suffocation and maybe, even, a heart attack. No government likes to admit that a foreign intelligence service has committed murder on its own soil; it makes them look incapable of protecting their own citizens, and can cause major diplomatic problems and calls for revenge. Much better to hide the facts if you can!

But then, could the British government itself be to blame? This would seem to be more likely than the Iraqis taking any action in a hostile foreign country, and there already seemed to be ample evidence to point this way. The fact that David Kelly was living under great stress, was reported by his family, and was assumed by the Hutton Inquiry, but this did not seem clear to many independent witnesses who had either met him, or talked to him on the telephone, immediately before his death. On 9 July, one week before he died, he was visited at home by another journalist, who had not written the original article. This journalist had warned him that his name would be published the following morning, as the person who had ridiculed the "Dodgy Dossier." Later that evening, he was telephoned by the Ministry of Defence, who advised him to leave home, at once, as hordes of journalists were on their way to interview him the following morning. According to David Kelly's wife, they had then quickly packed two suitcases, got into their car, and started to drive down to Cornwall, to stay in a cottage that had been offered to them by two of Mrs. Kelly's friends. As it was late at night, they had stopped at an unnamed hotel in the Somerset seaside resort of Weston-super-Mare. However, David Kelly, himself, was never heard to mention this overnight stay.

Instead, that evening, when he was supposed to be driving down to Cornwall, David Kelly was seen and spoken to by sixteen independent witnesses in a public house, just a mile away from his home. Fifteen were his regular friends, who he met every week to play the game of cribbage. The other witness was the landlord of the public house. Indeed, David Kelly was very relaxed and in fine spirits that evening; with his playing partner, he had won that evening's match, and he did not leave for home until half-past ten. It seems therefore, that the Kelly's did not leave their house until the following morning. Even then, David Kelly stopped off to visit a colleague, not far from his home, to deliver some malaria medication to him as they were both already booked to fly out to Iraq again at the end of the following week. Were these the actions of a man under severe stress and afraid of the press? None of these witnesses, who could testify as to Dr Kelly's relaxed mood, were ever called to give evidence to the Hutton Inquiry. Was it Mrs. Kelly who had invented the immediate journey to the south-west of England, and the story of the overnight hotel stay in Weston-super-Mare, to show that they had obeyed the instructions of the Ministry of Defence?

Once down in Cornwall, the Kellys visited various tourist sites, and a local couple who looked after the cottage that they were staying in, when it was left empty. David Kelly talked to the husband for more than an hour, and appeared to be very relaxed and happy. On the Sunday, he drove back to Oxford to stay with his daughter, so it would be easy for him to get to London, by train, to give his evidence to the two House of Commons Committees. Mrs Kelly returned to their own home, by train the next day. On the Monday, the first Committee Meeting decided that he was not the main source of "the leak" about the Dossier, so why should he have been at all stressed and worried by this? He had just been largely exonerated! Afterwards, he had even laughed and joked with some friendly colleagues who had accompanied him to the Committee Meeting.

Yet, just two days later, the Hutton Inquiry had decided that he had committed suicide, because of his extreme stress and depression. Not only that, but the suicide was allegedly carried out by two methods which, because of his disabilities, he would certainly not have chosen, as he would have known that they would have been virtually impossible to carry out. The helicopter, equipped with advanced thermal-imaging equipment, did not detect his body even when it had flown over the site where it was found, only a few hours later. His body therefore seems to have been moved and then moved again, before being photographed. David Kelly had also somehow, amazingly, as he was dying, wiped off all his own fingerprints from all the items that he was carrying, including the tablet wraps and the knife that he had used to supposedly commit suicide!

Might the true circumstances of David Kelly's death lie in a statement made by one John Scarlett, then the Chairman of the Joint Intelligence Committee, and later to be promoted to be the Chief of the Secret Intelligence Service, known as M.I.6, and subsequently knighted? On 7 July, Scarlett had suggested that David Kelly should "take part in a proper security-style interview" and, later that day, it was agreed in a meeting chaired by the Prime Minister, that such an interrogation should take place.

Were the Prime Minister's orders then carried out? A natural day to carry out this secret interrogation would be on the day after his two appearances before the House of Commons Committees, when he might be in a weakened mental condition and certainly before his next planned visit to Iraq at the end of that week. Given his regular habits, it would have been as easy for British government agents to intercept him in a quiet street that he was walking down, back towards his home, as it could have been for the Iraqis. He could have been put into a car, and taken somewhere to have been questioned.

Was the suspicion perhaps that he had become too close and too sympathetic with the Iraqis? Would that, perhaps, mean a hostile interrogation, which could have triggered his "hidden" heart problems, and could he have then died from a heart attack? Or could it have been even more sinister than that, as it was decided that, at all costs, he could not be allowed to go back to Iraq again? Mrs. Kelly admitted to having had some "visitors" at her home the afternoon of her husband's disappearance, but no names or further details were ever given, and these visitors were never called to give evidence. Could they have perhaps collected the tablets that were kept as part of Mrs. Kelly's stock, for the joint pain that she suffered from, and had these been planted, along with the bottle of water found next to David Kelly's body? Could these "visitors" also, later, have asked Mrs. Kelly not to report her husband's disappearance until midnight?

Was David Kelly's body kept somewhere, until it was moved and then carefully placed on Harrowdown Hill, after the helicopter had flown over, in a carefully staged "tableau", contrived to lead to a suicide verdict? Were these the true circumstances that led to the apparent panic at the top of government, resulting in the then Prime Minister being contacted urgently, whilst flying over the Pacific Ocean, about the unexpected death of such a relatively unimportant middle-ranking official? Was this why a suicide was immediately assumed as the cause of death, even before any proper inquiry or Post Mortem had been carried out? Was this the reason that the Hutton Inquiry was convened so quickly, and made to supersede the tried and tested methods of a Coroner's Court? Was this why this Inquiry made so many preconceived assumptions, failed to properly investigate all the circumstances, failed to call relevant witnesses, and failed to establish the real causes and the story behind the tragic and unexplained death of Doctor David Kelly?

7

But what was the basis of the claims of the Dossier, before all the lies and hype had been added? Edwards thought that, on the basis of his experience, probably Saddam Hussein had been playing what he had thought was a clever game. He was afraid of the Iraqi majority Shia Muslims, afraid of the Shia Iranians against whom he had started a war in 1980, and afraid of the West, who might try and topple him. Knowing that his every move was scrutinised, he seems to have carried out a "confidence trick." Purchases of certain components, needed for the serious development of chemical and biological weapons, were still continued, even after his defeat in the First Gulf War. But nothing seems to have been done with these components and the previous Iraqi development program of "Weapons of Mass Destruction" was never restarted. But Saddam Hussein wanted the West, and others, to still think that he had the capability to develop these weapons and, indeed, that he was probably still doing so. This was in order to provide a deterrent to protect himself, and to stop any possible military action that might be taken against him.

Instead these tactics "backfired" badly against him, and rational people like Edwards's former colleague Michael, who had access to the secret information on the Iraqi purchases of certain sensitive equipment, could only conclude that the capability to make these advanced weapons was still there, and that they were still being developed. So Saddam was caught out by his own "confidence trick." The governments of America and Britain tried to prove that Saddam was still making these weapons and was a "clear and present danger" to their countries, then the Western political leaders conspired to try and made something out of this belief. After Iraq was invaded, the West was genuinely shocked when none of these weapons were actually found. But, as a result of his trickery, Saddam Hussein was deposed, captured and eventually hanged.

The results of the Second Gulf War were disastrous. The violent and unnecessary removal of Saddam Hussein, by the invading Western forces, not only destabilised Iraq, leading to civil disruption and many deaths, but also prompted the so-called "Arab Spring." In other Arab countries, a disenchanted population tried to remove their own unpopular and undemocratic rulers. Only in one country, Tunisia, was that movement really successful. In Egypt, the army eventually reasserted its power. In Syria and Yemen, long civil wars resulted, with massive destruction and heavy loss of life. Iraq, that artificially created country, itself descended into a long war of opposition against the invading forces, which then turned into an intermittent civil war between the Shias, Sunnis and Kurds. Discontented, and now unemployed, senior Iraqi military and intelligence officers, worked hard to establish an even more radical, anti-Western version of Al Qaeda, the Islamic State. This would then need another war to remove it.

The only country that really benefitted from the Second Gulf War, was the Islamic Republic of Iran. For the West, the strong Law of Unintended Consequences now brought this major setback. With the Shia majority now ruling Iraq, their Iranian Shia brothers could establish a powerful "Iranian Crescent", through Iraq to Syria, and on to Lebanon and Yemen, all the way to the shores of the Mediterranean and the Red Sea. "Proxy Wars" began in the Middle East, with a now fearful Saudi Arabia and its Sunni allies, with the support of the West, on one side, and Iran, with its new allies of Russia and China, on the other.

The West's invasion of Iraq and its long-standing interference in the rest of the region had only resulted in their ultimate defeat, loss of influence, growing instability in the region and the strong and unexpected strengthening of the anti-Western Islamic Republic of Iran. The Western leaders' own ignorance, treachery and greed, had been the ultimate causes of this disaster for the Western countries. Despite all their efforts, and with the deaths, the destruction and the heavy costs, the West had just "Reaped the Whirlwind of History!"

The treachery of politicians, investors and businessmen, was evident; they put their own private profit before the good of their country, by profiteering from the war and taking the bribes to make it happen. Their actions created many victims; the dead and the injured of their own countries, as well as the future generations who inherited the burden of the debt created by the vast amounts of public money that they had expended. Then there were the dead and the wounded of many other countries. But, there were also the many silent victims of this conflict; the Truth being the main one. There were also the indirect victims, like Ambassador Joseph Wilson and his wife, and Dr David Kelly; people who believed firmly in the Truth, but who inevitably got in the way of the politicians, and their lust for power and money.

As for Edwards, he remembered very well what his friend and former colleague had once quietly said to him. Whenever he went for a walk in his own local woods, he remained nervous and ever watchful. He always tried to make sure that he was aware of who was behind him, and who was in front of him. A "Walk in the Woods" can, indeed, sometimes become a perilous undertaking!

IN THE SPOTLIGHT

"She was the People's Princess........"
– Prime Minister Tony Blair on the death of Diana, Princess of Wales.

1

She had flushed a shade of deep crimson. She was the only woman, except for the busy waitresses, in a large room full of men. She was seated, as befitted her position, as the wife to the Heir to the Throne, at the centre of the top table for the lunch. Soon she was due to make a short speech, and then to make the presentation. It was strange that she could still get embarrassed, as she had already given birth to her first child, some years before. Earlier, she had been more composed and very charming, when Edwards had been personally introduced to her; that had been along with a select group of his senior colleagues, in a smaller room, to the side of this very large room, which had been meticulously prepared for a large formal lunch.

The occasion was held on a spring day, in the mid-1980s. One of Edwards's close colleagues was about to receive a well-deserved award, from the leading construction institute. If had been awarded for his technical and managerial skills in completing the contract, on time and at the first estimated cost, for the building of a major project in the Middle East. It was a high-status project; a new university complex, which had been named after the ruler of the Middle Eastern country, where it was located. Edwards had, from some time before, been closely involved in finding the finance for it, so that it could go ahead.

Edwards did not begrudge this man his award at all; indeed he very much liked his colleague, who was to receive it, and he was delighted for him. Edwards respected his abilities to get on with and motivate people, his lack of ego and his excellent organising and management skills. He was very pleased that his colleague had been recognised in this way. Today was a day of celebration and, appropriately, it was a sunny, warm day outside the leading London hotel where, in a private dining suite, this lunch and the award ceremony were now taking place.

The first time that he had heard about this project had been several years before; then Edwards had only been employed by this major group of construction companies, for about a year. His job was to advise the senior management of all the companies in the group on matters financial, and to find the finance for many of their potential projects, to enable them to go ahead and be built. One of the first people he had met was the Marketing Director of one of these construction companies, for which he was now responsible. Edwards had immediately liked the man; he was Lebanese, a Christian and had a very sociable personality. His high-level contacts in various countries, not only in the Middle East, were undoubted.

Having met him several times, and having enjoyed their conversations, his new colleague had disappeared. Edwards had called his secretary to ask where he was. "He is in the Middle East," she had replied, naming the country involved. It was only after he had returned, and Edwards had met him again, that he discovered what he had been doing out there. Talking to the Ruler of this country, he had convinced him that he needed a new university complex for his country and that, furthermore, it should of course, be named after the Ruler! From that excellent start, in deploying his colleague's superb marketing skills, Edwards had assisted in this project, which would prove to be, in the end, the largest overseas building contract ever won by a British construction company.

It had been Edwards's job to find the finance to enable this large project to take place which, with the help of his colleagues, and after many long telephone conversations, and many meetings with British government officials and banks, he had managed to do. Edwards always said afterwards that he thought that this fine effort, made by the Marketing Director, was "the greatest example of creative Marketing that he had ever seen!"

One morning, unaware that this man already had a visitor, he had knocked on the door of this Marketing Director, and had entered his office. As always the man was charming; he stood up behind his desk and introduced Edwards to his visitor. He was the son of the then British Prime Minister! They chatted together for a while, and then Edwards mentioned that he would have to leave, to attend a meeting at the Group's head office in Central London. "Would you like a lift?" the young man had asked. Edwards accepted, happy not to have to take a crowded underground train to get to his meeting. They walked down together to the car park, situated under the building.

When he saw the car that he was about to ride in, Edwards was amazed. It was a top-of-the range Lotus sports car. It was a little difficult to get into, but he did enjoy the ride! Only later, did he begin to understand the role of this young man and his mother, in winning this new university project that would now be successfully built by a British company. But then, with so many other countries and their companies competing against Britain for similar construction projects, deploying such "Agents of Influence," in order to try and win such major contracts, was a natural thing to do. Why should Britain disadvantage herself, by not doing what all these other countries were always doing? Winning overseas business, after all, was a form of undeclared warfare, with countries and their companies, in an intense competition, for success!

2

Edwards's business life was very busy with extensive foreign travel, and the years rolled by very quickly. He had always been interested in keeping up with current affairs and now, because of his job, he had to be aware of what was happening in so many different countries of the world. These were the countries where his group of companies were already involved in major construction projects, or where they had the potential to become so. When he could, he also tried to keep up with events that were happening in Britain. Like the rest of the British population, he became all too aware of the difficulties in the Royal Marriage of the Heir to the Throne.

What had started off in Saint Paul's Cathedral, on a bright, summer day, full of hope and happiness, in July 1981, had now deteriorated into an unhappy marriage. Although the Royal couple had two sons together, their marriage would eventually result in a divorce in August 1996. Between those two dates, what had appeared at first to have been a happy relationship, had descended into arguments, bitterness and other love affairs, which had led into an eventual period of separation. This had then been followed by a divorce. The reason for this decline in their private relationship, would only become known after a number of years. Stories began to be leaked out into the press.

Then various revelations and admissions were finally publically made, by the two people involved.

What, eventually, became clear, was that the Prince of Wales even had doubts, just before his marriage, as to whether it should really go ahead. But, by then, he was too strongly locked into a situation, which had started with the wish of his family, and the whole country, that he should marry and provide children to succeed him. His bride was an ideal candidate, from an aristocratic family, somewhat shy but beautiful, loyal to him and the country, and with no serious previous relationships. Indeed, in the time honoured fashion, she had to endure the indignity of being medically examined, before she was married, to show that she was still a virgin!

But the Prince had a secret that he tried to keep to himself; over the years he had had many affairs, but now his life was concentrated on one, soon to be divorced mistress, whom he really loved. Unfortunately, in the past, she had been deemed unsuitable for him to marry, and hopefully bear him some children, one of which would then, in due course, inherit the Throne. So the scene was so surely set, for the tragedy that would follow.

In 1992, a book was published which claimed to give the true story of the Princess and her failing marriage. It was written by Andrew Morton, but based on notes that she had secretly provided to him. Then, In November 1995, the Princess had reached the point where she agreed to be interviewed on the B.B.C. Panorama program, about the intimate details of her married life. It drew an immense television audience, both at home and abroad, and would be repeated countless times and studied over the years. In a highly emotional state, she told the story of the "three people in her marriage", and how it had affected her both physically and mentally.

This was then followed by another television program, which had interviewed her husband, and tried to cast him in a better light. However, he still refused to admit how he had really behaved. Being very unhappy, the Princess indulged in various love affairs, all of which proved to be short-lived. She began to believe that she was under surveillance, and even feared for her life. After she was finally divorced, she was free to move on, and in 1997 she became romantically involved with Dodi Al-Fayed, whose father owned the famous Harrods store in London. Amongst other properties, he also owned the Ritz Hotel in Paris.

Dodi's father had never really been accepted by the British Establishment; rumours about how he had made his wealth, after his humble beginnings in Alexandria in Egypt, abounded. Those that probably should have known, often claimed that his money had first been made by dishonest means. Dodi was both a Muslim and an acknowledged playboy. He had also been married before, but was now divorced. As the affair became more obvious, and seemingly much more serious, criticism of the Princess began to be voiced. Rumours of a possible marriage between them began to spread, within the closed circles of government. She was, after all, still the mother of the potential King who would inherit the Throne, on the death of her previous husband.

The thought of a future King having a mother married to a Muslim, of doubtful pedigree, did not go down well in some quarters in Britain. This new affair had begun to become an embarrassment for the Royal Family, for the British Government and for the British establishment. The love affair seemed to have progressed very quickly and then, in the press, candid photographs appeared of the loving couple, and talk of a marriage began to be publically aired. There were now even rumours of a potential engagement that could imminently happen between the couple, and even that Diana was already expecting his child!

Various powerful people began to consider what could be done? The conspirators were not members of the Royal Family. They would have been some senior courtiers to the Family, who did not want to see their charges embarrassed further, permanent members of the "Deep State," and perhaps senior politicians of the newly elected Labour Party government. It is a strange thing, but newly appointed Ministers in a newly elected government, often want to protect the Royal Family who have, technically, elevated them to their new positions, and in so protecting them, they may feel that they are also, somehow, protecting themselves?

3

The two male swimmers, in full scuba-diving gear, slipped quietly from the inflatable dingy, which was handled by their female colleague, and who would then keep the small craft stationery, for their return. Around their waists were strapped two canvas bags, which contained two limpet mines. Their mission was simple; to attach the two mines to the hull of the ship, that was moored alongside a jetty in the port. This ship had been causing just too much trouble for their government, and their orders had been clearly given to them. Once the two swimmers were well clear, one smaller mine was timed to explode, to clear everyone from the vessel, then the second, more powerful mine, would detonate, ten minutes later, to finally sink it.

It was July 1985, and this scene was taking place in Auckland Harbour in New Zealand. The two men and the woman were highly experienced agents of the D.G.S.E., the French equivalent of the British Secret Intelligence Service, better known as M.I.6. Other agents of the D.G.S.E. had smuggled the mines into New Zealand, on board a yacht. More French secret service agents had been involved in the well planned reconnaissance operation for this mission, which was known in their Paris headquarters as "Operation Satanic."

Unfortunately, the operation went wrong; after the first explosion, the crew and others on board the ship did abandon it, but then some went back on board, to assess the damage. A Portuguese photographer, who had gone below decks to retrieve his camera equipment, was caught in the ship, after the second blast. The ship sank and he was drowned. The name of this vessel was the Rainbow Warrior, and it was owned and operated by the international environmental group called Greenpeace.

The Rainbow Warrior was on its way to take part in a protest against a planned French nuclear weapons test, on the island of Moruroa in the Tuamoto Archipelago, part of French Polynesia, in the southern Pacific Ocean. France had carried out nuclear tests there since 1966, to improve and perfect her nuclear weapons, and would carry on doing so until 1996, even in the face of rising international protests. The Greenpeace plan was to sail the Rainbow Warrior as close as they could possibly get to the test site. They thought that this would force the French Government to postpone their nuclear test, in fear of those on board the ship being killed. Now, the secret agents of the French Government, had stopped that plan happening.

Most of the French agents managed to flee from New Zealand, but the three man crew of the yacht that had brought the limpet mines into the country, were arrested by the Australian Police when they docked at Norfolk Island, an Australian island halfway between Australia and New Zealand. They were released on bail, pending the results of forensic tests, but were then secretly picked up, offshore of the island, by a French submarine. Meanwhile, the New Zealand Police had identified and arrested the two frogmen, who had planted the limpet mines. They were both charged with conspiracy, arson and murder, but then pleaded guilty to a manslaughter charge, which was accepted by the Court. They were both sentenced to ten years in prison.

Later the French Government would pay compensation to Greenpeace, the family of the murdered photographer and to the New Zealand Government. As part of the deal, the two French agents were transferred to a French military base on Hao Attol, to continue their imprisonment. But they were both released and returned to France, after less than two years. This incident caused a great deal of embarrassment for the French Government; the Defence Minister resigned and the Head of the D.G.S.E. lost his job. It was, of course, clear from the start, that the operation had been approved at the highest level. But it was only years later, after he had died, that it was finally admitted that the then French President, Francois Mitterrand, had actually fully approved "Operation Satanic."

As a result of the growing international protests, from many organisations and governments, about what they had done, the French Government temporally stopped their nuclear weapons testing program. But it was impossible to keep their nuclear "Force de Frappe" up to date and efficient, without continued testing. Despite increasing protests from other governments, the international community, and various environmental organisations, the testing program had somehow to be restarted.

In the late 1990's, a new British Labour Party Prime Minister was swept into office, by a landslide General Election victory. He spoke passable French and, having already been made aware of the difficult French position from his briefings by the British intelligence agencies, during his previous nearly three years as Leader of the Opposition, he seems to have decided what he wanted to do. As a firm pro-European, he was very keen on urgently improving the relations between Britain and its closest European neighbour. It was much better for the two large and democratic European countries with nuclear weapons, to co-operate, rather than to try and operate independently in this area of technology.

The "Five Eyes Agreement" is a secret agreement, which came about as a result of the very close and secret co-operation between Britain and the United States, once the Americans had joined the fight against the Nazis in the Second World War. Later, the other Anglophone countries of Canada, Australia and New Zealand were added to the Agreement. It allows for an unprecedented level of intelligence co-operation between the countries. Unless intelligence was classified as solely for distribution within just one country, it was almost automatically shared with the other participating countries. In the area of Signals Intelligence, or electronic surveillance, including emails and telephone calls, the co-operation between the American National Security Agency at Fort Meade in Maryland, and the British Government Communications Headquarters at Cheltenham, Gloucestershire, was so close that they were virtually one agency. The extent of this joint electronic surveillance, using orbiting satellites and other systems, could cover the whole world.

If the Americans were unable to listen-in to an American citizen because of, say, unfortunate legal restrictions, they would ask their British colleagues to do so instead. The British would then, of course, share the intelligence that they had gained with their American colleagues. The same reciprocal assistance was always available to the British, from their American friends, if they ever required it. The same co-operation applied to the area of defence technology; in 1940, in case Britain would be invaded, the wartime leader Winston Churchill had dispatched a metal trunk full of documents, to Washington, under the care of Henry Tizard, a British ex-pilot and now Chairman of the Aeronautical Research Committee. It contained full details and designs of all the top secret work that British scientists, engineers and designers had done. This included the development of advanced radar, the design for a jet engine, work on the decryption of coded enemy messages, chemical warfare research, rocket research and, of course, papers on how to develop a viable atomic bomb, light enough to be carried by an aircraft.

The new British, Labour Prime Minister knew that, over the years, the Americans had reciprocated. Not only had they shared the secrets of how they had eventually developed atomic weapons, but they had exclusively sold to Britain the missiles to carry them. They had also, in later years, shared with Britain some of the results of the research into advanced computer development, which had started with the British developing a computer to be able to read encrypted German messages, during the last war. The Americans had now been able to develop a software program that could successfully, and very accurately, simulate the explosion of a nuclear weapon. This advanced computer program was flexible enough to try out different and improved designs for nuclear weapons. It was reliable enough, in its results, to be able to dispense with the actual physical testing of nuclear weapons altogether! It had then later been shared with their close British allies.

This advanced computer program had brought to an end the need for the Americans and for the British to carry out actual nuclear weapon testing. It was this technology that the new British Prime Minister was determined to share with his French allies. He needed, first, to gain the approval of the Americans; after a series of carefully argued secret meetings in Washington, and the final approval of President Clinton, this was obtained. The highly secret computer program was handed over to the French; they would now never again have to carry out an actual nuclear weapons test!

A few weeks later, the new British Prime Minister was invited to visit Paris, to meet the French President Jacques Chirac. He was treated, not as a mere Prime Minister, but as a most important Head of State. He noted how grateful the French were; he knew that in the field of international intelligence and diplomacy, "one good turn deserves another." He wondered how he could now use this great favour to the French, to get something valuable back from them, in return, in the future? But, some people in the British "Deep State," had also noted this new gratitude from the French, created by Britain solving a major military and politically embarrassing problem for them, and were perhaps ready to use it more quickly?

4

Edwards had eventually left the world of construction, and was now a financial adviser to a Government organisation that helped British companies sell their products and services overseas. This organisation consisted mainly of civil servants, but also with a small number of outside people with strong, international commercial experience, such as Edwards. One of the civil servant members of this organisation, seconded in from elsewhere, was a senior intelligence officer. He was always in contact with other senior members of the British intelligence agencies. His name was Michael, and his job was to provide the benefit of certain appropriate secret knowledge to senior members of British companies. These were usually people who had already been through the vetting process, which then allowed them access to classified material.

These business people could always ask to see Michael, to put to him a particular question, or to seek general advice about a particular situation. Sometimes a full briefing, based on the collective knowledge of the British intelligence agencies, could be arranged, to help British companies win major contracts overseas. This was nothing more than other countries did; French companies were well known for their close contacts with their intelligence agencies. The Americans, with their vast experience and expenditure on intelligence, were always willing to brief selected senior members of their major companies. This took place either in one of their numerous embassies located in the country concerned, or at a classified briefing, before the company executives travelled to that country.

Edwards had got to know Michael very well and, indeed, had been asked to give his confidential advice, using his financial background, on several cases that he was dealing with. It had become Edwards's habit, to go and visit this colleague in his office, every Friday afternoon. If he had a visitor, or was engaged on some urgent task, Edwards would, of course, postpone his visit. But usually, by Friday afternoon, Michael was free and his week was winding down, towards the weekend. Edwards would smile at the man's Personal Assistant, who was also security cleared to the highest level, in her outer office, and ask first whether Michael was free. If she said yes, he would enter his inner office and close the door behind him.

The two colleagues would then discuss, for about an hour, various matters and countries that had come up during the week. It was an informal, but pleasant weekly arrangement, which they had; usually held over cups of strong coffee. His colleague was very well educated and worldly-wise, and Edwards always enjoyed the rather challenging conversations that he had with him. On one particular Friday afternoon, Edwards knew that he would be away on holiday the following week, and that his colleague would then be away himself on holiday for the two weeks that followed. This would be, therefore, the last chance for them to meet for over three weeks, and Edwards had a number of questions ready to ask, in order to get his invaluable advice.

But, on this occasion, he was surprised by his colleague's demeanour. Michael was normally a well-balanced and calm individual but, on this particular Friday afternoon, he seemed a little agitated.

"I cannot understand it," he said to Edwards. "Everybody seems to be so on edge. Something is going to happen, but I do not know what it can be. They all seem a little frightened by what may happen!"

By "Everybody," Edwards clearly understood the very senior staff in the intelligent agencies that this man was in constant touch with. Edwards found it strange; Michael had never said anything like this to Edwards before. Nothing more was said about this unusual situation; they had their normal conversation, and then Edwards left Michael's office. Before he left, mutual good wishes for a happy holiday were exchanged between the two men. They were not to meet again, privately, for four weeks. When they did, nothing was mentioned between them of Michael's strange comment during their last meeting. They were both too shocked and horrified, by what had happened, to mention it!

Edwards had met Colonel Sir David Stirling, the creator of the concept of the Special Forces and founder of the Special Air Service, in the middle of the 1980's. He had then, unwittingly, been recruited by David to help out in a clandestine mission, with one of his people, behind the then Iron Curtain! Since then, Edwards had followed avidly the exploits of the British Special Forces. He had met a number of people who had served in both the Special Air Service, carefully recruited from the British Army, and the Special Boat Service, recruited just as carefully, from the Royal Marines. They were, of course, very reticent to talk about what they had actually done but, once they had admitted their background, some wonderful stories sometimes came out. He had also become aware that certain

Special Forces people, after they had retired from active service, were still used for non-attributable "Special Operations."

The nature of these activities varied, but they could include certain very sensitive requirements, which required total deniability by the Armed Forces and the Government. The authorities had to be able to say, with some semblance of truth, that they did not know about these clandestine operations, and were in no way connected, with what had been done. Edwards also took a close interest in military developments as far as the equipment, used by the Armed Forces, were concerned. He became aware that a new weapon had been developed for the British Special Forces; it was a very powerful, but compact and portable, spotlight, which emitted, for just a fraction of a second, a flash of light so intense, that anyone on the receiving end of this weapon would be temporarily blinded and disabled. He had noted that this new equipment, designed for non-lethal use, could be used, for example, for storming a terrorist hide-out, particularly where hostages had been taken.

Edwards had met his colleague, when he had made the unusual remark, on the Friday afternoon. The following Monday, the first of September, was a Bank Holiday. Edwards had taken the rest of that week off to look after his children, as his wife was out of the country at an international conference. In the early hours of the morning of Sunday, 31 August 1997, a tragic car accident had taken place in the Pont de l'Alma road tunnel in

Paris. A reconditioned Mercedes limousine, driven by the acting Security Manager of the Ritz Hotel in Paris, Henri Paul, had crashed, at speed, into one of the concrete pillars inside the tunnel. The car had, in the past, been stolen, and had then been crashed several times. It was still being repaired from one of these crashes, and the seat belts, on the back seats, had still not been replaced. The question of why this car had ever been used for this, its last journey, has never been answered?

The front seat belts were in position, but Henri Paul was not wearing his; he was killed instantly. Trevor Rees-Jones, a bodyguard hired to protect the other man in the car, had worn his seat belt and had survived but, because of his injuries, had no recollection of the accident. In the back of the car, Dodi Al-Fayed was killed instantly. Princess Diana, who was with Dodi in the back of the car, was gravely injured. She was taken to the Pitié-Salpêtrière Hospital, where, after desperate attempts to deal with her awful injuries, she died. Both French and British senior officials had turned up, inexplicably, and very quickly at the Hospital; several of them appeared to be senior intelligence officers.

It was afterwards claimed that a blood test, on Henri Paul, had shown that he was three times over the permitted alcohol limit to drive a car. Unfortunately, the contents of this blood test were then lost, so that these results could never be checked. His parents claimed that he never drank alcohol before he was due to drive, and the bar till receipts from the Ritz Hotel showed that he had only purchased two small, alcoholic drinks, during that whole day. Henri Paul was a secret agent; he worked for both the French and British intelligence services, on a part-time basis, reporting on the guests staying in the Ritz Hotel. On that Saturday afternoon, he had disappeared for several hours; some people believed that he had met with one of his intelligence service handlers, and had been given his instructions. Maybe, during this meeting, Henri Paul had been plied with the mixture of alcohol and prescription painkillers that, it was then alleged, were found in his blood test? A bank account was found, in his name, containing a very large sum of money that he could not have possibly saved, from his small salary at the Ritz Hotel.

What was the reason that he had taken that night, such an unusually long route, through the tunnel where the crash happened, between the Ritz Hotel and Dodi's flat? Had he been asked, perhaps, to drive this route, in this particular car? At his flat, it was believed, Dodi was going to formally propose to Diana, and give her a very expensive engagement ring that he had purchased, the previous day, from a leading Paris jeweller. Unfortunately, all of the ten traffic cameras, along this unusually long route that Henri Paul chose to drive, were of no use. After the tragic event had happened, the French authorities reported that unfortunately, that night, they were all out of order!

Then there was the evidence of various eyewitnesses; several reported seeing a small white Fiat car, entering the tunnel in the other traffic lane, at the same time as the Mercedes. There was evidence that the speeding Mercedes had clipped it; white paint was found on the Mercedes. After some time, this Fiat car was found by a French newspaper; it had been sold and repainted with red paint. The previous owner appeared frightened and refused to talk. Witnesses also reported that a dark Peugeot car was "tailgating" very close behind the Mercedes, forcing Henri Paul to drive faster. It was claimed by the French authorities that this car contained newspaper reporters, chasing the Princess; but all of these reporters had been tricked when Diana and Dodi had, unexpectedly, left by the back door of the Ritz Hotel, just minutes before. In fact, only a small number of reporters had realised, too late, that they had been tricked, and they did not arrive at the crash site until several minutes after the tragedy had occurred.

The same eyewitnesses reported that a powerful motor cycle, with two men riding on it, had entered the tunnel just in front of the Mercedes. The pillion passenger was turning around, to look at the Mercedes following him, as he entered the tunnel. Then, from the tunnel, the eye witnesses had seen an unexplained very intense flash of white light! It would have certainly blinded the driver, Henri Paul, and would have caused him to crash. Some eyewitnesses even reported an explosion, before the Mercedes car smashed into the pillar in the tunnel; could this have been a stun grenade, let off to again disorientate Henri Paul, so that he would crash?

In the Paris hospital, for no apparent reason, certain organs were removed from Diana's body. These included her womb, which increased speculation that she might have been in the early stages of pregnancy with Dodi's child. Her body was then embalmed, which would limit the number of forensic tests that could then be done, including a blood test that could have determined if she was pregnant. Her body was then flown back to Britain, where unprecedented public mourning had broken out. There, a highly emotional funeral service, was held in Westminster Abbey. Her body was then taken to her ancestral home of Althorp House in Northamptonshire, where it was buried in its grounds, on a small island, in the middle of an ornamental lake. She was just 36 years old.

But there was a postscript; in 1999 a Freedom of Information Act request was made in the United States, and the answer revealed that the American National Security Agency had put Princess Diana under total surveillance for some time, before her death. This had been done, presumably, at the request of the British Government, and the results would have then been passed back to them. The file summarising the results of this electronic surveillance on her, was deemed to be so sensitive that, for reasons of American National Security, it will never be released!

The French Government also had advanced means of electronic surveillance and had, no doubt, because of their important position, been listening in on the couple. The fatal accident had happened, just a few months after Prime Minister Tony Blair had been officially received in Paris, like royalty, by the French President. This was in recognition of the secret, valuable service, that he had rendered to the nuclear ability of the armed forces of the French Republic. Unknown to him, had some rogue members of the British "Deep State," used this valuable service to gain French co-operation in this tragic incident? Official inquiries in both France and Britain, concluded that the crash had been caused by an intoxicated Henri Paul who was driving too fast, because of the journalists who were chasing the car he was driving. It was claimed that he was an alcoholic, but a very full medical examination, carried out just a few days before he died, had shown no evidence of this claim. No other possible explanations were ever offered for Diana's death.

Some sixteen years after the incident, a British investigative journalist was given the names of two senior members of M.I.6, by one of her contacts in the intelligence services. They were described as "being in charge of the Paris operation." It was "only intended to frighten Diana, so that she would not get engaged to Dodi," she was told, and "it was not intended to kill her, but only to cause her minor injuries."

Edwards well remembered the beautiful, somewhat shy, but sympathetic young woman whom he had once met, over ten years before her tragic, early demise. He also could never forget the words of his well-connected, intelligence colleague, just two days before her death, that "something is going to happen, but I do not know what it can be." The so-called "Paris operation" was meticulously planned and ruthlessly executed. But the plotters, in their eagerness to do something, somehow seemed to have forgotten, perhaps, that the British Special Forces, even if retired from official government service, were trained to efficiently kill people, not just to discourage them!

THE IRON LADY

"You can turn if you want to. This lady's not for turning" – Margaret Thatcher at the Conservative Party Conference in October, 1980.

1

Edwards looked into the piercing, blue eyes of the lady he was sitting next to at the formal dinner. He was suitably dressed in his dinner suit, which he had acquired when he had gone up to university, his frilled white dress shirt and his black bow tie. She was dressed, appropriately, in a shimmering long blue dress, perfectly made up and coiffured. She wore no jewellery but carried what seemed to be a relatively large handbag for this evening event, which she had placed on the floor at her feet. She was seated to Edwards's right as the Guest of Honour at the dinner; Edwards was then the serving Chairman of the Party's Association in the City of London and had therefore the duty to receive and entertain this lady and say a few words to welcome her, before she gave her obligatory speech.

"What do you mean by that?" she had just asked, fixing him with her very direct gaze, after Edwards had made some statement about economics and the current Monetary Policy being pursued by the Bank of England. Edwards had realised quickly, when he had greeted her at the door of the hotel where they were having this formal dinner, that he was dealing with a person with a commanding presence. She also had a very sharp intellect and Edwards nearly kicked himself, under the table, for just saying something that he might not have been able to fully justify. He hesitated, thought quickly and then managed to come out with what seemed to him to be a sensible explanation for what he had just said. Fortunately the lady gave the slightest of nods; his explanation had been accepted!

Around them, in the large function room of the hotel, were a number of long tables drawn up into a square, at which sat other members of the Conservative Party Association. On either side of Edwards and the lady on the "Top Table" sat the other members of the Committee of the Association, suitably dressed with sometimes their wives or girlfriends. Edwards was still unmarried and his current girlfriend lived in Switzerland, so he had come alone to this dinner. The lady had only just become the Leader of the Party. Edwards was relieved because, the previous year, he had had to receive and entertain the previous Party Leader, who had then ceased to be Prime Minister shortly afterwards, when he was defeated at a General Election by the Labour party leader, Harold Wilson. Edward Heath was not an easy man to talk to; fortunately Edwards knew a little about classical music and they had managed to have a reasonable conversation about that subject. But Margaret Thatcher proved easier to talk to; as the dinner wore on he realised that as well as an outstanding intellect, she also had a light sense of humour and, despite what he had heard about her, she could react with a real feminine charm. By the time that the dessert course was served, she was even smiling at him!

He unconsciously called in his colleague, sitting on her other side, to help with the conversation with her, so that he could relax a little before standing up to make the toasts and then the short speech of welcome to his Guest of Honour, that was now expected of him. Coffee, cigars and liquors were served and when he thought that the appropriate moment had come, Edwards stood up. He first invited all the others present to stand for the Loyal Toast to the Queen. After that he proposed a toast to the Conservative Party. Then he gave the required short speech to thank the Leader for her attendance and invited her to make her speech.

Her speech was quite remarkable; she held the attention of all the people present, not just out of politeness, but because of what she said, which was both interesting and greatly encouraged them to continue their work for the Party, of which they were all members. She was a truly committed politician who, perhaps unusually, seemed really to believe in the policies that she wished to pursue. At the end of her speech, Edwards had to get to his feet again to thank her and to propose a toast to her health and future success. His last job that evening was to escort the Leader to the main entrance of the hotel, and to see her safely into her waiting car.

"I think that that went very well," commented another member of the Committee to Edwards, when he had returned to the function room. Edwards had been at university with him and he also, like Edwards, now worked in the City of London.

"I think that she is a remarkable lady," replied Edwards. "If anyone is to make it, she will be our next Prime Minister." He was wrong in that; it would be James Callaghan who would take over from the then successful Labour Prime Minister, Harold Wilson, in April 1976, owing to what was claimed, at the time, to be Wilson's ill-health. The Association would have to wait until May 1979 before Margaret Thatcher would become the first serving female Prime Minister of the United Kingdom.

Before that happened, Edwards was due to entertain her again, to dinner, at the same occasion, the following year. This time he was a little more relaxed. He thought that he now knew a little bit more about the formidable lady that he was to meet again. After that, he gave up his role as Chairman, and let others take their turn to oversee the annual dinner invitation, and then to entertain the Party Leader. But the memories of those two evenings stayed with him, and the impression that he gained of the woman, who would soon rise to the highest level in the land, after the Monarch.

2

When she at last became Prime Minister, Edwards could not but feel a sense of personal vindication. For several years, she had seemed to be taking a consistent and successful line, and winning all the political arguments against the crumbling Labour Government. Prior to the 1979 General Election, Britain had experienced the "Winter of Discontent," with widespread strikes by public sector trade unions demanding large pay rises. Rubbish was left rotting in the streets and the dead were left unburied, in what was the coldest and most miserable winter for sixteen years. The strikes were a result of the Labour Party Government's attempt to control inflation, by imposing rules on public sector workers, to keep their pay rises below five per cent a year.

The Labour Party Government's inability to control these strikes, helped to lead to Margaret Thatcher's election victory in the spring of 1979. Shortly after that, Edwards had left the City of London and had become an employee of a large group of British construction companies, advising them on how to finance the many projects that they were trying to build around the world. In his new role, he was severely challenged in trying to find the support to enable many of these major construction projects to be built, not only in Britain, but in many other, sometimes difficult, countries. In this role he was required to travel heavily, and to negotiate with banks and other institutions, to put together the finance to enable these major projects to take place and, thereby, for his group of companies, to obtain the contracts to build them.

Inevitably, his job also required an interaction with government, partly to help find the finance for these projects and to win them to provide work in Britain, but also to provide other support that was often needed to supplement his efforts. The British Government, like many other governments, provided export credit loans, guaranteed by the government, on attractive terms, to the buyers of major projects to enable British goods, equipment and services to be exported overseas. But there were other forms of British government support that were needed, including diplomatic support from the British Embassy in the country concerned. This was particularly the case when the buyer was a foreign government, or where that government was involved in a major project in some other way. Because of this work, he came to know well a number of civil servants of both junior and senior ranks.

Edwards quickly realised that junior civil servants were important; unlike in business, where decisions were made at the top and then had to be implemented by more junior staff, in the civil service major decisions were often made by more junior personnel and then implemented by their bosses. There was a skill which you had to acquire to work with government; Edwards called it "a bottom-up and top-down approach" to win a decision by working both with senior and junior officials, in which contacts with both were made, in accordance with the correct sequence, to get a positive decision when "they met in the middle." A consistent, logical and well-argued approach was always needed and clever, planned timing was essential. Once you had learned that with the British government, it was a skill that could be exported to work, in the same way, with governments of other countries.

These officials were the "permanent government"; the elected Ministers were only temporary and knew very little about how government really worked, and what they should do. They therefore relied heavily on their civil servants, to give them the various options that were available and to recommend the best option that the Minister should finally decide to adopt. Communications between the government and the public were largely controlled by civil servants, who wrote the replies to letters from companies and individuals and which, usually, Ministers took on trust and signed off for them to be dispatched.

Slowly Edwards became trusted; his reputation was now high enough to be eventually told, by one of his senior government contacts, "you know that you are now an honorary civil servant!" This elevation became clear one day when he received a telephone call from a senior official. "The Prime Minster has received a letter from one of your Directors, complaining about the support he is not getting on a particular project," he was told.

"This letter has been passed on to me, by the Prime Minister's Office, to answer it. Unfortunately I know nothing about this project. Can you help me please?" Edwards quickly identified the bumptious and unpopular Director who had sent the letter; the civil servant confirmed that it was indeed from him!

Using the name of the project that he had been given, Edwards identified the group company that was involved. He called its Managing Director and told him what had happened. He received from him a full description of the project, what was the current position of his company with the project and what they now actually needed. He called back his civil servant contact and explained. There was a pause and then the official said "You seem to have learned a lot about this project in the last half-hour. Would you now like to write the reply from the Prime Minister please?" So Edwards did just that and faxed the reply off to the official.

A few weeks later, he received a call from the Director concerned: "I have written to the Prime Minister and have received a reply that I do not like," came the loud voice, with the Yorkshire accent, down the telephone line.

"Well send it to me with your original letter," replied Edwards. When copies of the two letters arrived by fax, the letter signed by Margaret Thatcher looked somehow, vaguely familiar, to Edwards!

One of the projects that Edwards had become closely involved with, was the building of a major, second bridge over the Bosphorus at Istanbul in Turkey. He had several visits to Turkey to try and win this project, against stiff competition, from a number of companies from other countries. Finally, the other competitors were reduced to a Japanese-Italian consortium, who had submitted a markedly lower price than Edwards's group of companies. The Turkish Government required a Finance Package to be also submitted from every competitor, so that they did not need to find the money to pay for the new bridge straight away. Edwards had put together the complex Finance Package submitted by his group.

His final visit to Turkey on this project was one of what he described as "his Missions Impossible"; he was not allowed to alter the higher price of his group, but he somehow, had to persuade the Turkish Government not to take the Yen financing offered by the competing group, as the Yen would probably continue to strengthen against the Turkish Lire. It would, therefore, in the long term, prove to be very expensive for the Turks to repay their Yen borrowing. But all governments think short-term and he was not having much success. One morning in Ankara, he was sitting with the British Ambassador at his Embassy. "The only thing that we can do now is to get a top-level message to the Turkish Prime Minster from our Prime Minister," declared Edwards, mentioning the only final option that he could think of.

The Ambassador passed him a pad of paper. "Write it," he said. The next morning Edwards was at the British Embassy again; overnight the letter signed by Margaret Thatcher had been sent from London. He read it; it had not been changed by even one word from his draft.

I must now deliver this to the Turkish Prime Minister," said the British Ambassador. "Do you want to come with me?"

3

By the early 1990's, Edwards had left the construction industry. He now worked for a British Government organisation which helped to promote and assist British exporters selling their goods and services to many overseas countries. The staff of this organisation not only consisted mainly of civil servants, but also there were a number of senior people from the commercial sector, with the required high-level of experience of international business. Among Edwards's colleagues was a senior civil servant called Jack: he was highly intelligent and had already spent time working in various British Embassies overseas. He was very knowledgeable, with a good sense of humour and, although now married, appeared still to have maintained an interest in women! Edwards made a point of visiting him in his office at least once a week, to review the various foreign export markets that were now his responsibility.

One afternoon, over large mugs of coffee, Jack revealed that one of his previous postings had been as the Night Officer at 10 Downing Street. As such, he was responsible for running all the activities in the building at night and reviewing all communications coming in and going out. He also had the great responsibility of waking up the Prime Minister if some serious event or crisis occurred during the night, and which he judged they should immediately be made aware of. This position gave Jack access to all the files held in the Prime Minister's offices, in case any file had to be consulted during the night hours. Jack had served in 10 Downing Street during the time that Margaret Thatcher was Prime Minister and Edwards was therefore interested in any stories that Jack could tell him about working for this lady that Edwards had met several times some twenty years before.

"She often used to come in from some evening event or other at one or two o'clock in the morning," recalled Jack. "She used to put her head around the door of my office and ask me if anything important was happening? When I replied that all was quiet, she used to ask me to her private flat, upstairs, for a drink. Denis, her husband, had already been tucked up safely in bed for hours but, it was widely known, that she required very little sleep."

Jack smiled to himself. "I clearly remember that, as I climbed the stairs behind her, I always used to notice that she had a very nice bottom. I had to quickly remind myself who this bottom belonged to, otherwise I might have pinched it or put my hand on it!"

Jack and Edwards laughed together; "Maybe she would have surprised you!" said Edwards. "What do you think she would have said if you had done that?"

"Well, I would have liked to have thought," replied Jack mischievously, "that, since she and her husband occupied separate bedrooms, she would have turned around and said to me, "Oh! Dear Boy! Come straight to my room and get undressed. Then lie down flat on my bed and think of England!" But that was just in my dreams."

Edwards laughed heartedly, but Jack kept a straight face. "When we got to her flat," continued Jack "she sat me down and asked me if I wanted a whiskey, which was her favourite drink at that time of night? I used to say: Yes please, Prime Minister, and she poured us both a good measure of the best Malt Whiskey."

"What did you used to talk about?" asked Edwards.

"Well she used to sit down, kick her shoes off and almost always her first words were "Jack, you know, I am rather worried about Mark!"

Edwards laughed; he had met her son, Mark Thatcher, many years before, while he was meeting with one of Edwards's more well-connected and more innovative Marketing Directors in one of the construction companies he looked after. Indeed, he had then offered Edwards a lift to Edwards's next meeting in his Lotus sports car, which had been parked in the car park under Edwards's then office building. Mark had once got lost while rallying in the Sahara Desert and, unbelievably, they had also managed to get lost as Mark had driven Edwards into Central London!

"Then we used to talk about many things," continued Jack. "She was really a very kind person. She always used to remember about the members of your family and ask after them," he went on.

"I know," replied Edwards. "I sensed she was too when I met her and also with a good sense of humour, if you dared to joke with her!"

"But she was also resolute and determined to make things happen," continued Jack. "I can't help but say that I was a little in love with her. She was just like a strict mother, but who also made sure that her children were always looked after."

Once, Jack had told Edwards about a find he had made, in the bottom drawer of a filing cabinet, at 10 Downing Street. After all, overnight he held all the keys to everything and rather than be bored, he used to open up drawers and cabinets to read things which were often classified as Top Secret and above. One night, in the bottom of a drawer, he found a folder which concerned a former Labour Prime Minister. Inside there were some enlarged black and white photographs. The two people shown in them, a man and a woman, were recognisable, even though they were lying in bed together. The woman was clearly not the Prime Minister's wife!

The worrying thing was that the photographs had some Russian markings on the back, but no date. They had probably been taken by the Russians, using a hidden surveillance camera in a Russian hotel room, years before. They had, no doubt, then been used by the Russians as compromising material to try and control the man shown in them. When they had extracted from him all that they could, they had then given copies to the British Security Service to try to politically destroy this man, who was still serving as Prime Minister, and also to try and destabilise the United Kingdom. These secret items had undoubtedly contributed to his decision to resign early from his high office, for health reasons, and then to retire from active politics, by entering the House of Lords.

4

In his new role, Edwards was often invited as a guest to lunches and dinners by various banks and other organisations. He recalled two such events when the former Prime Minister was to give a speech. The first was a large event, organised by a major French bank in London to celebrate Bastille Day, the most important event in modern French history. After a very good lunch, the people present were asked to stand for the toasts; the first was a toast to the President of France and the second to Her Majesty the Queen.

After the toasts, Edwards's host, a senior French banker, had whispered into Edwards's ear, "You know, we really like your Queen, far more, than we like our President!"

Margaret Thatcher was then asked to give a speech; her speech was on a topic close to her heart. How the alliance of Western nations had defeated the dangers of the Soviet Union and Communism. The problem was that she seemed to be suffering from some memory loss; the speech just turned into a long and rambling address! Fortunately the Chairman, who had invited her to speak, realised that there was some problem and, at an appropriate moment, rose to cut her speech short and to thank her for coming to the event. Nevertheless, there was a huge round of applause for her; those attending chose to ignore the health problems that she was obviously suffering from. Edwards was genuinely upset; he realised that the former Prime Minister, who he knew had a remarkable intellect, was now suffering from ill health and possibly some form of dementia.

A year later, however, he was invited to a different occasion for lunch. Again Margaret Thatcher was to give a speech. But, by this time, she had obviously recovered. Her speech reviewed her time in office and was delivered in her old precise style, with the flashes of political brilliance and intellect that Edwards could well remember. She had become a Member of the House of Lords and it was there that she made a speech, criticising the Treaty of Maastricht and saying that, "it was a Treaty too far." She argued that, as all three major political parties were in favour of the Treaty, that the British people should be given the chance to have their say in a Referendum about its terms. In 2002 her third book was published; in it she stated that the European Union could not be reformed and that it was a "classic utopian project, a monument to the vanity of intellectuals, a programme whose inevitable destiny is failure." She argued that Britain should leave the EU, without it could renegotiate its terms of membership.

Following several small strokes, she gave up her public speaking. In 2005 she celebrated her eightieth birthday, with the Queen in attendance. Carol, her daughter, then revealed that her mother was now suffering from dementia and had to be repeatedly reminded that her husband, Denis, was now dead. But in 2004 she had, nevertheless, insisted on attending the State Funeral of Ronald Reagan, the former American President, who she had considered a great friend. In 2006, she again flew to Washington, to attend the Memorial Service on the fifth anniversary of the 11 September attacks. In 2007 she attended the unveiling of a bronze statue of her, opposite a statue of her great hero, Sir Winston Churchill, in the Houses of Parliament. She remarked, "I might have preferred iron, but bronze will do. It will not rust!"

After another major stroke, she died at the age of 87 in April 2013, at the Ritz Hotel in London, where she had moved to, as she could no longer manage the stairs at her home. The Queen attended her funeral at Saint Paul's Cathedral; of her former Prime Ministers, only Sir Winston Churchill had ever been accorded this singular, great honour. Thus passed into history "The Iron Lady," a name that had been given to her by her great enemy, the Russian-led Communist Union of Soviet Socialist Republics, but in which she revelled. Together with Ronald Reagan, she had finally defeated that enemy, by her staunch opposition to this evil, totalitarian state. It was widely recognised that, not only had she changed the economics and politics of Britain, but that she had really changed the whole world!

MANOEUVRES

"You can do anything in the world if you are prepared to take the consequences" – W. Somerset Maugham.

1

There was a great flash of lightening followed by a long, low rumble of thunder. Edwards glanced at his watch; the storm was right on time! He and his wife hurried towards the café near to the exit of the Singapore Botanic Gardens. They had nearly finished their visit in any case, having arrived there at ten o'clock that morning. It was now three o'clock and they were both tired and hungry. They had been in Singapore for a full four days and by now Edwards knew that you could time the regular afternoon storm, almost to the minute.

Singapore is a tropical island, only some seventy miles north of the Equator. As a result the temperature and humidity are virtually the same every day of the year. Each day, during the morning and early afternoon, it seemed to Edwards that the evaporation of water built up the overhead clouds to a point that, exactly at three o'clock, the water was deposited back down again, through a tropical storm that lasted about one hour. After that, the air cooled a little and then the sudden tropical nightfall gave some further relief from the intense heat.

The first Botanical Gardens on the island were established by Sir Stamford Raffles, the founder of modern Singapore and a keen naturalist, in 1822. Later, in 1859, the Gardens were moved to their present site; they were originally compromised of only 32 hectares, but were then extended. Initially designed as a "pleasure park" for the members of the Agri-Horticultural Society of Singapore, they then developed into more of a commercial enterprise, when the first rubber tree seedlings were brought from Kew Gardens in London. When Henry Ridley became Director of the Gardens in 1888, he started experiments in the planting of rubber trees and then convinced British estate owners in the Malay Peninsula, to plant them widely. As a result, Malaya quickly became the world's largest producer and exporter of natural rubber.

As they hurried towards the café for a meal, the first large raindrops began to fall. Edwards quickly opened the umbrella that he had brought with him, and had carried around all day. His wife was a keen gardener and had been particularly delighted by the National Orchid Garden. The growing of orchids had been introduced in the 1920's by Eric Holttum, the then Director, and the Gardens now had probably the largest collection of orchids in the world.

It was 1981 and Edwards and his wife had arrived the previous Sunday morning, on the overnight Singapore Airlines flight from London. Edwards was used to at least Business Class air travel but, as they were on holiday, they had been in Economy Class. Even there, they seemed to have very comfortable seats and an impeccable cabin service, and they had enjoyed their long journey. They were staying with a friend of his wife's from her school days who, together with her husband, lived in a large and rather luxurious flat, in a modern block, just off the northern part of the long Orchard Road in the Tanglin district of the city.

Their holiday so far had been ideal; a good breakfast with their hosts each morning and then an evening dinner at their flat or out in a restaurant, which Edwards always paid for. They had each day to explore this modern City State, which only covered some 280 square miles, on an island just off the southern tip of Malaysia. They had already visited the original Chinese area of Singapore with its narrow streets and rather dilapidated three-storey buildings. They had explored the more interesting shops in Orchard Road and one evening, with their hosts, they had visited the famous Raffles Hotel, built in 1887, but then much extended in 1899. At the same time, the main hotel building had been equipped with electric light and electric ceiling fans, the first hotel in the whole region to have electricity. In front of the hotel stood a statue of Sir Stamford Raffles, set to the side of the Singapore Cricket Club's Ground, known as The Padang, which, when the Raffles Hotel had been built, had led down to what was originally a popular beach. Now, due to land reclamation, the sea was some distance away and the whole area was surrounded by modern high-rise buildings.

The evening that they had visited the Raffles Hotel for a pre-dinner drink, they had entered the Long Bar. Of course, their drinks that evening had to be the famous Singapore Sling; a drink invented some time before 1915 by the then barman in the Raffles Long Bar, which by reputation, was the longest bar in Asia. They took their drinks out onto the Palm Court, surrounded by palm trees and tropical plants, and bordered by some of the luxury guest rooms which were entered from the Court. Above each room door was a large grill, and a ventilator, which tried to capture some of the cool air from the Palm Court. Inside each bedroom was a high ceiling fan which distributed it. A number of famous writers and film stars had stayed in these bedrooms, off the Palm Court, including Rudyard Kipling, Joseph Conrad, Noel Coward, Graham Greene, Ava Gardner, Elizabeth Taylor and of course, Somerset Maugham, who had declared the Long Bar his favourite bar in the whole world!

Back in their host's flat, Edwards had found a copy of Sinister Twilight by the British journalist Noel Barber, and was avidly reading it, during any spare time that he had. It was the well written and accurate story of the Japanese invasion of Singapore, in February, 1942, which had turned into the largest military surrender of British-led armed forces in history. Some 5,000

British forces had been killed or wounded and 80,000 captured by a Japanese force of less than half the size of the British. The British had seriously underestimated the capability of the Japanese, who had used light armoured vehicles and bicycles, to totally outmanoeuvre the British and travel quickly down the Malaysian peninsula, through the thick forests, that the British thought would protect them against any invasion from the north.

The war time British leader Winston Churchill had called it "the worst disaster" in British military history, and it had served to seriously undermine the legend of British invincibility across the world. After the end of the Second World War, this event certainly increased the call for independence, from Britain, of many of her colonies. But, more importantly, was that this defeat resulted in the terrible suffering of the captured British troops, who had been imprisoned under harsh and overcrowded conditions at Changi Prison, and at other camps on the island, with little food and medicine. Many of these prisoners of war were forced into slave labour, by their Japanese captors, and many of these would die of illness and malnutrition. This proved to be the real human cost of this truly monumental British military defeat.

After the eventual surrender of the Japanese, Singapore was handed back to the Britain and gained self-governance in 1959. In 1963, it became part of the new Federation of Malaysia. Two years later, after great political differences between the majority

Singaporean Chinese and the other Malay part of the Federation, with its largely Muslim native population, Singapore was expelled and became an independent country controlled by its majority Chinese population. It was, by the 1980s, a thriving City State with large port facilities, and the location of the offices of many banks and other companies in the financial sector. The Singapore people were required by their government to be highly disciplined, but were well looked after with excellent education and health care facilities. Everything worked very well; in fact, too well. Edwards sensed that, rather like the unchanging weather, life in Singapore was now really rather boring! On the other hand, Singapore was now a fully developed and politically stable island nation. However, Edwards and his wife were now to experience something more uncertain and worrying.

2

Early the following week, Edwards and his wife were booked to fly from Singapore to Thailand. They had a hotel reservation in the Thai capital, Bangkok, for the rest of that week and into the following weekend. But something was now really worrying Edwards about the next leg of their holiday. Every evening, in their friend's flat, they watched the local TV news channels. By the middle of the week, it was being reported, that a group of Thai military officers were trying to overthrow the current Thai Government. Edwards and his wife were appalled when pictures of tanks and other armoured vehicles patrolling the streets of Bangkok, suddenly appeared. They discussed the situation with their friends.

"Do you think we should fly to Bangkok or just cancel our visit and our hotel reservation?" Edwards asked them, somehow expecting them to be able to answer this difficult question.

Edwards's wife seemed determined to keep to their planned stay in Thailand, if at all possible. She was fascinated by Thai history and culture and still wanted to visit the country. But Edwards was worried that the current, unstable situation, could lead to riots on the streets of Bangkok; or, even worse, shooting and perhaps a civil war, on the same streets, breaking out between two Thai Army factions.

The husband of his wife's friend tried to give him some comfort. "Thailand has had more coups and attempted coups than any other country on Earth," he said. But this statement did not give Edwards any reassurance. He was really worried about his and his wife's safety, if they went ahead with their travel plans!

The following morning Edwards had an idea. "I will telephone the British Embassy here and ask for their advice," he said to his wife. His wife agreed; surely the British Embassy would be able to give them some sensible advice about what was happening in Thailand, and whether it was safe to travel there?

Edwards picked up the thick Singapore telephone directory. He soon found, of course, that as Singapore was still a member of the British Commonwealth, the British Embassy was called the British High Commission. He dialled the number and heard a recorded message, with their opening hours. These seemed to be limited and did not start until much later in the morning. So, instead of going out, they stayed in the flat so that they could call the High Commission later.

Five minutes after their opening time, Edwards called the Embassy again. He heard the same recorded message. Ten minutes later he tried calling again; this time the recorded message had been turned off, but there was no answer. He kept on calling; it was some forty-five minutes after their supposed opening time, that he at last received an answer. He told the telephonist what he wanted; she seemed bemused as to who he should speak to about this matter. "I will put you through to the First Secretary's office," she eventually decided.

A female voice answered; it was the Secretary to the First Secretary! "I am afraid that he is not in the High Commission today!" she said.

Edwards again explained what he wanted; some advice to two British Citizens, from their Embassy, as to whether it was safe to travel to Thailand. "I think it best if you speak to the Second Secretary," she stated and put Edwards through.

A male voice answered with a British Public School accent. For the third time Edwards had to explain what he wanted; in view of part of the Thai Army staging an attempted coup on the streets of Bangkok, did the High Commission think that it was safe for British Citizens to go to Thailand? There was a long pause. "What attempted coup are you talking about?" was the surprising reply! Edwards put the telephone down, in sheer disgust, at the lack of any proper response from the British High Commission.

That evening they discussed the situation again with their hosts. "I just don't know what to do," said Edwards. "The British High Commission was hopeless. They did not seem even to be aware of what has been going on in Bangkok!"

They reached no conclusion that evening. The following day was Friday; they were due to fly to Bangkok the following Monday. Instead of fretting in the flat, Edwards and his wife took themselves off to Sentosa Island, the resort island located just off Singapore's southern coast. To reach it they decided to use the modern cable car system which had been opened in 1974. Both of them were used to cable cars, from their holidays skiing in the Alps, but this was different. It was the first cable car system in the world to span a harbour; there was a slight feeling of uneasiness hanging high above the sea. But the views from it and the quiet and beautiful beaches of Sentosa, at least took Edwards's mind away from the problem of whether they should go on to Thailand.

That evening, after dinner with their hosts, they turned on the television news again. It was now really too late to change their travel plans. After a few items of local Singapore news, suddenly an item from Bangkok was broadcast. It showed the Thai King, His Majesty King Bhumibol Adulyadej, seated on his throne in his Royal Palace in Bangkok. At his feet, prostrate and grovelling, in their Thai Army uniforms, were the leaders of the attempted coup! The status of the Thai King in his country is close to that of a god, and he had at last decided that "enough was enough." He had summoned the coup leaders and harshly admonished them. They appeared broken men and they were then led away with bowed heads. Edwards's problem had been solved and his Thai holiday had been saved by this firm Royal action!

3

Their time in Thailand was enjoyable; all signs of the attempted coup had now disappeared. Their holiday coincided with the Thai New Year Festival known as Songkran; a traditional national holiday in Thailand. This Festival is usually held close to the beginning of the Thai Rainy Season and, appropriately, it is marked by water fights, and the pouring of water over children and elderly people, for good luck. There are parties and heavy drinking and many people dress up in traditional Thai costumes.

Edwards and his wife were drenched a couple of times in water fights while walking in the streets of Bangkok and once again, when they were in a boat on one of Bangkok's many Khlongs, or canals. They had taken to the water in a long canoe powered by an outboard motor and the boatman was steering them through a narrow passage, between other boats, in the main Bangkok floating market. Suddenly a group of laughing Thai children, all carrying pots of different sizes, decided that now was a good time to drench as many of the passing tourists as they could! Edwards and his wife took it all in their stride, laughing with the children; fortunately, the high daytime temperatures served to dry your clothes very quickly.

After the King had saved their stay in Thailand, they felt that a visit to the Royal Palace to pay their respects was called for. So they joined all the other tourists visiting The Grand Palace, a complex of buildings in the centre of Bangkok, and the official residence of the Kings of Siam since 1782. Situated on the banks of the Chao Phraya River, it contains numerous buildings; palaces, halls and pavilions set around open lawns, gardens and courtyards. The varying styles of the buildings were due to the site's organic development, with additions and rebuilding made by successive monarchs, over the many years of its history.

Edwards and his wife gazed at the majesty of the Emerald Buddha, made of Jade, and dating back to the fifteenth century. It was now housed in its own ornate temple complex called Wat

Phra Kaew, in the grounds of The Grand Palace. Found again, when it was already centuries old, in Northern Thailand, it was, years later, taken by invaders to what is now Laos. It was then, much later, brought back to Thailand by a victorious Thai General. It was placed in the former Thai capital of Thonburi, before being moved to the new Thai capital of Bangkok in 1784, by the then King Rama the First, to avoid the risk of capture by the Burmese who were, at that time, invading Thailand.

That evening, Edwards and his wife visited a traditional Thai restaurant; usually Thai food is served on a very low table, with the diners sitting cross-legged on the ground. But, in an effort to accommodate Western tourists, pits had been dug below the low tables and cushions laid so that diners could sit comfortably on the edge of each pit, and be able to cope with eating off the low table in front of them. After an excellent meal, a performance of traditional Thai music and dancing, with dancers from the Thai Royal Ballet, in their magnificent, ornate costumes, was held.

The next day, to get a break from the incessant Bangkok traffic, Edwards and his wife took a coach north of Bangkok to the ancient city of Ayutthaya. This great archaeological site contains the remains of palaces, Buddhist temples, monasteries and statues. Founded in about 1350, it was mainly destroyed by Burmese invaders in 1767. Touring these extensive ruins, Edwards realised how fragile the history of Thailand had been. The country had so often been under attack by its neighbours and, where it not for several historically strong Thai Kings, who had fought back, it would have certainly disappeared. But Thailand had, in the end, survived as an independent country, defeating all attempted invasions, including those by the Western powers. It was the only country in the region which had strongly resisted any Western takeover, or even Western political influence.

But the often violent history of this country, had spawned a certain political instability; hence the great number of coups and attempted coups in more recent decades. But throughout it all, the Thai monarchy had stayed strong enough to defend the country. It was really no wonder that the Thai King was accorded his semi-divine status, by most of the Thai people, and still exercised strong political power. The Thais remained, sensibly, very loyal to the idea of a Monarchy, which they closely identified with and which, if needed, could act to contain the unwise ambitions of generals and politicians!

4

It was just over ten years later and the world had moved on. Edwards now had two young children; a daughter of eight years old and a young son of just six months. In November 1989, the Berlin Wall, which had been built between the two halves of the city of Berlin, had been breached and the city had been reunified. In October 1990, the Communist state of East Germany would join the other part of the country, which had been called

West Germany, to become again a united German State. In July 1991, the so-called "Warsaw Pact", whereby the countries of Eastern Europe had, since just after the Second World War, been in a involuntary military alliance with the Communist Union of Soviet Socialist Republics, was dissolved. In each of these now fully independent countries, Communism would soon be replaced by a democratic government.

The U.S.S.R. itself, would be dissolved in December 1991 by its own President, the Communist Party leader Mikhail Gorbachev. He had introduced his new ideas of Glasnost, which freed public access to information after decades of censorship, and Perestroika which had included major changes in the economy and the Communist Party leadership. The individual republics, including Russia itself, were then allowed to follow their own independent policies, leadership and political systems. But within the largest of those republics, Russia itself, by mid-1991, there was resistance growing against Gorbachev's policies. You really cannot have such major changes happening, over such a short period of time, without some people becoming very unhappy indeed about it!

Edwards's wife spoke, read and wrote fluent Russian; she had learnt Russian at school and then at university, where she had studied both the language and its literature. She was in demand to act as both a translator of written material and as an interpreter. Once, she had been asked by one of Edwards's colleagues, who Edwards suspected had a close connection with the Secret Intelligence Service, which most people knew as MI6, to translate a short Russian phrase. Slowly the story came out; it had been said by Gorbachev to his trusted Private Secretary, who he had grown up with, in a small town in the North Caucasus. It was in Russian slang, and even more difficult to translate, because it was in the local dialect which they both understood. It had been said about the then British Prime Minister Margaret Thatcher. At last Edwards's wife had been able to translate the true meaning of this phrase, and this had really been a trigger for the British Government to develop at least some trust in Gorbachev and in what he wanted to do to change his country for the better!

Every year Edwards's wife used to attend a regular international conference, where she joined a panel of interpreters to work for a full week, in a foreign city. She was paid well, with her hotel and flights provided. As a result she had visited a number of the major cities in the world. It was now August 1991, and the previous year it had been decided that the conference for the following year, should be held in Moscow. Before she left Edwards had expressed a little concern; after all Russia had experienced some staggering changes over the last few years. But his wife had shrugged it off; she was looking forward to visiting a city where she could speak the local language everywhere. She had also already booked a week's holiday from her fulltime work to make this visit. Edwards had to continue at his job, so their regular Nanny, who lived locally and looked after their two children, had promised to commit a few more hours each day, to allow for Edwards having to return from work late, if this was needed.

Edwards's wife had flown to Moscow on the Saturday, in order to have the Sunday to prepare for the conference. On Monday, Edwards went to work as usual, totally unaware of the ominous events that were actually happening in Russia. It was known by only a few people in that country that, the day before, a group of senior military officers and Communist Party officials, had flown to the Crimea to meet Gorbachev at his seaside holiday home. They demanded that he issue a Declaration of a State of Emergency, to enable them to stop the changes that were happening, or resign immediately. He refused, so they put him under House Arrest and cut off all of the means of communication from his house.

Edwards had returned home that evening, fed his children, bathed them and got them to bed. Only then, did he turn on the television for the news. All the news channels were reporting that, in that very morning, all the Moscow radio stations had reported that a State of Emergency had been declared, and that a new Acting President of the U.S.S.R. had been appointed, to replace Gorbachev, who had become ill. At the same time, the conspirators had arranged for certain army units, loyal to them, with their tanks and other armoured vehicles, to enter the outskirts of Moscow, and then to begin to make their way to the city centre, in order to violently put down any resistance to their plans. As the evening proceeded, television pictures of these military manoeuvres, heading towards the centre of Moscow, began to be broadcast!

Edwards was horrified; he watched the news over and over again. By eleven o'clock in London, the army units had entered the centre of Moscow. By midnight, Edwards decided that he must do something; he had the telephone number of his wife's hotel and he decided to call her. He did not know whether the same television pictures were being broadcast in Moscow, or whether they were being censored. He knew that the time in Moscow was several hours ahead and that he would probably have to wake up his wife. Not knowing what would happen, he dialled the number of the hotel. A female voice answered, in Russian; he asked for his wife. The voice immediately changed to perfect English and he asked for his wife again.

"Do you know what time it is here?" asked the female voice.

Edwards said that he did. "Are you watching television?" was the next question from the hotel telephonist.

Edwards said that he was. "You need not worry," came the calm reply, all the way from Moscow. "What is happening is happening a long way from here. Your wife will be safe. Do you still want to wake her up?"

Edwards paused to think; he decided to thank the Russian telephonist for her kindness and reassurance. Then he told her not to wake his wife.

The next day he watched the early morning news anxiously; no shots had been fired in Moscow and no one seemed to have been killed or injured. The newly elected President, of the now increasingly independent Russian Federation, Boris Yeltsin, was now shown on top of a tank outside the Russian Parliament building, known as The White House. He was making a speech to a vast crowd of people. He asked the army not to take part in the coup and for a general strike to be called. Yeltsin had just returned to Russia, from an overseas trip, and the plotters had failed to detain him. This was their great mistake, as Yeltsin was even more of a reformer than Gorbachev. In fact, Yeltsin's speech had actually been made yesterday, but had not been made public or broadcast. The commander in charge of the tanks, surrounding The White House, had then declared his loyalty to Yeltsin. The attempted coup had appeared to have collapsed, as a result of this commander's defection. But it was still a very worried Edwards who had to go to work that morning!

By that evening, the position had become no clearer; an overnight curfew was declared in Moscow. Most commentators believed that this was in preparation for a military attack on The White House. Meanwhile the tanks around it had been moved and its defenders, mostly unarmed, were preparing to defend it. Edwards became increasingly worried that shooting could now break out on the streets of Moscow and that this could prompt another part of the Soviet Army, loyal to Gorbachev, to intervene and a civil war to start. If even only a part of this was to happen, tourists like his wife would be confined to their hotels and after a while, food supplies could become difficult to maintain. Moscow Airport could be shut down and all flights stopped; his wife could be trapped in Moscow for months!

But Edwards was not to know, that the attack on The White House had been planned by a Committee, appointed by the plotters, and that several members of this Committee, had mingled secretly with the crowds surrounding the building. They had reported back that the crowds would resist any attack and that it would result in heavy bloodshed. Any attack should therefore be cancelled. Meanwhile, three civilians were then reported to have been killed, trying to block a road tunnel down which military vehicles were advancing. Edwards went to bed that night very worried; he fully expected to wake up the following morning to television news reports of fighting in Moscow and substantial civilian deaths!

But, it did not happen; he did not know it, but the conspirators had been horrified by these first civilian deaths and the thought of many more. Their nerve had been broken and the attack on The White House had been called off. Their troops were ordered to withdraw and to leave Moscow. Some of the conspirators flew again to meet Gorbachev, in the Crimea, but he refused to meet them. His communications were then restored; Gorbachev then rescinded all the orders that the plotters had made, and dismissed them from their positions. That morning, before he left for work, a telegram arrived for Edwards from his wife in Moscow. It read simply "I am alright. Will return on Saturday as planned."

5

Three of the leading conspirators committed suicide and the rest were arrested; their attempted coup was over. The result was the exact opposite of what the plotters had intended. Instead of their efforts to strengthen and reinvigorate the U.S.S.R. being successful, further work on a new treaty to do just that was abandoned. Immediately, more power shifted to the individual Republics. But even more was to happen; a few days later, Gorbachev resigned as General Secretary of the Communist Party. Five days after that, its main ruling body terminated all Communist Party activities throughout the U.S.S.R. The Communist Party collapsed and the U.S.S.R. was soon to follow, as the various Republics within it, declared their own independence. This was despite an attempt to form a new Constitution and a new united Supreme Soviet Council. By early December, only three Republics, including Russia, had not declared independence.

Then Boris Yeltsin, on behalf of Russia and the leaders of the Ukraine and Belarus, declared the end of the Union of Soviet Socialist Republics, and all its political apparatus was dismantled. Within four months of the attempted coup, the history of Russia's last seventy-four years had been swept away. On Christmas Day 1991, Gorbachev announced his resignation as the President of the U.S.S.R., and its red Hammer and Sickle flag was lowered over the Kremlin buildings, for the last time. It was replaced by the tricolour flag of Russia.

It was a happy and relieved Edwards, along with his two children, who met his wife at the Heathrow Airport terminal building, on that Saturday afternoon. Only after they had got their excited children, at last, to bed that evening, did they begin to discuss her visit.

"It was all very interesting," she said, "to be there, while all this was happening. The local radio and television did not seem to be subject to any censorship and they were trying to report everything, that was happening, as accurately as they could. I had some time off on the Tuesday, so I went to The White House, to mingle with the crowds there, and to talk to some of the ordinary people."

Edwards gasped. "You took a great risk," he replied. "That was the day that the plotters were planning a military attack on that building."

But his wife did not seem interested. "It was wonderful to be able to speak to them in their own language," she said. "Most of them thought that I was a local Russian and told me things about their lives, that they would never have told to a foreigner."

Edwards decided to keep silent. After all, his wife had safely returned home and his two children now had their mother back.

In the years to come, an older and much wiser Edwards would slowly reflect on these two attempted coups. The illegal manoeuvres of part of the Thai Army in 1981, had been ended by the King and had proved to be only a tiny blip in the long history of the Thai Kingdom. But the illegal manoeuvres of part of the Soviet Army in 1991, had resulted in the complete undoing of what the plotters had planned. Where Gorbachev had led the way, it was Yeltsin, who had bravely stood on a potential enemy tank, and defended his reforms and freedom for the Russian people. Only four months after that event, the Communist Party and the Soviet Union were no more!

Edwards concluded that he still believed firmly in Monarchies; somehow their continuous and family orientated presence, seemed to bring stability to a country. The nations that had become Republics were, instead, led by ambitious and often corrupt politicians; they sometimes proved unstable and to be prone to be taken over by one powerful, autocratic leader such as Napoleon or Stalin. Attempted coups were relatively common, but a successful revolution did not often happen. The American, French and Russian Revolutions had occurred as a result of extreme financial, and other problems. The Americans had fought for independence from Britain, after Britain had imposed more taxes on them, because of the cost of the British wars against France. The French had fought the British and supported their American colonies against their mother country. In so doing they had bankrupted themselves, resulting in even higher taxes, and then their own Revolution. The Russian Revolution had resulted from the very high financial and human cost to Russia of the First World War. As long as the events in a nation continued along a reasonably consistent and benign path, it seemed to Edwards, as a loyal Englishman, that a Monarchy probably held out the best hope of a stable and prosperous nation.

HEART STRINGS

"It is easy to fall in love among the winding cobblestone streets and snow-covered castles of Prague, but is it a good idea?" – Dana Newman.

1

It was a sunny, Spring day; Edwards and his wife paused in the middle of the medieval stone-arched Charles Bridge, decorated by the numerous statues running along both sides of its parapet. They gazed, up the hill, to the mighty building on the opposite river bank, that they were approaching. The River Vltava flowed under the bridge below them and above them soared the boundary walls and buildings of Prague Castle. Begun in the ninth century, it was now the largest ancient castle in the world. Edwards glanced down, over the parapet of the bridge, to the river below. On the river bank that they were approaching, were moored what were obviously a number of floating restaurants. But, Edwards had to ask himself, given all the other restaurants that he had noticed, were they really extensively used by the relatively limited number of tourists which he had seen, who came to this beautiful capital city? The passers-by, crossing the bridge, were not well-dressed; they looked sullen and defeated. They did not greet each other, or smile or laugh to each other if they were walking with another person. Edwards was now beginning to understand why!

Two days before, they had arrived on their British Airways flight from London's Heathrow Airport. As soon as they had taxied to a halt, in front of the Terminal Building, their aircraft had been surrounded by a squad of uniformed Czechoslovak Border Guards. They held their heavy sub-machine guns ready to fire! Edwards turned to his wife in the seat beside him; "Have they come for us, do you think?" he asked her.

She smiled at him reassuringly; "They are just there to prevent anyone storming the plane and trying to fly it out to the West," she said.

They collected their hand luggage and descended the steps, which had been pushed against the aircraft, leading to the ground. The Border Guards had now formed two lines, on either side of the arriving passengers, to guide them safely into the entrance of the Terminal Building. Edwards turned to his wife as they walked towards it; "I really did not expect a Guard of Honour!" he commented. His wife just laughed quietly, but rather nervously. She knew that this was the normal reception for any airline passengers arriving in the Communist, Russian-dominated, Czechoslovak Socialist Republic, in the year of 1977. Europe was, at that time, divided between a Communist Russia and its client states within the Warsaw Pact military alliance, and the Capitalist states of Western Europe, most of which were members of the North Atlantic Treaty Organisation, known as N.A.T.O.. Between these two blocks there was a "Cold War" and physically between them, on the ground, was a militarised zone, which Winston Churchill had once called the "Iron Curtain."

Entering the country was a complex procedure; first Edwards had to queue to exchange the requisite amount of British Pounds, worked out for each day of his stay, for the Czechoslovak Koruna that he was forced to spend while he was visiting this country. He was not allowed to take any of this local currency out of the country, at the end of his holiday. Then they joined the separate queues for Passport Control; his British passport would be scrutinised for the Visa that he had bought from the Czechoslovak Embassy in London, and he would then be asked for the receipt that he had just been given for buying the Czech currency, which was needed to validate his Visa. He would then be asked for the address where he would be staying, and then he would be given a reminder that he had to report to the nearest office of the internal Czech Security Service, within forty-eight hours of arriving in the country, to be formally interviewed. Failure to do this would result in his instant deportation.

Meanwhile his wife was queuing at the separate counter for Czech citizens; her Czechoslovak Passport was just as closely examined and in particular, the special permit that had been stamped into her Passport by the Czechoslovak Embassy in

London. This gave permission for her free, safe passage into and out of the country of her birth. Edwards well remembered the day that they had spent, a few months after they had been married in the previous year, to obtain this precious rubber stamp. First, there had been the visit to his bank to take out in cash, the required large amount in British Pounds demanded by the Embassy, to pay for his wife's "previous education" before she had decided to stay in England in 1969. After she had finished a working holiday, picking fruit in Kent during the summer, she had decided not to go home. Then, rather fearful about carrying so much cash around London, they had taken a bus to the Czechoslovak Embassy, to hand over the money. They were then forced to wait for hours while the vital rubber stamp was placed into his wife's Czechoslovak Passport. But Edwards still did not trust this stamp; he had decided to travel with his wife to Prague for a holiday, to stay with her parents, just in case she was detained there, so that he could be at least on hand to protest at this situation.

The reason for his wife's decision to stay in England was that, during the previous year of 1968, the Russian army, together with the armies of some of its allied Warsaw Pact members, had invaded Czechoslovakia. Their aim was to suppress the government led by Alexander Dubcek who, very bravely, had decided to try and introduce political reforms away from the previous hard-line Communist regime. This invasion was despite the fact that Czechoslovakia was also a member of the Warsaw

Pact military alliance; this membership had been forced on the Czechs, like it had been on all its other non-Russian members, by the military power of what was then the U.S.S.R. - the Union of Soviet Socialist Republics, the then greatly enlarged Communist Russian empire.

A large number of Czechoslovak citizens were killed or wounded trying to resist this invasion, although the Czech armed forces were confined to barracks to avoid further bloodshed. Dubcek and his Ministers were arrested and flown to Moscow where, no doubt, they were told in no uncertain terms, what would happen to them if they tried to continue their reforms. They were then returned to Prague, so that they could slowly reverse their own reforms, before Dubcek himself was forced out of office in early 1969. The following year he was expelled from the Communist Party. But political dissent continued with clandestine activity, strikes and demonstrations. Edwards's wife had been in her first year at Prague University, which had been seriously affected by this disruption. So, she had decided to make the brave decision to stay and seek political asylum in Britain; becoming a British Citizen after the required amount of time. The Czechoslovak government did not, of course, recognise this change in her citizenship status.

Having completed the Immigration procedures, their luggage was then searched swiftly, but efficiently, by Customs officials who were looking for anything that the Communist government would not like them to bring into the country, like any dissident literature or banned books. Then they were finally allowed to leave the airport. The next day they took public transport, a bus and then a tram, from her parent's home where they were staying, to report to the offices of the Czech Security Service in central Prague. It was a large, dour and rather frightening building; when they had mentioned its address to his wife's parents they had recognised it immediately as the headquarters of the "Secret Police!" Again they had to split up; at the reception inside the main entrance, as a Czech citizen, his wife was told to report to a department on the first floor. As a visiting foreigner, Edwards found himself in the basement of the building, where all alien visitors had to come to be interviewed.

It was, so appropriately for Prague, a Kafkaesque experience; inside the entrance of this department sat an obese, ugly woman, in some kind of uniform, who added Edwards's name to a long list. He sat in a large waiting area with other foreign visitors, obviously from many different countries; there was an oppressive atmosphere and the foreigners did not talk to each other. Along one long internal wall there were some six doors; each one was numbered. Every so often, a buzzer sounded and their female "jailor" announced in a loud voice, a surname and a number; first in Czech, then in English and then in German. A foreign visitor would then stand up, knock on the appropriate door and then enter. They would never be seen again by their remaining, waiting colleagues!

After one and a half hours, Edwards's turn came; he knocked on door number three as directed. He was asked to do this by a notice on each door in a number of languages. In English, the simple command was "Knock and Enter!" He entered; inside, sitting behind a small desk, was a sturdy young man in a cheap suit, shirt and tie. He indicated to Edwards that he could sit down on the uncomfortable wooden chair on the other side of his desk. In broken English he asked for Edwards's British Passport. He examined it carefully; he then took a copy of the page bearing Edwards's photograph, using a rather old-fashioned copying machine in the corner of the room. Then the questioning started, politely but firmly. Why had Edwards come to the Czechoslovak Socialist Republic? Where was he staying and for how long? What were the names of his parents-in-law? Was he going to be staying at any other address while he was in this country? Did he have the money to keep himself while he was there? Did he have a return air ticket to get home and when was his flight?

Then there followed the more personal questions: when and where had he married his wife? Where did they now live? Edwards was careful in answering this too fully, although he knew that the Czechoslovak Embassy in London had already demanded their home address. What did he do in London? Where did he work? Again, Edwards was careful not to give a full reply. The intrusive questions continued; they were still polite but unrelenting. Edwards fought hard not to compromise himself, his wife, her parents, or his country, in the increasingly complex answers that he had to give. The young man suddenly seemed satisfied; he handed Edwards back his British Passport. Edwards assumed that the interview had been recorded, since the official had taken no notes. The man indicated a door at the other end of the room; Edwards gratefully got up, walked to it and exited. He was now in a narrow corridor; there was a notice stuck on the opposite wall with an arrow pointing to the right. He walked along to the end of the corridor and found himself at the bottom of the staircase that took him up to the ground floor, and to the exit from the building.

Outside, he waited for his wife as they had arranged. He examined the building he had just left. On the pavement in front of it were a series of manhole covers, with opaque thick glass oblongs cut into them. They were supposed to let some daylight into the basement where he had been. To the left of the entrance, he could see the artificial light coming up from the rooms he had just visited. But to the right of the entrance, there was darkness; a shiver ran through Edwards! He had suddenly realised that this was, probably, where the cells for the prisoners were located. The prisoners could no doubt hear the passers-by, but they had no way of contacting them and telling them about their unfortunate fate! Half an hour later his wife had re-joined him; she seemed relieved, but thoughtful. They did not speak much about what had happened to either of them inside this large, ominous building.

2

His wife's parents lived in a fairly cramped, modern flat on the ground floor of a three-storey block. It had two bedrooms, a small kitchen and bathroom, and a sitting and dining area. Outside there was a narrow balcony, on which his father-in-law tended his collection of potted plants. The block of flats was situated in quite a pleasant estate made up of similar blocks and some higher-rise blocks, which had smaller apartments. There was an attempt at a children's play area, but most of the equipment there was old and rusting. Grass and a few bushes had been planted between the blocks, but there was no gardener to tend them, so the more community-minded residents took turns to cut the grass and clip the bushes. But this estate was far better than most of the typical Communist-era type of housing estates, in other parts of Prague, which consisted of gaunt, high blocks of small apartments, with tarmac or scrubland between them. There was also a reliable bus service to take you, albeit with one change onto a tram, to the centre of the city.

Curiously, Edwards had already stayed on this same housing estate; it had been some five years earlier, before he had even met his wife, when he had made his first visit to Prague. After university, he had moved into a relatively well-paid job in the City of London. It had given him enough money to take driving lessons, pass his driving test, and buy himself a blue, modern-designed Citroën car. Using this he had driven, with three university friends, to Brno, the capital of Moravia which, along with Bohemia, formed the so-called "Czech lands." Slovakia had, of course, been added to these "lands" by the Treaty of Versailles in 1919, which had formed the new, rather artificial, state of Czechoslovakia. In Brno they had stayed in a large house, owned by the parents of one of his passengers, another Czech girl who had travelled to England after the 1968 Russian invasion, and had also decided to stay in Britain. She had joined the same university as Edwards and he had met her there. She had now married a British student, at the same university, and he had accompanied her for this holiday.

It was while he was staying in Brno, that Edwards became aware of the true, elite nature of the Communist system. This girl's parents were both leading academics and both were members of the Communist Party. Because of this, they earned certain benefits; they were first allowed to keep their large house, which covered three storeys. Other larger families, with numerous children, who were not members of the Party, were often forced to share their small flats with another family, because of the "housing shortage." But it did not stop there; Party members could shop in special shops, which were always well stocked with food and other items, often imported from Western countries, like Germany or France. Edwards had visited the local supermarket several times; the shelves were usually empty of even basic food items. There were, sometimes, some poor-quality food items available, which sold out very quickly, and which non-Party shoppers had to rely on to feed themselves and their families.

In health care, there was the same divide; if you, or as a child, your parents, were a member of the Communist Party and you were ill, you would have access to immediate, specialist hospital treatment and a private hospital room. For the rest of the population, the health service was largely a "hit and miss" affair and, to even see your doctor, you probably would have to bribe him. The gifted children of Party members were allowed to attend special schools, where they received a first-class education. Party members also had subsidised access to luxury spa and seaside holidays, in other Warsaw Pact countries. They were also trusted to holiday abroad to the "West"; special holiday tours to Western countries were organised exclusively for Communist Party members. So this was how the elite Communist Party members, who regarded themselves as the "vanguard of the people," rewarded themselves. It was on the way back home, from Brno, that they had broken their journey to stay in Prague for a few nights, and they had been invited to stay on the same housing estate by a couple, who were friends of the Czech girl's mother. For the first time, Edwards was able to see the beauty of this city, with some of its fine buildings dating back to before medieval times, but also with many modern buildings of architectural merit.

If you were considered important enough, there were not only these "carrots" offered to you to join the Communist Party, but also you were threatened with the "stick" as well! Edwards admired his father-in-law as a result of the story that his wife had told him. Her father was a senior official in the Ministry of Finance; he had risen to that position on merit, without being a Party member. One day he was told that, in his position, he should be a Communist Party member, and was invited to become one. He refused. The next time that he was invited to join the Party, it was made clear that there was no alternative and that "bad things would follow if he did not." He refused again. At the third attempt to force him to join the Communist Party, it was made very clear that he would lose his job, if he refused again. But he did refuse again and as a result, he lost his senior position at the Ministry of Finance. Instead, he was sent to work in a railway repair team. One day, a heavy railway sleeper fell on him and his ankle was broken. Somebody senior in the Communist Party must then have relented. Or, perhaps, it had been found that nobody else could fill his government post for, once his ankle was healed, he was given back the same senior role in the Ministry of Finance that he had before. But, he had still refused to join the Party!

Within his parents-in-law's flat, conversation was always muted; there was always the fear that an electronic device had somehow been planted, to listen-in to the occupants. The arrival of visitors from abroad would have increased the need for surveillance; Edwards and his wife were asked to keep away from the windows, in case they were being observed or filmed and any telephone calls to or from the flat were assumed to have been recorded. It was prohibited to watch any television program beamed from the West or to listen to any Western radio broadcasts; this would have been picked up by any listening device and the penalties for doing so were harsh! When they were walking outside the flat, his wife had told him that the caretaker of the block, a middle-aged woman, was believed to be an agent for the "Secret Police!" This was quite normal; all blocks of flats had such agents, who were paid to observe and listen to what was going on. Several times Edwards and his wife caught this woman, very thoroughly cleaning and polishing the floor just outside the door of the flat that they were staying in. They had merely smiled at her and wished her a "Good Day" in Czech!

The next time that they visited Prague, Edwards and his wife came by car. It was a long journey; Edwards drove down to Dover and then they took the ferry crossing to Ostend. By now it was dark, but Edwards liked the fast drive across the flatlands of Belgium, as the Belgium motorway system was always very well lit-up at night. Only when you reached Aachen and crossed the German border, did the driving get more difficult. Most of the German autobahns had no lighting, but no speed limits either! Edwards made a fast time, although they stopped several times during the night to buy a coffee and have a short sleep in the car. By the next morning, they had reached the small German medieval town of Rothenburg ob der Tauber. Here, they bought breakfast and found a reasonably-priced place to stay the night. Then, his wife insisted, that they must visit some of the local shops and see a little of this ancient town.

Refreshed, the next morning they continued towards Prague. They knew what now faced them; the crossing of the "Iron Curtain." The high barbed-wire fence, complete with watch towers, equipped with searchlights and machine guns, and manned by the Czechoslovak Border Guards, came into view. In front of this high fence, after passing the West German simple border post, was a wide piece of cleared land; Edwards had been told that this was a minefield, planted under this last piece of Czech soil, and that it was further protected by automatic-firing machine guns, which could sense any sign of movement, day or night! Then he had to stop his car at the high border gate. They waited for it to open; vehicles were allowed through in batches. Past that, there was another high gate, so once the first gate closed behind them, they could not escape. Edwards had first to enter the Czechoslovak Border Post to change his British Pounds for the Czech currency; only then could the long examination of both their passports and visas began. Then their car and their cases were carefully searched before, finally, they were allowed through the second high barrier.

About two kilometres down the road, was the second "internal border"; another high barbed-wire fence and a heavy barrier across the road. As they were entering the country, they were just waved through the opened barrier, by the heavily armed Czechoslovak Border Guards stationed there. The purpose of this second border was clear; it was to keep Czechoslovak citizens away from the main border area itself, and to check outgoing vehicles for the first time, before they even reached the real border itself! One of the Border Guards was restraining, with great difficulty, a huge Alsatian guard dog. No doubt, this would have been used to bring down any unfortunate citizen attempting to escape into the prohibited border area, on foot, in the vain hope of somehow then breaching the main border fence and reaching the freedom that the West offered! The alternative would have been, of course, just to shoot them down!

3

Like all systems totally rotten from the inside, when the time came for the Communist system to collapse in Europe, it collapsed relatively quickly. A new General Secretary of the Communist Party in the Soviet Union called Mikhail Gorbachev, was elected by the Party in March 1985. He was only fifty-four years old and followed a series of much older and often, obviously senile, General Secretaries who had been elected over the previous decades. Almost at once he began to put forward arguments for reform. The two principles he established were firstly the need for "Glasnost", which translated as a need for a new openness in government and some democratic reforms;

the second principle was "Perestroika," or the need to begin to restructure the Soviet economic model. Over the years, such economics had proved to be largely inefficient in producing the consumer goods that the Russian and Eastern European populations desired. Much of this inefficiency came about as a result of the general, centralised control of industry, along with vast financial resources being diverted into the military sector, to make increasing expensive weapons and to carry out advanced research into new military technologies.

But what was the real cause of these sudden changes, other than an increasing dissatisfaction, within the population, at the Soviet system? To understand this, one has to examine what was happening in the great rival to the Soviet system, the United States of America. In November 1980, a new conservative, Republican American President called Ronald Reagan, had been elected; as soon as he took office in January the following year, he made clear his views on the Soviet Union. He was not a traditional politician, having had previous careers as a sports broadcaster and a successful film actor, before being first elected as Governor of California in 1966. As President he openly called the Soviet Union "an evil empire," and started a new "Arms Race" with the Russian-led block. Reagan refused to accept the existing doctrine of "Mutually Assured Destruction," to deter and prevent nuclear war. Instead, he set down his own ideas of America being able to destroy sufficient of the incoming Soviet nuclear ballistic missiles, so as to be able to still strike back again with a second round of their own missiles in a massive double response.

In 1983, the Strategic Defence Initiative, more commonly known as the "Star Wars" program, was announced; rather like the American commitment to land men on the Moon, it seemed a vast program to develop anti-ballistic missile defences, including anti-missile missiles, orbiting satellites and powerful laser weapons. Very large sums of money were allocated to this program for both research and development, and the building of these new weapon systems. But, in truth, this was probably a remarkable "Confidence Trick"; years later it was admitted that not much money had actually been spent and that it would have taken decades and even more money, to complete any real working system. Part of this spurious program was also used to identify Soviet spies, working deep within the American military and government machine, who had received desperate messages from Moscow to find out all they could about the Star Wars program. They would then often take unwise actions to do so, thereby exposing themselves to be identified. But the Russians seemed to have fully believed this trick, until they realised that attempting to copy the Americans would bankrupt their country, and that an alternative path towards peaceful coexistence was what was urgently required!

In November 1989, the divisions within Europe began to crumble; Germany had been divided between the two winning sides after the end of the Second World War. West Germany had been allocated to the Western allies of the United States, Britain and France, and was allowed to develop into a new democratic country, while East Germany was given to the Soviet Union and became a Communist state under the domination of the Russians. Even in the old capital of Germany, Berlin, control of the city was divided between the four victors and there were American, British and French sectors, as well as a Russian one. A high wall was built by the East German authorities to help prevent their citizens fleeing to the West. In 1989, because of Gorbachev's reforms in Russia, the citizens of East Berlin at last rose up and not only crossed the Berlin Wall, but started to demolish it! Gorbachev made it clear to the repressive East German regime, that he would not support them if they began to shoot their own citizens. Three weeks later, the end of the so-called "Cold War" between the Soviet Union and the West was declared, and Germany was reunified in 1990.

In Czechoslovakia, dissent against Russian domination and the Communist regime, had largely centred around one man, Vaclav Havel, a Czech author, poet and playwright. For years, he had used his literary work to criticise the Communist system, and had started off several initiatives to try and overthrow it. Havel spent many years in prison for his political beliefs and had suffered constant surveillance by the Czechoslovak Secret Police. The illegal political party, that he had established, played a major part in the so-called "Velvet Revolution" in Czechoslovakia in late 1989 which, as part of the wave of peaceful revolutions throughout Central Europe, swept the Communist regimes from power and established personal freedoms and democracy. By popular acclaim, Havel was first declared President of his country, and was then continuously democratically elected to that role for a period of over ten years. He was instrumental in demolishing the Warsaw Pact, which had for years militarily supported Russia. He also played a great part in the expansion of the Western N.A.T.O alliance, to include all of the countries of Central Europe. Havel also oversaw the so-called "Velvet Divorce" in 1992, whereby Slovakia became an independent country, and the state of Czechoslovakia ceased to exist; it had been, in many ways, an artificial creation put together in 1918, after the dissolution of the Austro-Hungarian Empire at the end of the First World War. Havel then became the first President of the Czech Republic.

4

For Edwards and his wife and children, these events changed their possibilities; for the first time they could travel easily to his wife's original home, and there they could sense the environment of a new found independence and freedom. Fortunately, Edwards's parents-in-law lived long enough to see this "New Dawn," and for their hopes and dreams for freedom to have been fulfilled. In their visits to Prague, Edwards could now see the changes; the people around him were relaxed and happy, increasingly better dressed and becoming more affluent. Business opportunities began to open up and many Western entrepreneurs began to take an interest in doing business, in the now increasingly prosperous economies of Central Europe. One of Edwards's oldest friends, Richard, had introduced Edwards to a British property developer, who had expressed an interest in the Prague property market. He had a man out there already, looking out for opportunities for him, but he was not happy that he was giving him a good service. Given his experience of the city, he had asked Edwards if he could go to Prague for him, for a week, and see what he thought? His air fare and other expenses would be paid to him, along with his time. Edwards, of course, accepted.

Following some nine years of separation, caused by his father's addiction to gambling, Edwards's parents had got back together again, and had moved to the once-fashionable seaside resort of Torquay in Devon. Edwards's mother had visited Torquay many times, with her mother, during the heyday of Torquay in the 1920's and 1930's, when Torquay and its surrounding area had been dubbed "The English Riviera." His parents had lived there together for over twenty years, but, Edwards's father had then passed away, a few years earlier. He had developed cancer, but that had been treated and he appeared to have been cured. But then it had reasserted itself. Meanwhile, Edwards's mother had become increasing immobile and had moved into a nursing home in Torquay. Edwards had managed to largely forgive his father for his gambling addiction that had led to his and his mother's privation, and a struggle to live for a long period in his teenage and early adult years. When his father was moved into a hospice and finally into a specialist nursing home, he had taken the long journey down to Torquay to visit him, and also his mother, numerous times.

His father and mother had fortunately managed to celebrate their fifty-fifth Wedding Anniversary and then their last Christmas together. Then, in the next January, Edwards received an urgent telephone call: it sent him driving down to Torquay, as fast as he could drive, with the thick winter fogs along parts of the road. He had arrived just fifteen minutes before his father had died; but fortunately he had been able to hold his hand and he knew that his father had known that he was there with him. After that he had the unenviable tasks of telling his mother the sad news of her husband's death, and then of clearing out the apartment that they had both lived in for so many years.

With his mother now alone, Edwards and his family tried to visit her as often as they could and had a telephone installed by her bedside, so that they could talk to her every evening. It was now nearly two years later; the evening before he was due to fly to Prague, he called his mother. He explained that he would be away for a week and he clearly remembered his mother asking him if he really had to go on this visit? He had spent a busy week in Prague and had then flown back on the Friday afternoon. When he arrived home from Heathrow Airport, his family were out for a walk and when they returned, Edwards was coming down the stairs, after changing his clothes and unpacking his case. His eight-year old daughter looked at him sadly; she seemed to have been crying. His nine-month old son was peacefully asleep in his pushchair. Straight away his wife looked straight at him.

"I did not want to interrupt your trip or cause you any distress," she began. "But, on last Tuesday morning, the nursing home called to say that your mother was not well and that you should get down there as soon as you could. I told them that you were abroad and could not do this. The next morning, they called me again to tell me that, sadly, during the night, she had peacefully passed away."

Edwards sat down, in shock. When he had recovered a little he turned to his wife. "It is strange," he said. "I woke up in the middle of Tuesday night. I could not get back to sleep again for a long time. It was almost as if I knew, unconsciously, that something was wrong!"

His wife nodded sympathetically. "You will have to drive down to Torquay on Sunday," she said. "They want to see you down there on Monday morning, to talk about the funeral arrangements that we will want, for your mother."

5

Time passed and it was now in the early years of the twenty-first century. Edwards now worked part-time as an adviser to a former government-owned high-technology group. Years before, he had met and established a friendship with an American who lived, with his wife, in California. He preferred to be called by the nickname "Indy." Indy was charming and well-travelled; he had been a banker, but had then established his own company to carry out various kinds of deals, particularly in Central and South-Eastern Europe. Indy was an independent adventurer and capitalist, and he visited London regularly. Edwards had always tried to meet up with him during these visits. But, gradually, Edwards began to realise that his American friend had a secret life; he was actually a covert and intrepid, American intelligence agent. He introduced Edwards to several of his contacts around the world, who usually occupied vital roles in various countries.

As well as meeting in London, Edwards and Indy had also met at various international conferences about trade and investment. It was at a conference in Vienna that they had indulged in a drinking session together, after dinner, in the bar of the hotel where they were both staying. Indy suddenly excused himself and came back, a few minutes later, with a very attractive and well-dressed lady, younger than both himself and Edwards, but also of mature years. She was educated, charming, alluring and friendly; Edwards recognised immediately that she and Indy already knew each other, and that she could well have been one of his operatives. She spoke very good English, with what Edwards thought was a Central European accent. She was probably Czech; this was not unusual as Vienna had the largest Czech population after Prague itself. Many Czechs had fled there over the years, to escape the brutality of the Communist regime.

After about half an hour, their conversation together had warmed up, then Indy politely excused himself again; he said that he was tired and wanted to go to bed. Edwards saw that Indy had manufactured this opportunity for him, perhaps as a playful gesture, to mimic a "honey trap," knowing full-well that Edwards's own experience of Communist Central Europe had taught him to avoid such entanglements! As Indy expected, Edwards had politely but firmly resisted this lady's too obvious advances. Edwards was always on guard against attempts to gather "kompromat," as the Russian intelligence agency the K.G.B. called it, or also known as compromising material, to help an enemy intelligence agency persuade innocent people to work for them. But it amused him to see that it could also be deployed as a friendly, jocular gesture, by an imaginative, covert American agent!

On his next visit to London, Indy had asked to see Edwards; when they met privately, he said that he had a confidential and very personal request.

"An old college friend of mine has spent a lot of time in Prague," he began. "He has now asked me if I can help him on a very personal matter? But I think that you are the one who might be able to help him."

"What is it that I can do?" asked Edwards, always willing to try and help his American friend.

Indy took a deep breath. "He has met a Czech lady in Prague," he said. "She is younger than him and very beautiful."

Edwards smiled; he knew what was coming. The Czech women in Prague were usually very good looking and it was just too easy to fall in love with them! "Go on," he said to his friend. He also sensed that, maybe, Indy's "college friend" was in the same covert intelligence business that Indy himself was in!

"They are now in a relationship and he wants to marry her and take her back to the United States with him," continued Indy. "But, being a jealous guy, he just can't get the thought out of his head that she might have been, or still is, how shall we say, interested in meeting Western businessmen for a good time!"

Edwards nodded; he understood Indy's friend's problem. "So how can I help?" he asked.

"If we used an American businessman, she might become suspicious," went on Indy. "But a British businessman, regularly visiting Prague, would be ideal. I can give you her name and her telephone number and you could call her and say that you will be in Prague next week and that you would like to meet her. You can suggest meeting her in the bar of your hotel, and that you will carry a copy of the Financial Times to identify yourself!"

"But I cannot just cold call her," said Edwards. "How am I supposed to have got her name and telephone number?"

"We know that she had a "close friendship" with another British businessman, who regularly used to visit Prague, some years ago," replied Indy. "That has now stopped. But you could say that you knew him, and that he had mentioned her to you and gave you her telephone number."

"So you expect me to fly to Prague to see if she turns up in the bar of my hotel?" asked Edwards.

"That is not necessary," responded Indy. "We will have someone that she does not know, in the bar, at the time chosen, to see if she turns up. They will know what she looks like."

"That is fine," Edwards said. "I am happy to call her, even if it takes several calls, and invite her to meet me. Then I will let you know the place, date and time of our supposed meeting."

"My buddy will be very grateful," was all that Indy would say.

So Edwards carried out this task; he gave himself a "cover name" and telephoned the lady in Prague several times. He mentioned the name of the British businessman that he had been given and struck up a friendly conversation with her. His knowledge of Prague, and of doing business there, certainly helped. He said that he would call her again, before he was next going to Prague, and that they really must meet up. He sensed that she rather grudgingly accepted. Two weeks later he called her again and said that he would be in Prague the following week; he set up a meeting with her in the bar of a central hotel that he had stayed in before. Then he informed Indy of the place, date and time for this none-meeting. He heard nothing more, so three weeks later, he contacted Indy to ask him what had happened?

"She did not turn up," said Indy, with a note of triumph in his voice. "We had someone watching inside the bar. My buddy was very pleased and sends his personal thanks to you for all that you have done for him."

Edwards did not think again about this curious incident, but years later, he did chance upon the name of Indy's colleague, that Indy had once given to him. What he read confirmed what Indy had told him; he had now become a very successful investor in Silicon Valley with an attractive Czech wife. They frequently featured in press reports, and from carefully perusing these, Edwards could confirm to himself that this now, "Silicon Princess," was the lady to whom he had spoken to all those years before, and with whom he had set up a nefarious meeting in the bar of a central Prague hotel. She now lived and worked with Indy's friend, as his wife, in the United States. As Edwards read more, he became very pleased that he had been able to help this particular American to find happiness!

Edwards now realised that both Indy and his colleague had bravely contributed, over the years, with their important covert work, to the final downfall of the Soviet Union. They had both seemed to have also been involved, with others, in promoting innovative ideas during the Presidency of Ronald Reagan; this process may well have involved the partly-hoax Star Wars program, which had so strained the finances of the Russian state. The result was that the Russians had to eventually abandon their efforts to try and copy the advanced military technology ideas of the Americans, and instead seek the path of peaceful coexistence. From what he had read, Edwards was able to see that Indy's friend had seemed to play a major part in this effort. As a result, America had succeeded in defeating their long-standing, major opponent. This carefully plotted, complex game of chess, proved, in the end, successful in achieving the historic end of the Russian Communist regime, the Soviet Union and the Warsaw Pact!

This also resulted, at last, in the freeing of the countries of Central Europe, including Czechoslovakia, from their oppressive Communism regimes and from the rule of the cruel, Russian, totalitarian state. The nations of Central Europe were now free to join N.A.T.O. and the European Union. As far as Edwards and his family were concerned, they were now able to easily visit a free, democratic and increasingly prosperous Czech Republic. They were also finally able to enjoy all of the delights that the beautiful city of Prague offered and the reflected happiness of its population in the new living conditions, freedoms and life experiences that they now had.

THE PLAYBOY

"…his dream must have seemed so close that he could hardly fail to grasp it. He did not know that it was already behind him…" from the last chapter of *The Great Gatsby* by F. Scott Fitzgerald.

1

"That's the third front door key you have lost!" said the father to his son. The older man was standing in his shirt, socks and underpants while the maid ironed his trousers. He turned to Edwards, who had taken up the invitation to sit down after his long walk, with this man's son, along the Promenade.

"That boy keeps on losing everything; that's the third key, the second pair of trousers and the second mobile phone that he has lost over the last two weeks," he said.

Edwards did not know how to reply; after all, the son was the Chairman of the company that he now worked for! They were all in the large living room of the penthouse flat, in a luxury apartment block, on the seafront. The door to the large balcony was open and the warm, fresh, sea air was blowing in. Outside, the waves rolled up onto the beach and the Mediterranean Sea was a sparkling blue.

Edwards had walked with the son, James, from Edwards's hotel, along the long Promenade. James had suggested some exercise, before the party that was due that evening, which they were all going to attend. About half way through the walk, James had spied an ice cream stall.

"Let's get some ice creams," he had suggested enthusiastically. "I used to get ice creams from there when I was a boy!" Unfortunately, James never carried any money. He did not have to; he was already a multi-millionaire, successfully working with the wealth that his father had passed on to him! So Edwards had to find the money, from his own wallet, to purchase this typical seaside treat.

James had now disappeared to get properly dressed for the party; he appeared again smartly but casually dressed in a brightly coloured shirt and slacks. His father took one look at him: "That shirt is not suitable for this party," he said. "Go and change it right now!"

Edwards had flown in two days before. He had been given the key to his room at the Hotel Reception and found his own way to it, because there did not seem to be any porter available, taking the lift to the correct floor and, at last, finding the room he had been allocated, along a long corridor. It was a comfortable room with an en-suite bathroom and a small balcony overlooking the sea. He had been told that it had been previously occupied by one of his colleagues, in the company that he now worked for, who had returned to London the previous day.

Everything seemed to be fine until he began to unpack. He opened the wardrobe only to find some clothes, including a couple of business suits, hanging inside. There were also a couple of pairs of shoes on the floor of the wardrobe. In a drawer, he also found some underclothes and socks. Nonplussed, he picked up the telephone and asked to speak to his other colleague who, he knew, was still in the hotel.

"I think that David has left some of his clothes here," he said. There was loud laughter on the other end of the line.

"Those will be James's clothes," he was told. "He will come and knock on your door early tomorrow morning, wanting a shower and a change of clothes, after his regular run along the Promenade, from their family apartment, where he is staying."

Fortunately, Edwards had got up early the following morning; he had just finished his shower when there was a great pounding on his room door. He opened it, and his Chairman staggered in wearing a vest and running shorts. "Can I have a shower?" he asked. Edwards found him a clean towel and he proceeded to use Edwards's bathroom. Then he changed into a business suit, while Edwards took in the sea air on his balcony.

"Let's go up to the top floor now," James said, his toilet completed. "They provide a good Buffet Breakfast up there and I will have some people arriving to meet us shortly." So they both took the lift up to the top floor Executive Lounge. Sure enough, their guests were there already waiting for them. Edwards could not fault James on his work ethic; he just sometimes exhibited some strange behaviour and did some unusual things.

That evening they attended the party; it was held in a very large mansion a few miles away from the sea. The house had a spectacularly large atrium entrance hall in which the party took place. There must have been well over two hundred guests and rows of seats had been provided for them on both sides of the vast entrance hall. In the middle there was a small orchestra providing a musical accompaniment, and on both sides there were tables groaning with food and drink.

James and his father were honoured guests and Edwards was introduced to their wealthy host, who, he knew, had made a fortune out of his agricultural business in this country. This charming man then took Edwards by the hand, and introduced him to some more people, including some very attractive women, who he obviously expected Edwards to strike up a conversation with.

During the course of the evening, Edwards found himself sitting next to James's father. "I really hope that my son will find himself a nice girl and settle down soon!" muttered the old man quietly to Edwards. "There's a girl over there he has known since he was a boy. I have tried to bring them together but he won't have anything to do with her." The party went on well into the small hours; then James, his father and Edwards were collected by the same car and the driver who had brought them, and were taken back to their respective beds.

2

Edwards had been introduced to James about a year before by Brian, who was now a long-standing friend. Brian was an established Barrister in the Middle Temple, specialising in commercial law with an international clientele. But he also had handled some high profile criminal cases. When mentioning Brian to other people, Edwards used to joke about Brian's education. "He had a terrible education," Edwards used to say. "Eton, then he read law at Oxford and ended up teaching at the Harvard Law School." Brian had been very prominent during his time at Oxford University and his high-level contacts, both in Britain and overseas were, as a result, truly amazing.

Before introducing James to Edwards, Brian had told him about the circumstances under which he had first met James. He had been introduced to James one evening, by one of his international contacts who, was himself, a most interesting and well-placed man. Both men had taken a taxi to a block of luxury apartments in Chelsea. Before entering the building, Brian's contact had cautioned him.

"Whatever happens, do not be put off," he had said. "Just act normally, as if nothing was wrong."

They had taken the lift to the penthouse apartment and Brian's contact had pressed the doorbell. The door was opened by a tall, beautiful blonde woman; she was completely naked! Brian's companion asked for James, and they were shown into the flat's large living area. A sexual orgy was obviously taking place; completely naked men and women were lying together on the thickly carpeted floor, or on the various chairs and settees, placed around the room. There was a plentiful supply of food and alcohol, and also various other substances, scattered around the large room on numerous tables.

The beautiful, naked blond led the two fully-clothed men to a very large settee. It was, at first, difficult to see James; he was buried beneath both another naked, well-spoken, English blonde and a stunning brunette who, they found out later, was from Italy. When the two women had moved from their respective positions astride James, at either end, Brian's companion was able to introduce James to Brian. In accordance with his instructions, Brian had behaved perfectly normally, as if nothing unusual was taking place. He shook James's hand and then, for some reason, rather regretted doing so!

The two men, both still in their full three-piece suits, were then invited to sit down to talk to James. His two lady friends were dispatched to help entertain his other guests. Brian and his companion did not take off their clothes; they were, of course, offered some alcohol, which they accepted and a variety of other things, which they politely declined.

Fortunately, the circumstances in which Brian had introduced James to Edwards had been somewhat different. They had met at James's offices in the Mayfair district of London and, over a simple lunch, the deal had been concluded. Edwards was currently looking for a new position; it would soon be the beginning of the twenty-first century. After leaving his role as an adviser on exports working for the government, he had joined a medium-sized London company as a Director. But the owner of that company had proved difficult to work for, and had failed to continue to sufficiently financially support the company he owned. Edwards had found that, as part of his day, his time had been regularly taken up with having to speak to a number of the company's creditors, and trying to find some excuses for why they had not yet been paid!

Over their lunch, James seemed to be anxious to learn about the broad experience, that Edwards had now gained, in international business. He then explained his plans; he wanted to set up a new company which would take his current activities in Britain, and expand them, into other parts of the world. As the lunch drew to an end, James offered Edwards a role as Managing Director of this new company, with a task to develop the international opportunities that it should have available. He mentioned a high salary that he would pay him, and some other incentives that he could offer. Edwards wisely said that he would think about it carefully and they parted on very good terms.

Edwards thought no more about it until, one week later, a letter arrived at his home, formally offering him the position that they had talked about over lunch, and stating the attractive terms of employment on offer. He waited for another two weeks, to see if things would develop any better in his current employment, and he then decided to accept James's offer, all be it, with some trepidation.

3

But he need not have worried; James was pleasant, but rather challenging to work for. He expected total commitment and long hours of work, but Edwards settled down quite quickly into his new role. He was given his own office and secretary and set about arranging to recruit an international team of experienced people to help him. They were to cover the world, as he had agreed with James. He gradually built up his team. There was a man who spoke fluent Arabic to cover the Middle East, a man for Africa who had lived there for many years, a long-standing friend of Edwards called Derek, who was very experienced about doing business in Asia, a former colleague who now lived in Sydney to cover Australia and New Zealand, and finally, a man who lived in Canada, to cover North America. The post for South America was left open until a suitable candidate could be found. Edwards, himself, was to look after Europe. The team were housed in one large room in James's Mayfair offices and Edwards soon joined them in this room, with his secretary, to improve communication and to be in overall control.

Edwards tried to manage his team and give them general direction. They were all very knowledgeable about their individual regions of operation, and therefore he decided to keep his control fairly loose and to give them their own space to develop the right opportunities in their area of responsibility. He was not surprised when his old friend Derek, who looked after Asia, mentioned to him that James had expressed a wish to fly out to this region of high economic growth, and meet Derek's many contacts there. The trip was arranged for a two week period to cover visits first to Bangkok, then to Jakarta, Hong Kong and Tokyo. Edwards's friend was to lead the delegation with James and two of James's assistants, to look after him and to "carry his bags."

For the two weeks, following their departure, there was virtual silence from the team on this overseas trip. Then they returned, and Edwards asked his friend Derek for a brief on how the visits to the four cities had gone. His friend asked to meet with Edwards in a nearby hotel, to ensure privacy, and they sat together one morning, over a large jug of coffee.

"He is completely mad!" was Derek's opening remark. "Knowing his predilections," he continued, "I had warned him, while we were sitting together on the aircraft flying to Bangkok, to avoid any "white powders" in Thailand. They have very severe penalties there, if you are caught carrying illegal drugs or using them."

"Yes, I know," replied Edwards. "It can be a hanging offence, although they have not hung any Westerners yet."

"There is always a first time," commented Derek. Then he went on, "So on the second evening, there we all were waiting for him to come down to dinner. He did not appear; so I go up to his room to find him. The door is locked and I bang on it, but there is no reply. I cannot think where else he can be, so I get the Concierge to come up to the room, and use her pass key to open the door."

By this stage, Edwards was sitting on the edge of his chair. "What did you find?" he asked.

"James was inside, lying on the bed," continued his friend. "He was completely naked and unconscious. On the bedside table, beside him, there were traces of a white powder. Next to him, also naked, was a Thai girl. She woke up when I entered the room, and started screaming. But I managed to get her up, get her dressed, and got rid of her by giving her a large amount of Thai money."

Edwards was horrified. "Whatever happened next?" he asked.

"He had obviously overdosed," replied Derek. "So I got him up and walked him around the room, supporting him, while the Concierge called for a doctor. Overall, it cost me a lot of money to have it all hushed up and kept away from the Thai Police."

"It sounds that you saved his life, one way or another," said Edwards.

"When he came to, I gave him a right rollicking," replied Derek. "The next day, he did have the decency to thank me for saving him from dying from the overdose or from being imprisoned, for a very long time, in a very uncomfortable Thai jail!"

4

On some days, Edwards had to work long into the evenings because of the pressure on him to provide an efficient international network to generate the new business opportunities that James required. His office was on the second floor of the

Regency building, in Mayfair, in which James's company was located. On leaving, he had to walk down the staircase and he had to pass the door of James's large office, which was on the ground floor. James was always still working, behind his desk, until late into the evening. As soon as he saw Edwards, he used to call to him.

"Sit down and let's have a chat," he would say.

Each time this happened, Edwards did sit down and spent about half an hour, with his Chairman, reviewing the day. Edwards had realised one thing; despite, or perhaps because of his great wealth, James was incredibly lonely! James always needed someone to talk to, that he could rely upon, and who would tell him the truth, rather than pander to what they thought he would like to hear. He always asked after Edwards's family, and Edwards used the opportunity, in an amusing way, to suggest to James that maybe he should have a wife and children too. But James always laughed; he obviously did not want to ever abandon his bachelor life style!

Some evenings, James would invite Edwards and some of his colleagues to a dinner to meet some important people that he was due to entertain. Edwards found that, inevitably, he was always placed next to the most important guest around the table. He realised that James was really rather shy when dealing with politicians, senior bankers or other very successful people. He would rely on Edwards to lead the conversation off, and then interject with some of his, often brilliant, but unusual, ideas.

These meetings would take place at a leading London restaurant; the choice of venue for dinner would depend upon how James was feeling that particular day. This proved sometimes difficult, as guests usually liked to know, well in advance, where they would be having dinner that evening. James's personal assistants were always forced to contact all his guests, in the late afternoon, to tell them where they were having dinner with James that evening. He would never make up his mind, until the last moment, and then there was the problem of finding a vacant, large enough table at his chosen restaurant. But James always tipped very well, so head waiters usually were able to accommodate his last-minute decisions.

After the meal had been eaten, the talk would inevitably turn to visiting a Night Club. At that point many of James's guests would make an excuse and leave. Unfortunately, Edwards was not in that position and, for a few hours, he had to accompany his Chairman on his night-time visits around London. It usually proved to be quite amusing; wherever he went James seemed somehow to immediately attract the attention of young, well-dressed and beautiful women! Expense was no problem; the Champagne, and any other drink that you desired, would flow in bucket loads and James always paid for everything. Perhaps, that was his secret in attracting many friends?

At about two o'clock in the morning, Edwards decided that he had had enough and made his excuses to leave. Fortunately, James's company had a special arrangement with a private taxi firm. Edwards had their priority telephone number, so that he could call to request a car and driver to arrive, as soon as possible, to any location where he had ended up. Needless to say, the bill for this would ultimately be met by James, as well as the large bills for that evening's entertainment.

If he wanted to entertain in a more intimate setting, James would invite his business guests to his house, which was only a short walk from his offices in Mayfair. It was a large house and inside it was decorated with no expense spared. James always gave Edwards at least a day's notice of these domestic events, and the fact that he wanted him to be at his house to help entertain his guests. This was fortunate, as Edwards knew, by now, exactly what would happen. In order to build up his strength for the evening, Edwards would make the short Tube train journey to his Club, and then sleep in one of the comfortable armchairs in its large rooms, available to Club Members only, for at least a couple of hours. Only then would he return to his office and prepare for that evening's event, by examining the guest list provided by James's senior private secretary.

Edwards would walk to James's house and then check that all the required staff were present and ready to receive the guests. These were expected to arrive from seven o'clock onwards. It was his responsibility to greet the guests and make sure that they were supplied with all the drinks and luxury nibbles that they wanted. James had promised to be there at eight o'clock, but Edwards knew that he would never arrive on time. At half past eight, he would telephone James to remind him that his guests were at his house and that he should come around there immediately. James would promise to do so, but he would never turn up until ten o'clock!

By then the guests had become increasingly animated and Edwards had to carefully pace himself in order to remain sober. After James had eventually arrived, a further round of drinks would then be served, before they sat down to dinner at about eleven o'clock. After dinner, coffee, digestives and cigars were on offer. It was by now well past midnight and some of the guests had started to leave; but other guests were staying on, perhaps because they knew what would happen next?

At precisely two o'clock, the front door of the house would open and, led by the same, very smartly dressed Madam, the carefully selected, beautiful young ladies, who would be available to the remaining guests, for the rest of the night, would arrive! At this point in the proceedings, Edwards always made the necessary telephone call to order the car and driver to take him back home. He would arrive home about three o'clock, and quietly let himself into the house, so as not to disturb his sleeping wife and children.

5

The highlight of the year was the summer visit to the South of France, ostensibly to attend an annual conference, which was held there. James kept his yacht down there; he owned his own 130 foot boat, but he often hired a couple of smaller yachts and also made these available to his guests, if required. The main activity of the conference was at Monte Carlo, but James's favourite anchoring place was over one hundred kilometres to the west, in the middle of the bay at Saint Tropez. From the town of Saint Tropez itself, fast motor boats could then be used, to ferry his guests out to his yacht and back again. His own private jet and those of his more wealthy guests, could land at the small airport at Saint Tropez. His less well-off guests and members of his staff, would take a commercial flight into Nice Airport and then be flown by helicopter to Saint Tropez.

One year, Edwards was invited. He took a cramped, commercial flight to Nice and then braved the helicopter ride to Saint Tropez. Edwards had already decided that he did not like helicopters; they were too noisy and he could not get over the fact that they did not have any wings! The fast boat trip from the harbour at Saint Tropez to James's yacht was the most enjoyable part of his journey.

On his vessel, James always ensured that there had to be at least twice as many pretty girls, than the number of his male guests. For Edwards, this proved to be perhaps the most embarrassing part of the trip. The Champagne flowed like water, but Edwards, as a happily married man, found that the obligation to be draped by at least two bikini-clad, beautiful young women, proved a little too much. Some of the girls were, of course, intelligent and he did find a few that were very amusing to talk to. James had his favourite "Number One" and "Number Two" girls who, together, both slept with him on his yacht. But this valuable privilege could, of course, be changed, as and when he determined, and if he wanted a change of sleeping partner.

James remained on the Cote d'Azur for one month every year; Edwards had visited for only a few days, staying at a pleasant hotel in the town of Saint Tropez. It was a short break from his office routine, but he soon had to return to London. It was later, when James had returned from his holiday in the South of France, that Edwards began to feel that something was not quite right. James began to be locked in long meetings, behind closed doors, with his father. Edwards received reports of angry exchanges between them, from one of James's personal secretaries, whom Edwards had got to know well.

She was a girl from the mining valleys of South Wales, who had left school when she was only sixteen. She had then moved to London and established for herself a career in sales and marketing. She was petite, charming and highly intelligent and, Edwards thought, had the most beautiful pair of eyes that he had ever seen on a woman! She would later become the much publicised mistress of several well-known married men and would go on to write a successful book, about her series of numerous love affairs, as "the second woman."

Edwards sensed that James was not being open with him; there was something definitely wrong. He now avoided Edwards as much as he could. Finally, one day he asked to see Edwards in private.

"I am sorry to say," James began, "that my father has decided that I should stop spending so much money."

Edwards nodded; he had expected something like this. But James definitely did not want to disturb his present life style. "I am afraid that we will have to break up your team, because they are costing me too much," James continued. "But you can choose just two of them, to continue to work with you, and I will promote you to the Chairman of the international company I have established. I will even give you some more money."

Edwards tried to defend his team. "We are just at the point of achieving some major deals," he said. But James would not reconsider the matter; he was obviously under strict orders from his father.

"Can I think about it please, James?" Edwards asked. Edwards knew that he had recently received an offer to work, on a part-time basis, advising an established, former government owned organisation, in the area of high technology.

At home, that evening, Edwards pondered the matter; he was really getting rather tired of the "jet-set lifestyle" that always surrounded James. He finally decided to accept the well-paid offer from the government organisation, and tell James that he wanted to leave him. The following morning he sought another private meeting with James and told him of his decision.

"How much time will you have to give to this former government organisation?" asked James.

"Just three days a week," replied Edwards.

"Then what if you work for two days a week for me, as Chairman of the international company?" asked James.

Edwards thought for a moment. "I am sorry James," he said. "It has been great fun working for you, but I am getting older now. I will be paid sufficiently well for my three days a week of work that I will not have to work any more days than that. It will enable me to now spend some more time with my family."

James looked very disappointed; for once he had not got his own way! But Edwards could already "see the writing on the wall." James's father had made his decision; his wayward son could still enjoy his life-style, but he must now concentrate on his existing British business. His father had probably determined that, to try to continue to extend his business internationally could prove, for James, just one step too far! In the end, Edwards had to decide, that he and his team could never get him to concentrate sufficiently on any real international opportunities, and now he would have much less money, from his father, to try to do so.

So, even his remaining team's hard-working and combined efforts, could never really bring any real and final success. They would also now not be allowed the funds to really achieve this. This situation could also, importantly, prove a real risk to their personal professional reputations. Unfortunately, it would prove to be the end for Edwards of this "jet-set" lifestyle. But, now that he was getting older, he had really begun to feel the strain!

SPOOKS

"Once you have lived the inside-out world of espionage, you never shed it. It's a mentality, a double standard of existence" – John le Carré.

1

Edwards had been sent by his Chairman to Washington D.C. He was staying at The Mayflower Hotel and attending a Conference on International Trade in the Business Suite of that same hotel. His Chairman had insisted that several of Edwards's current colleagues should also attend, and they had all flown out together, Business Class, from London. With his current Chairman, Edwards knew that "no expense would be spared." He was a multi-millionaire, unmarried and a playboy! Some six months before, he had employed Edwards as the Managing Director of a new company, that he had created, to take the activities of his established British group into the international arena.

The fact was that Edwards's Chairman, James, was originally funded by his father, who had been a very successful businessman. James had been successful in his own activities in Britain, but his father still maintained a great control over his son. James was, of course, always very busy and so he had said that he would have to arrive late for the Conference, on its second day, perhaps only to show how very important he was? That morning, he had arrived on an overnight flight from London. He always said that he "could sleep anywhere," and his First Class, flat sleeper seat, must have been very comfortable. When he met Edwards, in the hotel, James was full of energy and ideas, just as he always seemed to be.

Edwards, who was older than James, took a more cautious view of life, as a result, perhaps, of his long experience. "What happened yesterday?" James immediately asked Edwards, so Edwards told him.

"What are the plans for this evening?" asked James, always interested in the evening's entertainment. Edwards considered quickly; he thought that he would surprise James.

"We are having dinner with the Central Intelligence Agency!" he said. James's mouth gaped open. "You know that I am always serious and always tell you the truth." added Edwards.

That evening, Edwards had indeed invited two of his American friends to dinner, at the hotel, to meet his Chairman. Tom was a firm-jawed, no-nonsense American, born in Florida. He had served in the U.S Army in Vietnam, during the long war with the Communist North Vietnamese. Then he had joined the

Central Intelligence Agency at Langley, Virginia. He was the only American that Edwards knew that had then gone on to serve also, in a senior role, at the National Security Agency, at Fort Meade in Maryland. The N.S.A. was responsible for the global monitoring, collection and analysis of communications, information and data, and of course was much larger than its British equivalent of the Government Communications Headquarters in Cheltenham.

Tom worked closely with Mark, who was younger. As well as still working for the American government, from time to time, they were now both involved with projects, of their own, in the private sector. Mark had a background in Defence Research and Technology, and had served under President Ronald Reagan as the Technology Adviser to the White House. He had gone on to set up his own consulting company, but still retained the highest levels of American Security Clearance. He now secretly advised the American Department of Defence at the Pentagon, the C.I.A and the N.S.A. Mark had recently visited London, together with a very Senior Adviser to the Pentagon, and Edwards had arranged for them to visit the headquarters of the much smaller, British equivalent of the American Defence Advanced Research Projects Agency, where Mark had, years before, started his career.

This British organisation was located in Farnborough, Hampshire and they had all spent the day there, being shown around by its senior staff. The following evening Edwards and Mark had been invited for an open-air dinner and to view the Beating the Retreat military ceremony, dating back to the 16th century. This was held at the Horse Guards Parade ground, just off Whitehall, in the very centre of political power in London. It had been a beautiful, dry evening and Mark had been impressed and grateful to Edwards to have been able to attend this, so typical, British event.

2

Nick was a contact of Edwards's long-standing friend Derek. Nick had married into the rich aristocracy and no longer had to work for a living. He spent his time between his London flat in Dolphin Square, a country estate in deepest Sussex, and his wife's luxury American home in South Carolina. Nick was built like a front-row rugby player, but he liked his wine too much. He was short-tempered, with high blood pressure; unfortunately, his life would end prematurely as a result of a massive heart attack.

One evening Nick, Derek and Edwards had been drinking at Edwards's Club, located near to Whitehall. Derek had left early and now Edwards had to deal with Nick by himself. At last, Edwards had persuaded Nick to leave; they had weaved out of the Club together. But Nick was much the "worst for wear." He closely embraced one of the ornate Victorian lampposts, outside

Edwards's Club, and slid slowly down it, to the ground. Edwards realised that Nick needed a taxi to get him home and hailed one.

With great difficulty, he managed to raise Nick up and pour him into the vehicle. Nick said something but, by now, his voice was so slurred, that Edwards had to ask him to repeat it three times. At last he managed to understand what Nick was saying.

"I have no money!" he had said.

Edwards took out a large-denomination banknote from his wallet. He handed it to the taxi driver. "The main entrance to Dolphin Square, Pimlico please," he said. "And please make sure that this gentleman gets home safely."

The main problem with Nick was that he was trying to live up to his father's success. He was still in great awe of his father, although he had died some years before. Modestly born, his father had left school, at the age of sixteen, to become a junior bank clerk. But he had risen to become a very senior, international banker, a Director of the Bank of England and a Knight of the Realm. Before the Second World War, he had been involved in the necessary, secret, financial planning, in case the conflict should ever arise. During the war, Nick's father had been engaged in highly secret work, and his son was therefore always interested in all matters dealing with the clandestine world of espionage.

Nick had read his father's papers and diaries, that he had inherited, and he wanted to write a book based upon them. One of his father's secret wartime duties, according to Nick, had been to act as an interlocutor with the Duke and Duchess of Windsor. The Duke was the former Kind Edward the Eighth, who had abdicated his throne in December 1936, to marry the divorced American Wallis Simpson. The Duke was believed to be a Nazi sympathiser, having visited Adolf Hitler. They lived in exile, just outside Paris, but when the Germans invaded France, they fled south to Portugal, a neutral country in the war. Worried about what the Duke might do, the British government persuaded him to become Governor of the Bahamas in the Caribbean and there, according to Nick, his father continued his contact with the Duke, to make sure that he was well supplied with money. According to Nick, one of his father's other secret exploits, that he organised, seemed to have been to maintain contact with certain, probably dissident, German senior military officers. This was carried out by clandestine meetings, in the middle of the North Sea. It was arranged that one small boat from England, would meet another small boat from occupied Europe, at an agreed location, where both sides could talk in total secrecy.

Early one morning, Nick reported to Derek and Edwards that he had been awakened with a heavy banging on the door of his flat in Pimlico. He opened the door, and several armed Metropolitan Police Special Branch officers burst in with a Search Warrant. They searched his flat, looking for his father's papers.

Fortunately, Nick had them hidden away in another location, otherwise he believed that they would have taken them and then impounded them, forever. He just stood there, until they left empty-handed, telling them loudly and repeatedly, what they could do with themselves! Fortunately for the authorities, Nick had died before he was able to write, and then publish, any book about his father's secret activities. Derek and Edwards never did find out what had happened to Nick's father's papers, which had set out his secret life and work.

Because of his father's background and Nick's obsession with espionage and the "secret world" of intelligence, on one of Nick's visits to America, Edwards, at his request, had arranged for Nick to meet Mark in New York. Nick had invited Mark to lunch at his New York Club, the Knickerbocker. "The Knick" as it is known, was founded in 1871 and boasts a membership list of many past and present Presidents, Bankers and successful business millionaires.

Mark had arrived for the lunch; meeting him, in the reception, Nick noticed that he was carrying a large bag, similar to the document bags often carried by lawyers. The problem was that this bag was chained to Mark's wrist! Bags were not allowed in the Club's dining room, but Mark refused to give it up to the Club staff, who had insisted that it had to be left safely in the reception area.

"This gentleman is from the C.I.A.!" Nick had shouted at them loudly.

Mark had then produced some kind of Security Pass to the Club Manager, who had now arrived, due to the altercation that Nick was causing. The bag went with Mark to the dining room and he, with the bag still chained to his wrist, rather awkwardly, began to eat his lunch.

Half way through the lunch, Nick later reported to Edwards, there had been a strange noise. "That bloody bag had swelled to nearly twice its size!" said Nick. "Mark looked down at it, and then he made an excuse that he had to go to the Rest Room," he continued. "When he came back, the bag was back to its normal size again. I could only assume that there was some kind of secret communications device hidden inside it, which he had to deal with, when the bloody thing went off!" Edwards was very entertained by this true story and reported it to Derek, who had introduced him to Nick in the first place.

3

That evening, in Washington, Edwards had booked a table for four in the hotel's restaurant. He was waiting for Tom and Mark in the hotel reception when they had arrived. As usual, James was late. They were already sitting down at their table, ordering their drinks, when he eventually joined them. Edwards introduced him; he could tell from his offhand manner that James just did not believe what he had told him about these two American gentlemen. But James seemed a lot calmer and remained unusually quiet, seeming just to listen to the conversation of the others. "He has probably taken some white powder, up his nose!" thought Edwards.

As the meal proceeded, Tom also seemed to relax. "I must tell you about my time in Vietnam, when I was much younger," he said to Edwards. "I had my day job in the U.S. Army, of course, but I then had another job as well. Often, at night, I had to cross the border to get behind enemy lines. There I could meet with my secret agents."

Edwards could see that James appeared to suddenly have woken up and had become very interested. "The Soviet Union, of course, supported the Viet Cong with money and arms and, in return, the Russians were told about North Vietnam's war plans, through the Soviet Embassy in Hanoi," continued Tom. "The Russians would then have some vodka-fuelled parties in their Embassy, with their so-called Warsaw Pact allies and inevitably, stupidly, tell them what they had learned about the planned Vietnamese tactics." Tom looked straight at Edwards. "So I used the Poles in their Embassy in Hanoi," he said. "The Poles have never had any reason to love the Russians, and they were only too pleased to tell me everything that they had learnt from them."

James mouth gaped open. "Amazing!" was all that he could say.

After that revelation, James was only too pleased to take the stage. He started talking volubly. He asked about any kinds of private sector projects that Tom and Mark were now involved with. They described to him, in limited detail, some of their projects. James immediately boasted of his ability to finance them and made all kinds of rash promises. He said that he would return to Washington soon, to meet with them again and help them with finance for these projects.

Edwards saw that Tom was looking at James rather quizzically; it was now Tom that perhaps had the doubts about the person that he had just been introduced to. After the excellent dinner they all, of course, parted as the "Best of Friends." There were renewed promises from James to return to Washington soon, and firm assurances that he could finance any and all of the private sector projects that Tom and Mark were currently involved with.

4

It was over twelve months later that Edwards had, at last, been able to return to Washington. This time, he was with his Canadian colleague and friend Theo. Edwards had recruited Theo to work with him to look after North America. He was part of the world-class team that Edwards had been asked by James to put together, in order to take the business of James's British group of companies, into the international arena. Theo, like some Canadians, was rather conservative and reserved. But he had some very good contacts with the Canadian Government in Ottawa and many commercial contacts both in Canada and the United States.

Theo lived in a small university town, just south of Toronto, with his wife and children. He had come first to London, for four weeks, to work with Edwards and to learn more about James's business. He met James, and then asked to speak to Edwards privately. After work, they moved to a nearby Wine Bar for a private discussion.

"Is James completely mad?" Theo had asked Edwards immediately.

"I think that our Chairman is well intentioned," replied Edwards. "But his mind is just too over-active and it is not helped by what he takes."

It became their habit to make a visit to the same Wine Bar, after work, twice a week. They found that the Wine Bar had a stock of excellent Chilean Merlot wine, which had now reached drinking perfection. Edwards found that he could reduce Theo to a state of hysterical laughter, by telling him about some of James's exploits. One evening, he confided in Theo that James was actually an alien, from another planet, in a far-distant galaxy.

The planet was called Zog. James was really the secret supreme leader of this planet, and Edwards dubbed him with the name of "The Emperor of Zog." Theo had nearly fallen off his bar stool with laughter!

A few months after Theo's visit to London, Edwards had grown very worried about a transaction that James had been trying to do. Somehow, he had acquired full details of an advanced surveillance technology, made by an Israeli company. He had also talked them into issuing him with a letter that said he was their Appointed Agent, to sell their products in certain parts of the world. With this letter, James had now started discussions with a certain foreign government, so that they could acquire this technology. He told Edwards about this opportunity, and Edwards quickly realised that it would not be in the interests of Britain, or its allies, for this particular government to acquire this advanced surveillance technology.

He knew that he had a duty to James, who employed him, but he also considered that his duty to Britain was stronger and more important. If he said anything to James to try and stop him, he also knew that James would just ignore him, and still try and go ahead with this particular sale. Edwards thought about what he could do; in the end he decided to ask for a meeting with his former colleague Michael. Edwards had worked closely with Michael, while he had been a temporary Civil Servant. He knew that Michael was a serving senior Intelligence Officer, and

Edwards had worked on certain things for him that he could never talk about.

They met at Edwards's Club, that provided the quiet and secure environment to discuss such matters. Edwards explained the position with James carefully to Michael.

"Just leave it with me," was all that Michael had said.

The days went by; it was now a Monday afternoon over a week since he had met with Michael. Then, the older of James's secretaries told Edwards that James was very upset. She was close to retirement, and James treated her almost as a "Mother figure." She told Edwards that James had told her that he had been woken up at 6 o'clock, on the day before, the Sunday morning, with a pounding on the front door of his luxury house, which was only a short walk from their offices. Three men were outside demanding to speak to James. They were not the kind of men that you would argue with!

They had grabbed James by his arms and carried him to his living room, where they had sat down with him. They identified themselves as agents of the Israeli international intelligence service, known as Mossad. They told James, in the most certain of terms, that he was no longer allowed to represent the Israeli company, or to try and sell its surveillance technology anywhere. Then they had left, leaving James in a very nervous state. Needless to say, thanks to Michael's contacts, Edwards's problem of loyalty had now been permanently solved!

5

Edwards had travelled from London to Ottawa, to meet with Theo in the Canadian capital. There they had some useful meetings with a number of the departments of the Canadian Government. Then, they had taken the train to Toronto for some more meetings, before flying down to New York for a few more days of intensive work. Altogether, Edwards would be away from home for nearly two weeks. Washington was to be the next stop on their itinerary, and then they would fly down to Texas, to meet with a major American company there, where Theo had some senior contacts.

Edwards had telephoned ahead to see if Tom and Mark could meet him again, for dinner, when he arrived with Theo in Washington. This time they met for dinner at another Washington hotel, where Edwards and Theo were staying. Edwards introduced Tom and Mark to Theo. As the meal proceeded, the friendly Americans joked with Theo about Canada.

"I just think that we Americans might invade Canada one day," commented Tom to Theo, trying to keep a straight face. Edwards remembered that the border between the two countries, including the border with Alaska, was some 5,500 miles long.

Edwards turned to Theo. "Well, if that happened, Theo, I think that the Canadian army is just about big enough to put about ten Canadian soldiers for every one hundred miles along the border!" he joked.

But, as the meal continued, Tom became more serious. He fixed Edwards with his penetrating dark eyes. "Is that guy James ever coming to Washington again?" he asked.

Edwards realised that Tom was very annoyed with James, particularly about all the unfulfilled promises that he had made. He thought carefully about his reply, but he also had to be honest with Tom. "I really do not know," he said to Tom. "He has been very busy travelling to other parts of the World, including South East Asia. At the moment I do not think that he has any plans to come here."

Tom seemed to accept this, but then he thought for a moment. "If you find out that he is coming back here, please let me know on what date and where he will be staying," he said.

"Of course," replied Edwards.

"I have a small stock of unmarked weapons at home," went on Tom. "If I hear that James is coming back, I might just draw one of those weapons from out of my stock. I might then go and visit him, just tie his hands and persuade him to take a midnight swim in the Potomac River!"

Edwards looked at Theo. Theo had realised the meaning of what Tom had said, and also that he had meant all that he had said. He was horrified; he had gone deathly pale and was sliding slowly and gently down his chair, in fear and shock. If Edwards had not grabbed him there and then, he would probably have fallen off his chair, on to the floor. Edwards thought quickly; despite himself, he felt rather sorry for James, if he ever did meet Tom again!

"I do not think that you really mean that, Tom," he replied, looking directly at the man as he spoke. He knew full well that this man was serious and perfectly capable of carrying out what he had said. He would have probably have got away with it; he had decades of experience of operating undercover, using clandestine methods to draw on. In any case, his friends and former colleagues, in the secret and permanent "Deep Government" of the United States of America, would certainly have protected him from any consequences.

Then, Edwards spoke again. "I really don't think that this stupid bastard, James, is worth any of your time and effort, Tom," he said to his American friend. "Even just to carry out the simple task, that you have just described, is a real waste of your valuable time!"

A grin began to spread across Tom's face. "Yep, you are right about that!" was all that he would say, in reply.

HIGHLAND GAMES

"Ah, the power that gift would give us, to see ourselves as others see us." – Robert Burns.

1

It was the beginning of a fine day in the awe-inspiring scenery of the Western Highlands of Scotland. Edwards stopped the little red car, pulling it into the side of the road. The car had already travelled nearly four hundred and eighty miles that night. Finally, he had driven over part of the great expanse of Rannoch Moor. Behind the parked car, the sun was just rising. Ahead of the car, the high mountain peaks, on either side of the Pass of Glencoe, were just beginning to be seen in the clear, dawn light. They rose suddenly and dramatically, out of the flat moorland. Edwards stifled a yawn; he had driven without a pause, except for a necessary short refuelling stop, just north of Carlisle. His new wife was beside him; they had left London after they had finished their dinner the previous evening. It was a hired car that Edwards had collected from a local garage the previous afternoon, just before they had closed for the day. He no longer owned his own car, having sold his old, blue Citroën DS, some years before. He had done this so as to move into the modern Barbican residential development in the City of

London, which had only very limited parking spaces, to share a large flat with a friend.

Beside him, his wife had started to wake up. She had sensed that the car had stopped and was beginning to wonder why. "What about some fresh air?" he asked her. They both got out of the car and then let the cold, early morning air, fully wake them up.

"What do you think of the view?" Edwards asked his wife, as the sun's light began to strike the tops of the peaks of Glencoe in front of them. Between the mountains, the great valley of the Glen itself, still shrouded in darkness, could just about be discerned.

She looked, thought for a moment, and then replied: "I am suffering from cultural shock. It is such a magnificent sight!"

Edwards had been to Scotland many times before, but he understood that for his wife, who had, as yet, never been north of the Scottish border, this was a completely new experience. It was now the second-half of the 1970s, and they had been married over six months before in the Registry Office of the ancient Guildhall of the City of London. This had only been possible because Edwards had then been resident in the City. Unfortunately, their honeymoon had been limited to only one night away, at a hotel on the banks of the River Thames, just east of Reading. Now, Edwards was taking his wife away for a proper holiday, and he had chosen to take her to an area that he already knew well; to the spectacular North-West coast of Scotland. They both climbed back into the small car, and Edwards restarted its engine.

"It is just over forty miles to go to Fort William," Edwards told his wife. "We can get some breakfast there."

Edwards was used to driving long journeys overnight, and then into the following day. Before he was married, he had had, for several years, a Swiss girlfriend who lived just north of Zurich. This journey had been over six hundred miles, including the slow ferry crossing between Dover and Ostend. He chose to go to Ostend because the Belgian high-speed motorway system was always brightly lit at night. It was only when you had passed Aachen that the German autobahn network was only partly lit, but it had very few speed limits. He used to leave London, after a day at work, and only briefly stop to refill his car or to eat at suitably convenient motorway service stations. His visits to Scotland also involved such long, non-stop drives. A good friend that he had met at university, now taught at Kings College, Aberdeen, and Edwards regularly drove the five hundred and fifty miles between London and Aberdeen, overnight, to stay with him.

Having driven through the "Weeping Glen" of Glencoe, they passed the village of Glencoe itself. Then, they drove through

Ballachulish, to take the road along Loch Linnhe, to the Highland town of Fort William. The Pass of Glencoe was so named after the massacre in 1692 of thirty members of the Clan MacDonald, by mainly Clan Campbell highlanders, who were serving the British government. The MacDonalds had apparently refused to swear allegiance to the new British monarchs of William and Mary, and this was the excuse for the revenge wrought by their long-time enemies, the Clan Campbell!

When they arrived in Fort William, Edwards parked the car on the High Street and they entered McTavish's Kitchen, a restaurant that Edwards had visited some years before, and which he knew provided a good Scottish Breakfast. This consisted of a full English Breakfast, but with the addition of a good portion of Scottish Haggis! The "All Day Meal" there still consisted of the traditional "Haggis, Neeps and Tatties" - a combination of Haggis, diced swede and mashed potatoes, just as Edwards had remembered it.

Edwards had not told his wife that, some six years before, he had stayed in Fort William with the girl that was then his fiancée. He was now quite skilled in the game of intimate relations. The reason that he had not told his wife was, really, that he felt responsible for the break-up of that relationship. He had stayed with this girl just outside the town, in a cheap Bed and Breakfast place, that had a spectacular view of Ben Nevis, the highest mountain in Britain. This had been the second part of their holiday; the first part had been passed staying in a cheap hotel in Edinburgh's New Town, and from there, they had enjoyed the tourist sights of Scotland's capital.

It was while that they were staying near Fort William, that Edwards had driven them along the "Road to the Isles", the A87 which took them to Kyle of Lochalsh. There they had taken the short ferry ride, with the car, to the island of Skye. He had then driven along the main road to the island's capital of Portree; to the left of this road rose the spectacular, blue-tinged heights of the Cuillin mountain range. It was when they were coming back from Skye, that they had discovered the hotel. It was set back from the road and easy to spot; it was painted white, just before you crossed the road bridge, across to the small village of Dornie, that divided Loch Long from Loch Duich. They were hungry and had stopped for the traditional Scottish meal of "High Tea." But, as their dining room was already set for dinner, the hotel staff had asked them to eat in a conservatory filled with tables and chairs, jutting out from the main hotel building.

Edwards did not mind about this; he gazed out of the glass of the conservatory. Never before had he seen such a magnificent view. In front of him lay the quiet, reflecting waters of Loch Duich. On a small island to his left, linked to the shore of the loch by a short, but picturesque bridge, stood Eilean Donan Castle, the ancient stronghold of the Clan Mackenzie. At the end of the loch rose the mountains of Glen Shiel, known as the "Five

Sisters of Kintail." This view, on a good day, was astoundingly beautiful. Edwards immediately dubbed it as: "the Finest View in Scotland." It was to this very hotel that Edwards and his new wife were now heading. Edwards had booked the best room in the hotel; it was a large double bedroom, with its own en-suite bathroom, with large windows and a door to the room's private balcony. This room gave Edwards and his wife, even from their double bed, "the Finest View in Scotland."

2

This was not Edwards's first stay in this hotel; in the years since he had discovered it, he had stayed there several times. Twice that had been with his university friend, who was now resident in Aberdeen. He was a driven academic; he had taken his first degree, then his Master's, and then a Doctorate in Economics at the same university that Edwards had attended. Edwards had kept in touch with him; he had worked first in London for a government "think tank", but had then taken up a teaching post at Kings College, Aberdeen. Founded in 1495, with its Chapel and other historic buildings located in the medieval town of Old Aberdeen, close to the beach, this was the fifth oldest university in the United Kingdom. It had been founded even before the University of Edinburgh.

Edwards had stayed with his friend in his house, built in the local, grey, Aberdeen granite stone, like so many other buildings in this city. It had a neat back garden that was replete with small, granite headstones, bearing sayings from the strict Scottish Presbyterian faith, and illustrating this sect's strong work ethic. Edwards remembered one of these in particular; it had simply read "Capture the Morning!" They had taken his friend's Volkswagen car and driven west to the Highlands. Edwards was used to competing against this car when, several times during his visits, as a game, they had raced against each other in competition, along a set route, through Royal Deeside, just to the west of Aberdeen. It was here that the Royal Family had their summer home at Balmoral Castle. In the winter, the driving here could be difficult, and even dangerous. Edwards had got used to looking out for the "Black Ice" on the road surface, which glistened like diamonds in the winter sunshine.

They had stopped for a few days at the hotel that Edwards had discovered on the banks of Loch Duich. It had good food, and a bar that was stocked with some one hundred different kinds of Scottish, single malt whiskeys! They even set up a competition between them, to try and taste as many as possible. One evening they were sitting in the bar, when a drunken, local Scotsman entered. Sitting close to them, partaking of more whiskey, he was talking to the barman. Edwards and his friend heard him mention, several times, about a great Ceilidh, or Gaelic party, that was going on that very evening. It was happening in Plockton, a small village some ten miles away, on the shores of Loch Carron.

Immediately, Edwards's friend suggested that they should join this party. They jumped into his car, and he then drove along the steep, winding, narrow roads to reach this charming village, known for its warm micro-climate, and the palm trees growing along the short promenade, alongside the Loch. But Plockton was dark and completely silent; there was absolutely no sign of the expected, great Gaelic Ceilidh. Disappointed, the two friends concluded that it was just a figment of a drunken Scotsman's imagination, and returned to their hotel.

His friend living in Aberdeen spoke fluent German; he had acquired some friends living in Munich and used to visit a particular German girl living there, quite frequently. She had announced that she would visit him in Aberdeen, and would bring another German girl with her. Edwards was invited up to Aberdeen to join them. He could never quite work out what the real relationship was between his friend and this girl; were they just friends or lovers? But it seemed just friendship as, when he arrived in Aberdeen, she was occupying a separate bedroom, with the other German girl.

To give his two foreign visitors some experience of Scotland, Edwards's friend had booked two twin rooms in the same Loch Duich hotel, for a few nights. After a few days taking in the sights of Aberdeen, he had driven them all, via the Great Glen of Loch Ness, to the Western Highlands. There, they had taken in a day-time view of Plockton, and travelled to Skye, across the short car ferry crossing. They had also driven north, past Loch Torridon and then through the great Beinn Eighe National Park, where you still hoped to spot the Golden Eagles, flying high above the isolated glens and mountains. Eventually, they arrived in Gairloch, where they had stayed for a couple of nights at the comfortable Gairloch Hotel. Edwards well remembered trying to play a game of golf on the windy, public golf links at Gairloch, right by the side of the sea loch. It had proved amusing to hire a set of golf clubs, and then to try and teach two German girls to play golf, in such breezy conditions!

The third time that he stayed at the hotel on the banks of Loch Duich, had been with his Swiss girlfriend, who he had met in London, while she had been seconded for some six months to the London branch of her Swiss bank. Before she had returned to Switzerland, he had taken her on a holiday to Scotland. While the scenery of Switzerland was very beautiful, Scotland's highlands provided scenery of a different type of beauty. He thought that she should have the opportunity to see it. Edwards had told his new wife about this visit but, then, he felt that he could blame the Swiss girl, for the final break-up of this romantic relationship!

He had taken his Swiss girlfriend on drives that he already knew; one day south to Fort William to see Ben Nevis, a small mountain by Swiss standards! Then up north on the A830 road towards Mallaig; they stopped at the haunting monument, a tall column topped by the statue of a Highland warrior, at Glenfinnan, at the head of the beautiful Loch Shiel. It had been put there to commemorate the doomed Jacobite Rising of 1745, and was located just where "Bonnie Prince Charlie" had first landed in Scotland. But, at the Battle of Culloden, where nearly two thousand Highlanders had died, the Prince had finally failed to re-establish the House of Stewart back again onto the British throne. On another day, he had taken the Swiss girl across the seemingly endless, lonely beauty of the Beinn Eighe National Park. They had met just two other cars, going the other way, during the whole day on the narrow, single-track road, with occasional passing places. He commented to her that this was quite a busy day in what was, probably, the loneliest part of Scotland, itself acknowledged as the greatest wilderness in Europe.

3

Edwards and his wife arrived at the hotel on Loch Duich; they were to spend a week there. On their first full day they took an easy excursion; just along the road to Eilean Donan Castle, situated on its own little island, just off the shore of the loch. They crossed the footbridge to the island and entered the building, some parts of which dated back to the thirteenth century. For hundreds of years, it had been a centre of feuding and fighting between the various Scottish clans of the area, until, finally, the Clan Mackenzie had managed to hold it. In 1719, the castle was largely demolished during the Jacobite wars, and was then finally rebuilt in the early twentieth century. It was still occupied by a representative of the Clan Macrae, close allies of the Clan Mackenzie.

The following day they paid a visit to Plockton; they were fortunate as it was a pleasant summer's day. Strolling along the palm-decked promenade, there was even a feel of the Mediterranean coast about this remote settlement on the shore of Loch Carron, surrounded by mountains. Although it was located high in the western wilds of Scotland, there was a thriving Artist's Colony in the village, and they visited the various shops, offering for sale the locally produced paintings, mainly of the beautiful surrounding area. They were served the Scottish meal of High Tea in one of the little cafes, looking out over the long, narrow sea Loch, which was warmed by the Gulf Stream - that great, ocean current that brought warm water up from the Gulf of Mexico. The air was clear and invigorating; it gave them the appetite to also eat their dinner when they got back to their hotel that evening!

The last trip that they had taken was across the car ferry at Kyle of Lochalsh, to Kyleakin, on the south-eastern corner of the Isle of Skye. Then they drove the nearly fifty miles, past the Cuillin mountain range, to visit Dunvegan Castle, on the north-west corner of the island. After that, they made a visit to the Piping Heritage Centre at Borreraig, a few miles from the Castle. This overlooked the clifftop, memorial cairn, marking the site of the MacCrimmond's Piping School. The MacCrimmonds were the traditional bagpiping family serving the Clan MacLeod, whose seat was at Dunvegan Castle. They had, for centuries, provided one of the main piping schools in Scotland. They composed and played many pieces of Piobaireachd, the ancient, classical bagpipe music. There, Edwards had bought himself some recordings of these traditional compositions; long, introspective tunes which, to him, so mirrored the wild and beautiful scenery that surrounded them.

Dunvegan Caste is built on a rock some fifty feet above the sea; there have been fortifications on this site for many centuries, and the first fortified house had been built there in the fourteenth century. The castle had been added to, over the years, and the present building, with its mock battlements and drawbridge, was completed in 1840. Among the heirlooms that it contains was the Fairy Flag, which had belonged to the hereditary chiefs of the Clan MacLeod for centuries. Its origin was a mystery but, when it had been scientifically analysed, some decades before, it had appeared to have been made from silk, in the Middle East, many hundreds of years before. The historic stories surrounding this artefact are remarkable, and serve to represent the ancient Celtic legends of Scotland. It is said that the flag was given by the fairies to an infant MacLeod chieftain, to protect him and his Clan. Amongst its many attributes are that, if it is waved in battle, it has the power to increase the numbers of the warriors, fighting for the Clan MacLeod, many times over.

Over the following years, Edwards and his wife visited Scotland again, a number of times. They now had a young daughter, and they took her with them, on visits to a number of the Scottish islands. The Isle of Arran is known as "Scotland in miniature" and is located in the Firth of Clyde, on the west coast of Scotland. In a straight line it is not far from Glasgow and its varied highland and lowland scenery, and its lovely coastline, has made it a major holiday destination for the inhabitants of that city. With its beaches, ancient standing stones and castles, there is much to see. Edwards and his expanded family stayed at Brodick, close to where the ferry from Ardrossan had landed them, with a fine view of Brodick Castle across the bay. This castle was the traditional seat of the Dukes of Hamilton; rebuilt in the early sixteenth century, it had been greatly expanded by them in the mid-nineteenth century. The castle stood on a small hill, surrounded by its extensive gardens, which first sloped down from the castle itself. Edwards always recalled how his small daughter had insisted on rolling down the soft grass of this hill, over and over again!

A few summers later they had stayed on the Isle of Mull, at a hotel near Craignure, where the ferry from Oban usually docks. They visited the island capital of Tobermory, and the island's tiny Little Theatre, to see a play, as Edwards's daughter now attended dance and drama classes at a leading London theatre school. One sunny day, they circumnavigated the island, stopping at Calgary Bay on its wild, western shore. The beautiful, white sand and the sparkling, blue ocean, would have done justice to a nearly deserted, Caribbean island. You could not believe that you were far to the north, on the shore of an island in the Western Hebrides of Scotland. On another day, they took the small ferry over to the Island of Iona to visit its ancient Abbey, which contained the graves of countless Scottish kings from many centuries before. Then they had walked over this tiny island. On another beautiful day, they had taken the boat trip to the Isle of Staffa. Edwards led his small family up the steep, narrow pathway, cut into the rock, and they entered the awesome cavern of Fingal's Cave. Perched on a narrow ledge of rock, they clung together as, far below them, the foaming sea cauldron that had inspired Felix Mendelssohn to write his "Hebrides Overture", ebbed and flowed with the pounding waves.

4

And then, some ten years later, had come "The Great Game!" The Great Game was a long-standing political and espionage confrontation between Britain and Russia, that had lasted for most of the 19th Century. It was now the mid-1990's and Edwards was employed by a government organisation with the responsibility to help British exporters sell their goods and services overseas. Among his civil service colleagues was a senior, serving intelligence officer. Edwards had grown close to this man and he had arranged for Edwards to be cleared to read certain Top Secret material. Because of his financial expertise, Edwards was even asked to help in the interpretation of some of what he had read, and to feed back his comments into the intelligence assessments. His colleague's name was Michael and one January day, Edwards was asked to meet with him privately in his office.

"There is something that might interest you," said Michael. "In the summer there is to be a major conference in Scotland. It is to be one of the annual Advanced Summer Schools run by the North Atlantic Treaty Organisation. I wonder if you would like to help organise it? There will not be much work for you to do; there are already a number of retired civil servants organising it. But you will become an Organising Committee Member and therefore entitled to free accommodation and food, for yourself and your family, for the two weeks of the conference. Would you be interested?"

Edwards was a little taken aback, as he did not know how he could really help? The North Atlantic Treaty Organisation, or N.A.T.O. for short, was the main Western Alliance that, for decades, had helped counter the military and political power of the Warsaw Pact alliance, led by the Russian, Communist Union of Soviet Socialist Republics. Communism had now largely been defeated; in 1989 the Warsaw Pact was disbanded, as its members gained their full independence from the U.S.S.R. Then, on Christmas Day, 1991, the U.S.S.R itself had collapsed, and the end of Communism, certainly within Russia and its satellite countries, had been hailed by the world anxious to see the end of the "Cold War", that had dominated international politics since 1945.

"What is the conference about?" Edwards asked.

"It is somewhat different this year," replied Michael. "This will be the first N.A.T.O. Advanced Summer School where the Russians and their former Warsaw Pact colleagues will be invited. The theme is to try to help them to convert their large military manufacturing capacity, into civilian production. If you like, we have to convince them to beat their Swords into Ploughshares."

"But that is a huge topic," replied Edwards. "I do not know whether I can contribute to that in any way."

"Nevertheless, we would like you and your family there!" said Michael breezily.

Edwards consulted his diary. "What dates are we talking about?" he asked. Michael told him. "Unfortunately, my children do not break up from their schools until the end of that first week," replied Edwards.

"That's alright," said Michael quickly. "We will pay for you, to go up by train, for the first week. Then you can come back at the weekend, to collect your family, and go back up there. By then, the proceedings will be much more relaxed in any case, and the Russian delegates will have settled in."

Edwards had failed to register properly the last remark that Michael had made. It was only much later, that the reason for this remark became clear. Meanwhile, Edwards contented himself with meeting the existing members of the Organising Committee, and trying to contribute, in any way that he could, at the number of meetings that then took place. It was an enormous task to manage this major event, with some one hundred delegates attending. A major hotel, close to the town of Pitlochry, in the beautiful hill country of Perthshire, and close to the River Tummel, had been selected to hold the conference. The hotel had been completely taken over for this important event. It had its own conference centre, attached to the hotel, where the proceedings of the conference would take place. The hotel was huge, built in an impressive Scottish Baronial style, surrounded by acres of its own gardens, and with spectacular views of the surrounding countryside from its vast public rooms.

In the end, Edwards thought that he had really done very little to help the retired civil servants on the Committee; they had plenty of time on their hands, and they had done most of the organising work. Edwards had suggested a number of possible speakers, from the financial world, that he knew well, and some of them had accepted an invitation to speak at the conference. As the time for the conference approached, a room booking for

Edwards and his family were confirmed, and a first class return rail ticked provided to Edwards, to get him to Pitlochry for the first week. He had decided to drive back to Pitlochry, with his family, for the second week of the conference. It was just a few weeks before his trip up to Scotland, that Michael had asked to see him again. This time Michael revealed the true thinking behind Edwards's Scottish visit.

"We know that your wife speaks fluent Russian," he said. "We just ask for two things: first that you keep careful note of the proceedings and anything that you observe. This work is to be the subject of a strictly confidential report to me, once you return. The second is that during the second week, when you are up there with your wife, can you ask her please not to reveal that she speaks fluent Russian. Instead, use every opportunity to be in the public rooms of the hotel and get as close to the Russians as possible. We would like her to listen in to their conversations and judge their demeanour. Any results from your wife's observations and translations can also then be part of your report to me please."

Edwards smiled; he had almost expected something like this. "We will do our very best to help," he promised.

"They will not talk to each other in their hotel rooms," Michael went on. "As in Russia, they will expect those to be bugged to listen in on their conversations. They might go for long walks together, but that will very much depend upon the weather. But, in the public rooms, they should be more relaxed and talk to each other. We just want to get an overall impression of their thoughts and feelings about this conference, its aim and what was said," he continued.

Edwards nodded: he now understood the game that he and his wife were in.

5

During the first week of his visit to Pitlochry, Edwards tried to meet as many of the delegates as he could. About half of them were Americans, both men and women. The Russians provided some one-third of the delegates. The rest of the delegates were the British and some Europeans; most of them were from the newly-liberated countries of Central Europe. Edwards was given a small suite of rooms; a double bed for himself and his wife and, in a separate adjoining room, two beds for his children: his daughter and his newly arrived, three year old son.

For the first couple of days things went well; he and the rest of the delegates settled into the routine of attending lectures and presentations, held in the hotel's conference centre. The food served was excellent; sit-down breakfasts and dinners, with a buffet lunch, served in the large hotel lounge, during a break in the proceedings. Edwards did make a point of introducing himself to most of the Russian delegates attending, and welcoming them to the conference and to his country. He tried to match their faces to their names and the brief descriptions given in the list of delegates. He sensed that they were a little uncertain in their new surroundings. He also noticed that most of them seemed to speak good English, and therefore could certainly follow the conference proceedings. But they did not fraternise too much with the other nationalities, especially with the Americans, who largely behaved towards them in the same standoffish way.

It was the second evening of the conference when the trouble started. It was not the Russians that caused the trouble, but the Americans! Edwards was in the hotel bar that evening, quietly buying himself a gin and tonic before dinner, when he began to hear their strident complaints to the barman. It was mainly the American women who were complaining bitterly to him, about the lack of Diet Coke! Angry, raised, American voices were dominating the bar. Quickly, Edwards realised that this was about the choice of a particular drink not being available. The level of emotion expressed showed more; there seemed to be a strong addiction to this magic liquid which was just not available! As a member of the British Organising Committee, Edwards felt that he urgently had to help sort out these growing complaints. He quietly spoke to the barman.

"There is nothing I can do, sir," responded the man. "We have never kept Diet Coke here. We have never had any demand for that stuff!"

Edwards was worried; he could hear the disparaging remarks being made between the Americans, growing ever more in volume. He was afraid that Britain had another American revolt on its hands; this time not in Boston Harbour about tea, but now a "Pitlochry Diet Coke Party!" He immediately sought out the hotel manager, in his office, and put this very serious position to him.

"I can try and get hold of some Diet Coke tomorrow morning," the man pondered. "But I don't think that there are any large stocks in Scotland!"

"Can't you try in England?" asked Edwards, growing more desperate.

"Well, there is one place in Newcastle, who might have some," replied the hotel manager. "But then it will take them at least a whole day, to get any of it up here!"

Edwards went away; there seemed nothing more that he could do. Then he had an idea; he knew that Michael was senior enough to do something, and that he was intelligent enough to understand the serious situation that Edwards was now in, up here, in Pitlochry! He had Michael's home telephone number; he could call him and ask him urgently to source a supply of Diet Coke in London. Then Michael could use his military contacts, to get a Royal Air Force helicopter to fly up these emergency supplies, to try and content their American cousins! The hotel had a helicopter landing pad, a short distance away from the main building, so that VIP guests could arrive there in style. So therefore, so could emergency supplies of Diet Coke! The Royal Air Force could be seen as rescuing their American guests from a possible disaster! But he had to put this idea aside, as it seemed just too impractical.

The next morning, at 10 o'clock sharp, he was in the hotel manager's office again. The Scotsman smiled at him. "I have just found some supplies of that bloody stuff in Edinburgh," he said. "They are putting it on a lorry, and it will be here with us by mid-afternoon!" Edwards breathed a long and audible sigh of relief; the Transatlantic Alliance would now hold firm!

6

In the late afternoon of the following Sunday, Edwards arrived back in Pitlochry with his wife and two children. His children loved the big hotel and its grounds; fortunately the hotel provided a very efficient nanny service for young children, and Edwards and his wife made extensive use of this so that they were both free during the day, and in the evenings, to mingle with the other guests. One evening before dinner, they espied a collection of the Russian delegates, sitting together in the large, main reception room of the hotel. They were gathered around a Russian man who appeared to be their leader, and to whom they were addressing their remarks. He was in his late-forties and was short, but stoutly built, with a large head and a round, friendly face. His curly dark hair was already tinged with grey, and he seemed to be held in great respect by his Russian colleagues. Edwards and his wife sauntered over to a nearby sofa, sat down and picked up some magazines, put out for the guests to read, on a table in front of them. Edwards did leaf through his magazine but, he saw that his wife only pretended to read hers, and was carefully listening to the numerous Russian conversations going on close to her.

After dinner, Edwards and his wife returned to their small suite; their two children were already safely asleep next door, having been fed and put to bed by the hotel's nanny service.

"Tell me what they were saying," asked Edwards quietly. "Perhaps you should write down what you heard straight away now. But first give me a summary, please."

"It was very interesting," his wife replied. "They were being very open about their views on what was going on here. They called that little man "Professor" and he seemed to be the most senior person present. They were not happy; some of the remarks were about the American delegates. They thought that they behaved like children, were obsessed by their material, consumer values, and were not at all friendly to them. They liked more the British and some of the Europeans. But, of course, the Eastern Europeans did not like them; the Poles, the Hungarians and the Czechs, that are attending here, have all got their own reasons for not liking the Russians. After all, the Russians have invaded all their countries in fairly recent history!"

Edwards understood these more personal views. "But what about the Conference?" he asked. "What did our Russian friends think about that?"

"They thought that it was well put together," replied his wife. "Unfortunately, they thought that they had seen through its real purpose! That was to try and deprive Russia of its ability to make military equipment and weapons for its own defence. They understand, of course, the advantages of switching some production of the current large military sector, into making civilian consumer goods. But they did not think that this would be easy, particularly as the West will now want to sell its more efficiently produced consumer goods into Russia. It is a big problem if military production stops in Russia, or even reduces a lot, because so much technical expertise and financial assets have been tied up in it, and so many people are employed in the military production sector."

"That is very interesting," Edwards told his wife. "Was there anything more?"

"Not really," she replied. "Those were the main themes of the conversation that I heard. I will write it down now for you, so that I will not forget it. But, I cannot forget the feeling that I sensed; they were all very suspicious of the motives of the West, especially of the Americans, in trying to reduce the size of the Russian military industrial sector, and thereby trying to reduce the ability of Russia to defend itself. They thought that the Americans were arrogant and aggressive and wanted, in that way, to help to destroy Russia."

Edwards thanked her. "There is one more thing," she said. "I think that the little man that they called the "Professor" is very important. I have no doubt that, when he gets back, he will be called in to give a report on this conference to the Russian intelligence agencies in Moscow." She smiled at him. "Rather like you are doing for the British!" she continued.

One afternoon, Edwards and his wife took time off from the conference, to take their two children to the local Pitlochry Highland Games, which were being held in a large field on the banks of the River Tummel. For their children, it proved to be a thrilling experience and Edwards was also pleased to go as, despite his many visits to Scotland, he had never yet attended such an event. There were the typical Scottish events of Tossing the Caber, Throwing the Hammer and the Tug o' War, but there was also Highland Dancing, which his daughter enjoyed watching. Then, of course, there was a Scottish marching band, with bagpipes and drums, which Edwards particularly liked. Both of Edwards's children returned to the hotel tired but happy and, after their dinner, back in their room, they fell instantly asleep.

7

On the evening before the last day of the Conference, a formal, festive dinner was held. All the delegates were taken, by a number of coaches, on the short journey to Blair Castle. The construction of this castle started in the mid-thirteenth century, and it is the ancestral home of the Clan Murray and the seat of their Clan Chief, the Duke of Atholl. The Duke is unusual, he commands the only private army in Europe: the Atholl Highlanders, which still act as his personal bodyguard. The regiment was first formed in 1777 and helped Britain by serving against the American colonists, in the American War of Independence. The members of this small infantry regiment are still hand-picked by the Duke himself, who provides the finance for their activities. In the past, they have been lent to the British Army, if their services were ever required but, now, they fulfil mainly a ceremonial role.

The formal dinner was held in the impressive Great Hall of Blair Castle. As a member of the Organising Committee, Edwards did not enter the Great Hall until all the other guests had taken their places. The other guests were then asked to stand and, together with the other Committee members, Edwards and his wife and children entered, preceded by the Pipe-Major of the Atholl Highlanders, playing a stirring march on his bagpipes! Edwards found that they had been seated, by his fellow Committee members, at the same small table as the "Professor," who had his wife and small son with him. Edwards's son had been dressed in a frilled shirt and a small Scottish kilt that Edwards had bought for his daughter, some years before. It was amusing to see that the Russian boy had also acquired a Scottish kilt, and this "broke the ice" and enabled the two sets of parents to begin to chat to each other.

They spoke about normal family things and compared experiences of bringing up young children. The "Professor's" wife was much younger than he was and did not speak as good English as her husband. But Edwards's wife was careful not to reveal that she spoke fluent Russian. Suddenly, the sound of the bagpipes filled the Great Hall again, playing a series of Scottish marches and dance tunes, to entertain the guests over dinner. The little Russian boy got off his chair and started to dance to the music and soon Edwards's young son joined him. Edwards's daughter just sat on her chair, resplendent in the new dress especially bought for her for this evening, behaving politely, and trying to appear very sophisticated for her age. The two young boys danced together, trying to imitate the Scottish dancing that they had obviously both seen. Both sets of parents were delighted by this family entertainment!

The next day was the last day of the conference; the Russians had apparently asked for a slot to make a speech half-way through the morning. It came then as no surprise, when the "Professor" walked to the rostrum, and in his almost perfect English, addressed the crowded room. He talked first about how pleased the Russians were to have been invited to this conference. He understood why the main theme of the conference had been chosen, but that, because of the number of people employed in the Russian defence industry, also how difficult it would be to re-employ them all into making goods for the civil sector. Not only would it take retraining, but substantial amounts of capital investment. Towards the end of his speech, his tone became even more serious. He began to talk about the highly qualified scientists and engineers, like himself who, for years, had been employed in military research and development programs. He finished with a warning: "Unless you can find a way to re-employ these kinds of people to work on other things," he said, "some of them could be employed by other countries, for a lot of money, to help those other countries develop the kind of things that you, the West, would not want them to have developed!" Edwards immediately thought that he knew what this serious warning might be about.

Back in London, Edwards asked for an urgent meeting with Michael, to brief him on how things had gone at Pitlochry. At Michael's request, he then started on a full written report on the proceedings of the conference and what he had learned, including the comments that his wife had been able to translate from her overhearing of the Russian conversations. Michael had asked for this report to be classified to a high level, and Edwards complied, and tried to complete it as soon as possible. After a few days, he submitted it to Michael for distribution to senior officials, who had been security cleared to read Top Secret documents, in all the other government departments and agencies that Michael thought relevant.

About two weeks later, Michael asked to see him again. As soon as he was sitting opposite Michael at his desk in his secure, carefully "swept" office, Michael looked at him.

"Your report has really caused quite a stir," Michael said. "It was very good to get an impression of how this conference went from someone that was there. It was also excellent that your wife was able to translate and report on some of the real, private feelings of the Russian delegates, about what this conference was trying to do."

"Good," replied Edwards. "I am pleased that this exercise proved worthwhile."

"More than that," said Michael. "Your report on the speech of the man that you call the "Professor," that he gave on the last morning of the conference, was very important. What he said has caused us all a lot of thought about the real risks of the proliferation of Weapons of Mass Destruction, by the means that he so clearly described. You realise who he actually is?"

"I was hoping that you would be able to tell me," replied Edwards. "All I can say is that he was a most intelligent and interesting man to meet and to talk to."

"He is one of the leading scientists in Russia," Michael told him. "He was, of course, a staunch member of the Communist Party during the Cold War, and he was appointed to run a top-level, secret, scientific institute specialising in the development of new nuclear, biological and chemical weapons! He is still doing that."

Edwards gasped. "I should have guessed," he replied.

"We even know about his wife," Michael continued. "He was teaching in a university in Moscow, before he was transferred to this scientific institute. He was brilliant and was very young to be appointed as a Professor. His wife was one of his students. They married and then they moved to live near his new institute, which is located in a city in Siberia, that does not exist!"

"What do you mean by that?" asked Edwards.

"None of its inhabitants were ever allowed to talk about where they lived and what they worked on there," Michael replied. "The city still does not appear on any maps of Russia and no ordinary Russian even knows of its existence." Michael continued; "What the man you met has told us in his speech, is perfectly possible. Some of his more poorly paid, but still highly qualified colleagues, could certainly be attracted to go and work abroad, if they were offered a lot of money to do so. They could sell their dangerous expertise to the governments of certain countries that we certainly would not wish to acquire this expertise, and thereby then start to develop some advanced nuclear, biological or chemical weapons for themselves!"

Edwards just nodded. Michael sighed; "We must now devote more effort to watching this situation very carefully," he continued. "If we discover that this might be going to happen, in any particular case, we might have to intervene, with our new Russian friends, to try and stop this transfer of know-how and expertise. It is, after all, in both our interests, to try and stop the proliferation to other countries, particularly unfriendly ones, of this advanced military technology."

Edwards was very pleased that his latest visit to Scotland had resulted in such a serious, potential danger, being clearly identified. Now, hopefully, some action would be taken to try and stop the dire consequences of such an event, as the "Professor" had outlined, from actually happening!

But, as the years went by, Edwards became disappointed; he believed that a great opportunity had been missed. The West, collectively, seemed to have failed to understand the historic position of Russia and to take advantage of this to engineer a breakthrough in its relations with that country. Instead, the West failed to offer Russia, even an associate role, in future political and military developments and, by failing to understand the concerns that Russia might have, the West again drove a large wedge between itself and this enormous and resource-rich country. Instead of detente, a new "Cold War" was allowed to develop and Russia increasingly turned to the Chinese, the new major competitor to the Western world and to its democracy and its freedom. The Russians had always believed that they were really a European nation; the story of Tsar Peter the Great establishing St. Petersburg as a new capital in order to open up his country towards Europe, served well to illustrate this. Edwards distinctly remembered a direct, but rather crude, quote from a senior Russian General, at the very height of the previous "Cold War," that seemed, so aptly, to sum up the Russian position and the opportunity that had been missed to create from Russian a powerful and huge "buffer state" against the growing power of China. This quote was to the effect that "We will never allow the yellow hoards to piss on the paintings in the Louvre!"

ALARM BELLS

"A nation can survive its fools, and even the ambitious. But it cannot survive treason from within." – Marcus Tullius Cicero.

1

For anyone watching, it was almost a comical sight! The scene was set at an airport in the south of Spain. Outside the airport terminal, the July temperature was in the mid-thirties Centigrade but, inside, the air-conditioning was blowing fiercely. In the Arrivals Hall, an Englishman, in a light-weight business suit, had just passed through the one-way door from the Immigration and Customs area. Despite the heat outside, he was wearing a woollen, check-patterned, peaked cap, pulled well down on his head!

In front of him, just behind the barrier which kept the waiting crowd back from the busy exit, stood another man. He was also in a business suit. His strong, stocky build identified him as probably a rugby player. On his head was a smart, brown, homburg hat. The Englishman spotted him, walked over and stood straight in front of him. He raised his cap and said the other man's name. The white African, for that was what he was, politely raised his hat and said the Englishman's name. They then grinned at each other; how else could you safely recognise a stranger in a crowded airport, when you did not know what they looked like, without some form of recognition signal? The Englishman had suggested, on the telephone before his visit that this should be the ploy that they would adopt, in order to meet safely.

Edwards walked around the barrier and then shook Barry's hand.

"Let me take you to my car," said Barry. "We will drive a short way down the coast to a little seaside resort, so we can talk there over lunch. There is a good fish restaurant, by the side of the sea that I use a lot."

Edwards was booked back on a return flight to London that evening. But why had he taken the trouble to get up very early that morning, to get to the airport, to take a flight to Spain, just for the day? It was the early-2010's; Edwards was now working as a consultant. He advised a large, formerly government-owned, technology group, for up to three days a week. The other days he was free to carry out other work and he was given occasional assignments by an established, but very discrete, business advisory and intelligence company. This had been established, some years before, as a commercial entity, by former senior members of the Secret Intelligence Service, better known to the public as M.I.6. A disproportionate number of its current staff, were still former members of this organisation. The particular assignment that Edwards had now been given, was very sensitive; the questions that he had to ask and the help that he needed could only be done with a face-to-face meeting. Any other forms of communications were just too insecure!

Barry had parked carefully and then they had walked along a short section of the palm-decked promenade, before entering the restaurant, which jutted out towards the sea. Edwards waited for them to have started to eat their main course; an excellent fish dish, freshly caught that morning from the Mediterranean that stretched out in front of them through the picture windows of the restaurant. Then, in strict confidence, he briefed Barry on his assignment. A major British company wanted to know about the perception that they were now held in, by a number of foreign governments. This had followed a recent scandal where, it had been claimed by the press, this company had been implicated in paying bribes, in certain countries, in order to get business. The company believed that this adverse publicity, implying that certain politicians and government officials in these countries had taken part in corruption, would adversely affect them for any future business.

"Your country is one of those," Edwards told Barry. He went on to identify the business contract involved. Barry nodded; he already knew all about this deal. "We need to know what the company's position now is within the highest levels of government," Edwards continued. "What do the senior politicians and officials now think about doing further business with this company?"

"This is not an easy task," replied Barry. "But I do have two people who may be able to help. One is the former head of their intelligence services, who has now moved into the commercial sector. I am close to him; I once saved his life when we were both young men. We were swimming in the sea together, one day, when a great wave came. It nearly swept him out to sea. Fortunately, I was a much stronger swimmer than he was, and I was able to grab him and pull him back to the shore. I now call him "the Chief.""

Edwards nodded; he knew from the man's name, that Barry had just given him, that his friend was a black man. But he also knew how such incidents could bring a lifetime's very close relationship, despite the racial problems that Barry's country had once suffered from.

"But I need a cut-out," said Barry. "He would not thank me for approaching him directly. He will still be under close surveillance. I have another close friend, Roger. He also was in the intelligence services and worked with the Chief, very closely. He now has his own corporate advisory company in the capital city."

"But can we keep all of this on a secure basis?" asked Edwards, knowing full-well that Barry would understand what he had asked. He knew that Barry had served, with distinction, in the Special Forces of his country, before the majority black population had, at last, taken over the government. Indeed, Edwards had been told to meet Barry, who might be able to solve his problem, by another member of the same Special Forces, who Edwards knew back in London.

"No problem," laughed Barry. "Roger and I were at school together. We know each other so well we now have our own language, built up, for fun, over the years. Anyone who listens in to us, on a telephone call will, just, not be able to understand us!"

Edwards nodded again; he was satisfied. They went on to talk about the commercial terms of the transaction. How much would Barry and Roger earn from their efforts, and how would they be paid? Also, would the former head of intelligence have to be paid? Barry thought not. "He is above all that," he said. "He does work for the good of his country, as he sees it."

Edwards returned to London, that evening, fully satisfied with his day trip to Spain. But now he had to find similar intelligence sources in the several other countries that he had been asked to explore. A few months later, Edwards had completed his sensitive and clandestine task. His final report had been typed by himself, on his home computer, and printed out. Then he had hand delivered it to Adrian, the person in the business advisory organisation who had given him this assignment. Adrian was a charming man who had served for many years in the Secret Intelligence Service; but he had then retired early to join the commercial world. Edwards had invited him to his club, located just off Whitehall, several times and he had mentioned, very discretely, about his time in the Service. He told Edwards that he spoke both Arabic and Farsi, the language of Iran, fluently.

"I can't understand how the Service could have let you go," commented Edwards. "With what is going on in the Middle East these days, your language skills must have been critically important."

"But there are new youngsters coming in all the time, perhaps with similar skills," said Adrian modestly. "And I suppose that "the Office", as we call our organisation, did not have to pay them so much as they paid me," he added.

Edwards found out that Adrian's wife also served in M.I.6, where they had met, and that they had two young children. It had then seemed an even greater tragedy when a shocked Edwards had heard, only some six months after this conversation, that Adrian had contracted a fatal medical condition and had sadly died shortly afterwards.

2

In the interim, Barry had come to London and they had met again, discretely, at Edwards's club. Barry had lived in England for some years, before he had moved to Spain, and he still kept a small flat in a commuter town, just outside London, where he could stay.

"The Chief is coming here next week with some of his business colleagues and he has suggested that I should meet with them all on Tuesday morning, at their hotel," said Barry. "I have suggested that I bring you along to the meeting, as you are now my main contact in England."

"Of course," replied Edwards. "I would be delighted to meet them."

"He has asked me to meet him after that, privately, that afternoon," said Barry. "I do not know what it is about but, no doubt, it will be interesting."

So it was that Barry and Edwards reported at the appointed day and time, to the ground floor lounge of a luxury London hotel. Barry led the way to the group of four men, sitting in easy chairs, with a large jug of coffee and a number of cups on the table in front of them. Introductions were made by the Chief, of Barry to his colleagues, and then Barry introduced Edwards to them all. They sat down and more coffee and two more cups were ordered. A wide ranging discussion ensued; the group were now developing a new mine in the African country concerned, but they also had existing investments in other sectors of the economy. Edwards did his best to keep up with what was being said, and even managed to make his own small contribution, as he had travelled to this country several times in the past. "The Chief" did not say much, but Edwards caught him looking carefully at him when he was speaking. The meeting over, he walked outside with Barry, who had another appointment before his private meeting with "the Chief" that afternoon. Edwards was not to see Barry again during his present visit, as he was returning to Spain the following day.

It was now some five months after Barry's last visit; one morning Edwards received a telephone call from him.

"I will be in London again next week," he said. "I must meet with you privately, at your club. It is very important. Will Wednesday morning, at eleven be alright with you?"

Edwards readily agreed. Barry, as always, was on time and Edwards conducted him up the impressive staircase, to the large, comfortable lounge that his club provided for members to meet with their guests. It was never crowded in this big room, and a discrete conversation could be held in one of its many corners.

They sat, side by side, on two easy chairs drawn together, so that they could talk very quietly, by speaking directly into the other's ear.

"I have been speaking to Roger in our own language!" said Barry. "He is most concerned about something. After several, long telephone conversations, I think that I now understand what it is. He is asking for a contact with the British intelligence services. He has discovered evidence of a plot, by the Russians, to acquire a company in his country which has access to some very powerful technology. He says that it is really important and that the West, not only Britain, will really suffer if this company's purchase is not stopped."

Edwards had listened carefully but, now, he felt that he had to ask a question. "What kind of technology are we talking about?" he asked.

"I do not know," replied Barry. "He will not tell me the company name, or what it actually does, over the telephone. But it is all very real and he is actually scared for his life. I must remind you of his long background in intelligence work; he is not one to panic or to over-emphasise things. He says that, if it is found out what he is doing, he could be killed. He does not want to come to England and he does not want to meet anyone in his own country, because he knows that everywhere is under surveillance. He has suggested that it would be nice to see me again and I have invited him to stay with me, in Spain, for a week's holiday. He will be coming in three weeks and he would like a senior representative of British intelligence to meet him at my house. Either, they can fly someone in and I will meet them at the same airport that I met you, or, perhaps, they have someone in their embassy in Madrid, who can travel south to meet him?"

"That does not give me much time," said Edwards. "I, and the intelligence services, must act quickly!"

"There is one more thing," continued Barry. "The Chief would also like to be contacted by the same British intelligence officer. He is happy to meet discretely with them locally and to keep them informed, on a regular basis, about what is happening at the very top in his country. He is very concerned about some aspects of what is happening there and he thinks that the British government might be able to intervene, in some discrete way, to try and correct a few bad things that are happening."

Edwards nodded. He knew that the recent history of Barry's country was not a happy one. The ruling party kept on getting elected, but it was totally corrupt and bought many votes. It really did not seem to care about the people. Increasingly, as a result, there was a rising tide of discontent in the country. This could easily lead to violence, and a complete fracturing of the political situation that had, at least up to now, led to some general stability and a working accommodation with the white minority in the country.

For the next two weeks, Edwards was furiously trying to get his contacts to arrange for a meeting between himself and the Secret Intelligence Service. Meanwhile, Barry informed him that Roger had booked his flights, had obtained his Spanish visa, with Barry's help, and was coming for his holiday, with his old school friend. At last, a day and time was set and Edwards was given the name of a lady, who would meet him one morning at his club. He waited, expectantly, in the reception area for her to arrive. He had thought that it would be someone older; she was tall and slim, well-dressed, but, he estimated, only about thirty years old. He escorted her up the stairs and found a quiet corner in the large lounge for them to talk. It had a table, normally used to play cards, so that she could make some notes if she wished. He bought two coffees for them from the up-market dispensing machine that, he thought, really did seem to provide a fairly decent cup of coffee!

3

At least she tried to appear business-like. She had taken a small note book and a pen out of her handbag, to take notes. But she appeared completely ignorant as to what the meeting was about, despite Edwards having given a discrete, but concise, description to his contact, who he knew to be a trusted associate of this Service. Edwards, instead, had now to assume zero knowledge, so he started with describing Barry and how he had been introduced to him, carefully avoiding the commercially confidential reason for his day visit to Spain. He then described Roger and his background and gave all the information that he had about what he had discovered and what was happening with the Russians in his country. He outlined Roger's request for an urgent meeting at Barry's house in southern Spain; Roger would now be visiting there the following week! Could someone fly out, just for the day, to meet with him and to hear what this was all about? Barry would meet them at the airport and take them to his home to meet Roger. Or could, perhaps, the Service's representative in Madrid drive south, to Barry's home, to meet Roger?

She seemed perplexed. "I can see if anyone can help on this," she said. "But, really, the Russian team is in such a mess, I don't think they have the capability to take this on."

"But what about if someone goes to meet him from Madrid?" asked Edwards, surprised by this lack of interest. "That is much easier perhaps. Roger is a very experienced intelligence officer and he has said that this is very important for the security of the West. I would remind you that he was a member of their intelligence service for many years and therefore he should know what is real and important. Barry does believe that Roger is really risking his life by coming to us!"

She still did not seem convinced or, perhaps, she simply just did not know how to deal with something like this? Edwards understood that even the Secret Intelligence Service had a limited budget, but this lack of any interest seemed ridiculous! He realised that they were "tasked" by their political masters to do certain things and that, these days, they probably had less autonomy than perhaps they used to have. "I will have to talk to my colleagues and get back to you," was all that she would say.

Edwards then told her about "the Chief" and took his business card, which he had given to Edwards, out of his pocket to show to her. She made a careful note of the name, of his current company and all the other information, including telephone numbers, on the card. "All he wants to do is to meet someone from your Service, discretely, within his country itself, to form some kind of mutually advantageous, long-term relationship," said Edwards.

"That is difficult, too," was the reply. "We are so pushed at the moment, what with Muslim extremism and the Middle East. Recently, too, we have been asked to look closely at China. I don't think that we have any people who can spend time on Africa at all."

So this was perhaps the reason for her disinterest; the disastrous, apparent intelligence failure of 11 September 2001, still seemed to play a too important part in the minds of the intelligent services and their political masters? This was purely a reactive way to set the priorities of intelligence gathering; what was needed was an ever-updated proactive policy. By all means have regard to what had happened in the past, but also it must be appreciated that the world now presented an increasingly rapidly changing political, technological and strategic picture, and the intelligence priorities should be set with that in mind. Political control should never be exercised over the intelligence agencies; they must be independent, totally objective and be free to set their own agenda to tackle current and future threats.

"But it is a very important country in Africa that we are talking about," responded Edwards, still trying to change her mind. "We are talking about a very well-placed, senior man, who is willing to help us there. His country has large mineral resources and some parts of its economy are very advanced. It is pivotal for the whole of the African continent. What happens there could well set the trend for the whole of Africa!"

"All I can do is to ask someone," was the noncommittal reply. "I will get back to you. Meanwhile, in case there is anything else, I will give you my direct, secure email address so that you can contact me." Edwards made a careful note of her email address not thinking, that, at this stage, he would use it. He gave her all his contact details and asked again that his requests be very urgently dealt with.

But he was to be disappointed; two days later he received a message from her Foreign and Commonwealth Office email address. It said that the two matters had been very carefully considered, but they were unable to do anything to help. "I was only trying to help them!" muttered Edwards to himself. "And so were a lot of other people." He then had the difficult task of telephoning Barry and telling him the result. Barry could not believe it; in fact he was also very annoyed as his close friend Roger was arriving for his stay, at his house, that very weekend! Roger was expecting to have been able to unburden his dangerous knowledge, to someone who should have been able to do something about it.

Barry did not return to London for over three months. Before he did so, he called Edwards and asked to meet him at eleven o'clock on a particular morning, just the other side of the ticket barrier, at Blackfriars Underground Station. Edwards was waiting underground, at the appointed time, for him to emerge from the London Tube train system. But he did not; at five past eleven there was a touch on his arm, and Barry was standing behind him.

"I have some meetings in the City today," said Barry. "I have an hour or so between them now, so it gives us time to talk. Let's walk across Blackfriars Bridge; there is a good coffee shop there that I know, on the other side of the river. We can get some coffees there."

They walked out of the station together, crossed the road and began to walk across the bridge from the financial centre of the City of London, towards London's South Bank, along the bridge's eastern pavement. But, in the middle of the bridge, they stopped and stood, side by side, as if admiring the fine view of the river and Saint Paul's Cathedral and Tower Bridge downstream in the distance. The heavy passing traffic drowned out their voices and none of the passers-by took any notice of them, as Londoners usually do!

"Roger was very disappointed that your people were not interested," Barry began. "He told me what it was all about, while he was staying with me. It was a computer programming company, probably one of the best in the world, and it must be one of the most advanced companies in my country. Some years ago, they helped a major American software corporation develop their security algorithms, and they have continued to develop them for other similar companies as well. The Russians cleverly identified this opportunity to penetrate the West's computer systems security and decided that they must buy this company. They set up a local front-company to do so. Their clear aim was to capture all the security algorithms of the Western software companies that used this company to produce them."

"But surely there must have been some resistance to this happening?" asked Edwards.

"The Russians were determined," replied Barry. "They offered a high price for the company to the current owners and funded their local front-company, ready to buy it. That way it appeared that the company was not going to be taken over by foreign interests. But some people saw through it and objected; they were either threatened or paid off. Some may have even just "disappeared." Large cases, full of United States dollar notes, were brought into the country. Politicians and officials were bribed, with large amounts of cash, just to support this company purchase. Everything is now in place for the purchase to go ahead."

"If only the British could have made an official representation, at the highest level, and showed that they knew what was happening, it might have been stopped," he went on. "But now it will go ahead and the Russians will get the source codes to enable them to read or listen in to every sensitive Western communication that they want to. It is just like the British capturing the German Enigma machine in the Second World War, which enabled them to decode all the sensitive coded German messages. It is a disaster for the West and it will take years and a lot of money to now correct this situation!"

Edwards just did not know what to say. Eventually he lamely said how sorry he was that he had failed in his mission to try to stop this happening and then asked a simple question: "So, what happens now?"

"Roger is still determined, since this company purchase cannot now be stopped, to at least get the news of what has happened out to the West, in some way," Barry replied. "We discussed this. Maybe Roger can get the Chief to help him. They do, after all, trust each other implicitly. Maybe the Americans will be more open to listen, than the British have proved to be? This is all still work in progress. But we have now lost the opportunity of stopping this company being bought by the Russians!" he repeated grimly.

4

Edwards, like Barry, still had his own contacts in the City of London, although they were now fewer in number than in the past. He had fairly recently been introduced to two bankers, who seemed to be much more concerned with their own importance and making money, than in providing any kind of service to companies or individual customers. They had brought Edwards into a number of meetings, really to use his experience and respectability. He quickly discovered that the City had changed, in many ways, since he had worked in it during the 1970's. He had also worked closely with many banks and bankers, too, during the 1980's and 1990's. But now, sadly, the banking industry seemed so constrained in its activities, by its ever-present lawyers, that little initiative or innovation was possible. Perhaps this explained why these two modern bankers were now much more interested in getting their activities "packaged" within newly incorporated companies, and then getting these companies "floated", with a quotation for their shares, on the Alternative Investment Market, part of the London Stock Exchange. They rewarded themselves with large numbers of these company's shares, in the hope that they could make large amounts of money, when the shares increased in price after a public floatation.

It all seemed a long way from the gentlemanly activities of the merchant banks that Edwards had worked in, during the 1970's, when total importance had been placed on the unofficial motto of the City: "My Word is my Bond." These merchant banks provided vital services and independent advice to companies, pension funds and other institutions. But the advent of the "Big Bang", in October 1986, which was a massive deregulation of the City of London's activities, had resulted in major American and European banks entering the City, with very large amounts of money, and capturing most of the business that was available. This then led to the purchase of these established British merchant banks and stockbrokers, by these larger foreign firms, and the whole emphasis had changed to making them "money making" machines, rather than providing any kind of service. As for the large British banks, they had stopped providing many services to their customers and were now nothing more than a basic retail organisation, like any chain of grocery shops. But, whenever they could, unlike true retail chains, they closed down their branches to save costs, further depriving their customers of any kind of personal service or helpful advice.

Gerald was one of these "new breed" of bankers. that Edwards had been introduced to. He was a director of various companies including a high-technology fund, the activities of which, one day, he explained to Edwards. Peter, who worked closely with Gerald, was more "behind the scenes", cultivating ideas and contacts. Edwards met with them both a number of times, including over long and luxurious lunches which they always seemed to be able to buy him. "They must have investors who were prepared to indulge them with a large expense account!" Edwards thought to himself. But it was at a meeting with Gerald one day, when he chose to explain to Edwards the background to this particular technology fund that he was working on. The new Conservative government in 2010 had ushered in what was called a "Golden Era" of a close relationship between Britain and China, and much was now hoped to come from this initiative. On thinking about it afterwards, Edwards become more and more concerned about this technology fund's operations.

In September 1940, during the battle for the survival of Britain against the Nazi aerial onslaught, with the permission of the then war-time Prime Minister Winston Churchill, a British scientist called Henry Tizard had travelled to the United States on a highly secret mission. His intention was to obtain American assistance to exploit and manufacture in the United

States, the military potential of the advanced research and development work that Britain had been carrying out. This scientific portfolio included the development of radar, designs for proximity fuses, the design of the jet engine and work on the feasibility of developing an atomic bomb. Along with these very significant technologies, there were also designs for rockets, gyroscopic gunsights, submarine detection devices, self-sealing fuel tanks and plastic explosives. Because of the large domestic political support for America's neutrality in the war raging in Europe, Tizard decided that the best thing to do was to give the technology away. Then they could simply use America's spare industrial capability, to manufacture these technologies in large amounts, and then export it back to help Britain fight the war. The following year, the documents containing all these vital secret technologies were placed in a large trunk, and sent by ship from Liverpool to Canada, and then on to Washington D.C.

In Washington, Tizard then had a series of secret meetings whose purpose was to efficiently transfer this vital knowledge, over to the Americans. Tizard carefully selected the American companies, universities and research institutes, that were suitable to receive these advanced technologies, work on them further if needed or, if they were ready, just produce them in large numbers. But, for all these technologies, the British were offering them free of charge, in order to gain help from the Americans. The main successes of this mission proved to be the transfer and further development of radar technology, the joint development of the jet engine, and the development of the atomic bomb. When America finally entered the war, after the Japanese bombing of Pearl Harbour in December 1941, these British developed technologies proved to be vital for America and Britain to defeat the Axis powers of Germany, Italy and Japan. This technological co-operation helped forge the Anglo-American Alliance and the so-called "Special Relationship" between Britain and the United States, which remains vital to the present day. But this mission took place, and this close relationship developed between the two leading democratic countries in the world, with a common belief in individual freedom and the rule of law, and in the emergency conditions of the war needed to defeat the evils of Fascism.

What Gerald had described to Edwards was something very different; he had helped to create a Fund which took in a number of the current leading advanced technologies that Britain now had to offer. The idea was that these could now continue to be developed with financial funding from overseas. But the funding was not to come from the United States, nor for that matter, from another friendly democratic country. Instead the funding was to come from the totalitarian, undemocratic, pseudo-Communist People's Republic of China! Edwards was appalled; he knew that, for many years, Chinese government agents had sought to steal advanced Western technologies, even placing people in the waiting rooms of Patent Offices around the world, in order to copy Patent Applications as soon as they had been filed! But

Gerald's fund seemed to have high-level approval; its Chairman was a former well thought-of Conservative government Minister, who had now been elevated to the House of Lords!

5

As soon as he had realised the danger to Britain, Edwards asked for a further meeting with Gerald. "I really don't think that you should consider putting this together," he had told Gerald. "It really is not in the national interest to do so. All that the Chinese will do is to steal the results of the work that has been done by British scientists on these technologies, and use all that work for themselves. They will, of course, claim that they have every right to do so, since they have financed part of the further development." But, try as he might, he could not convince Gerald.

"People see working with China as a great benefit," he had replied. "Using their money, this means that we will not have to find the money ourselves. Once the technologies are developed, we will have China, the largest market in the world, to sell into."

Edwards had heard this argument about the immense potential Chinese market many times before. But he had also heard of companies and people with inventions, which had tried to deal with, or even invest into China. Very few of them had been successful in making any money, and usually their investment and their ideas had been stolen, or they had completely lost control of what they had set up there. The Chinese did not import manufactured goods from other countries in any great amount; instead they preferred to be self-sufficient and to manufacture all that they could for their own people, themselves. They had always firmly believed that the ancient Chinese civilisation was superior to the Western countries, that therefore they did not need them, and they always took a very long-term view that, in the end, China should and would dominate the world.

Edwards did not know what to do; Gerald would not listen to him and the Fund seemed to be protected by its high-level contacts and implicit government approval. Then he remembered the young lady that he had met at his club. He had noted that she had mentioned that China had now been made a priority for her organisation to examine, and he had already used the secure email address she had given him, to send her one small, but he hoped helpful, piece of information. Some months before Edwards had been introduced, by one of his contacts, to a Chinese gentleman who now lived in London. As far as Edwards could see he had no job or means of financial support, but, he was still able to go with Edwards's contact, on an expensive visit to an African country, where they had both met the government and viewed several potential mining projects. His English was very poor, despite the fact that he claimed to have come to Britain when he was a child and had been educated here. It was difficult to understand him and, when he spoke, it was in a very low and conspiratorial tone. The President of

China had recently visited London, and Edwards's contact had afterwards proudly informed Edwards, that his Chinese friend had been asked, by the Chinese embassy here, to serve in the security team for the President's visit!

This meant only one thing to Edwards; the Chinese man who he had been introduced to, was very possibly an undercover, Chinese government agent. How else could he live so well in London and even travel to Africa, unless he was being funded by the Chinese government? He wrote a carefully worded email with the full details of this man, and what he knew about him, to the secure email address of the young lady that he had met. He even included the mobile telephone number of the Chinese man that he had been given. That way, if the British intelligence organisations thought that he was suspicious, the Security Service, known to the public as M.I.5, could then track his movements and even listen in to selected telephone calls that he perhaps made to China. These could then be translated from the official Mandarin Chinese language, or the Chinese dialect that he might have used, to find out what he was discussing.

Gerald had sent Edwards a full Prospectus of his Fund, which contained a lot of detail on each advanced technology and the scientific team, located in one of the leading British universities that were working on it. The Prospectus had been very well put together and it made a very good case for why the Chinese government should invest in these British-inspired technologies, to take them forward to a situation where they could then be industrialised and mass produced. But it was clear that any such mass production would take place in China and not in Britain. The government in Britain now proudly claimed that it saw Britain as "a largely post-industrial services economy"; in other words, Britain should no longer make anything! Edwards was annoyed by the crass stupidity and assumptions of this political view and of Gerald's Fund, which now seemed willing to give away the hard-won achievements of British scientific research, for a relatively small amount of money, as far as the Chinese were concerned. No doubt, Gerald and his colleagues would earn large fees and profits from the transaction, but what was being given away were virtually the "Crown Jewels" of Britain!

Edwards was now determined to do all that he could to stop this happening; he wrote a long email to the lady that he had met, and attached the Prospectus that Gerald had sent to him. Although he had read all the books and seen all the films about the British agent James Bond, Edwards knew that the British intelligence services did not have all the omnipresent knowledge that was usually portrayed in this fiction. He realised that, as this situation was in the financial sphere, probably the lady and her Service colleagues were not even aware that such a proposal as that contained in the Fund's Prospectus, was seriously being put forward for the Chinese to consider. If they did accept it, and why should they not, then it would be very difficult to stop it happening afterwards. In his email, he emphasised the seriousness and the urgency of the situation. He unfortunately received no reply to this email; but he had not received a reply to his previous email either.

It was several months later when he met with Gerald again. They had several things to discuss but, towards the end of the conversation, Edwards brought up the topic of the technology fund. Gerald looked distinctly uncomfortable; "We are looking at it closely again," was all that he would say.

"But I thought that you were in advanced discussions with the Chinese already?" Edwards questioned him.

"Yes," replied Gerald. "We have visited them in Beijing several times. We have met everybody there, including relevant government Ministers and their officials. We have even visited some of their leading universities and met the Chinese scientists, who want to work closely with their British colleagues."

"So what has happened then? Are you now reconsidering it?" asked Edwards. But Gerald would not answer him.

There is an event known as a "Gypsy's Warning" in which someone has a quiet word with an employee or an acquaintance, suggesting that they best proceed with caution in respect of their current conduct or intentions, or otherwise they may be in for an unpleasant surprise. Edwards had to assume that someone, within the Fund's management, had received such a "Gypsy's Warning." It might have been Gerald that had received it but, more likely, it would have been given to the Chairman of the Fund who, so recently, had been elevated to the House of Lords. But Edwards still continued to try and monitor the situation and when he next met Gerald, a few months later, he asked him again about the Fund.

Gerald's instant answer, which seemed well rehearsed, was to the effect that "The Chinese had failed to come up with the money!" Edwards did not believe him, but the way that it was said, seemed to show that the Technology Fund had been forced to withdraw its unwise proposal to the Chinese, or that the Chinese had, for some reason, withdrawn their offer to finance it. Maybe, they had been given the message that the British government would stop any transfer of the relevant British technologies, and that this would then result in a serious embarrassment for both governments.

Whatever had happened, Edwards was now satisfied. He did not know, of course, how much his intervention had really helped in stopping these seriously detrimental actions? Maybe others, far more important than he was, had seen the danger? But, the thought of these proposed actions, had triggered the sound of alarm bells in his mind, and he had decided to do something about them. At least, some kind of warning had been given by him, and this very doubtful initiative had now been firmly stopped in its tracks! It had been foolish for Gerald and his colleagues to even contemplate obtaining Chinese funding, using Britain's most advanced and valuable technologies as a "bargaining chip." But, maybe, the thought of all the money, that they could personally have made, had distracted them? In these complex circumstances, the motive of treason was very difficult to prove. But such unwise actions, it could be claimed, could really amount, in the end, to such a heinous crime.

POSTSCRIPT

"The unexamined life is not worth living"
– attributed, by his pupil Plato, to Socrates. (Athens– circa 470–399 BCE).

First, I should write some Acknowledgements. Most of all I want to thank my readers who have bought and read my two previous volumes, and I hope that they have also now enjoyed the further true stories in this book. I would also like to thank my family and friends who have supported me with encouragement, and kind words and comments about my writing. My wife should be thanked for putting up with my long absences on the computer, while there were obvious and more important household tasks to be done. Our daughter has maintained a file of all my true stories, as a back-up if needed, while our son has acted as my brilliant IT Adviser, keeping me sane while my computer has been trying to drive me mad!

An acknowledgement is due to thank my good friends Brian and "Indy" and to my late, good friend Daniel who have commented on, and given their approval to, the stories in this book where they are mentioned and play such a large part. An acknowledgement and thanks are also due to my good friend Rob Green who has proofread this book and has creatively criticised its style and content.

I am indebted to and acknowledge the contribution made by the book "Billion Dollar Whale" by Bradley Hope and Tom Wright regarding the background to the huge Malaysian fraud mentioned in my story about Malaysia. I am also indebted and give thanks to Miles Goslett whose excellent book "An Inconvenient Death" investigated the mysterious "suicide" of my former colleague Dr David Kelly and provided background for my own story. I also acknowledge the investigative work of Sue Reid, in her August, 2013 article in the Daily Mail, regarding the death of Princess Diana. Finally, where I have used some short quotes from certain individuals or from their published works, I acknowledge and give thanks to those authors or, if they are dead, to their estates.

One of my very close friends has written, "Without an understanding of History, there can be no Wisdom and no ability to plan for the Future. The people are thus surely trapped in the constant Present and so are much easier to control." I cannot but agree with what he has written; if we cannot read and understand about the Past, how can we ever try to plan for the Future? The Past is the most certain, the Present is but a fleeting dream, and the Future has to be largely unknown. But we can try at least to plan for it. In this current world with its ever-increasing uncertainty, totalitarianism and Climate Change, to plan for the Future has become essential if we are ever to preserve the human species within democracy and freedom. Therefore, a full understanding of Humankind's history is essential.

In my three volumes of stories I have tried to write only the truth, to try to let my readers understand the uncertainty and difficulties of dealing in the "Real World," and to illustrate many of the problems that I really did face along my life's way. Because it would be outside the experience of many of my readers, I also hope that they will find my humble attempts at storytelling both entertaining, and educative. Unfortunately, I see the immediate future of our world as one of greater international difficulties; famine, war about the allocation of resources or politics, increased mass migration, rising health issues and catastrophic climate events. Therefore, it is essential for the human species to face these difficulties with calmness and hope, to struggle to find solutions, to limit corruption, and to fight against the narrow vested interests of individuals, countries, and large corporations. All of these vested interests will naturally resist, with all their strength, any and all developments which will go against their existing interests, or just reduce their power and their profits.

That is what Humanity now faces and I can only wish it well with all my heart. As I am now eighty years of age, this will probably be the last book in this series. I do have other true stories to tell, but I may not get the time to write them down. However, I have now put down in print the substantial part of my varied life experience. I have toyed with the idea of writing some fiction and, if I get the time given to me, I may still attempt that. But, it will probably be written under my real name. Some family and friends have asked me why I have not used my real name to write these stories? I have not done so partly because I am still working, free of charge, to try and help the world with sustainable ideas and technology. But, also, it is because in this modern world one can face vicious social media criticism; I want to protect myself and my family from attack. I have zero "social presence" as it is called, but this would not stop the attacks upon me!

Because of social media, the world now seems an unkind and ruthless place; rudeness, lies, conspiracies, abuse and violence abound. These are not the conditions that will help the Human Race overcome the vast problems that it now faces! There must be kindness in the world and a general willingness for people to work together with others, despite perhaps disagreeing with them on other matters. There must be a full understanding about the dangerous and imminent situation Humankind now faces, and full co-operation between nations, organisations and individuals, to face and overcome it. Anything that divides people and their world must be put aside literally, so that Humankind can survive!

As I have continued my writing I have realised something: that much of which is classed as fiction is not actually fiction- it is really an "illustration of fact." Many fiction writers base their stories on what they have experienced, and what they see around them; the works of Charles Dickens and Jane Austin are examples of that. It is only, perhaps, in the case of Science Fiction that we do see total fiction writing, or in those works where writers create truly "imaginary worlds" like J.R. Tolkien, and J.K. Rowling. Even then, the unconscious experiences of the writer, perhaps from their childhood, may well come to the fore and enable them to imagine and construct their fictional worlds, and then write about them. I, of course, have set myself the task of only writing about the truth as I have actually experienced it.

That is not, surprisingly, an easy task as one must first struggle to recall, and then frame your true stories, in such a way as to hopefully interest your readers. All the while, one is still trying to preserve the truth and the anonymity of your characters and, where necessary, the circumstances and places in which the events happened. I can only hope that I have been successful in the task that I have set myself, and that my readers have enjoyed the experience of sharing my stories and some of the events of what has turned out to be, fortunately for me, a varied and interesting life. With that I will terminate, I hope prematurely, my life story, as I still intend to work on, in my very modest way, to try and help the world face its new challenges, for as long as I can.

For those of you who would like to see me and hear what I have to say about my books and about other topics, I have been filmed in a series of YouTube videos. You can find this series by searching YouTube for:-

"@englishmanasks – Christopher Spencer"

If that is not successful, submit the same search to Google.

Fortunately, despite my age, life is still thrilling and interesting for me, and I still love meeting new people, travelling, reading, writing, learning new things and having new experiences. Good health is all important and I seem to have been lucky enough, so far, in this regard. I hope that these enjoyable experiences will continue for me, for as long as it is possible and for as long as my allocated time on this Earth allows!

Christopher Spencer.
August, 2024.

Illustrations provided by the Author:

Front Cover: The Greek Temple of Concordia at Agrigento, Sicily.

Back Cover: Sea Cliffs near Tintagel Castle, Cornwall.

www.ingramcontent.com/pod-product-compliance
Lightning Source LLC
Chambersburg PA
CBHW030541080526
44585CB00012B/220